Hermeneutics of Galatians and Its Doctrinal Engagement

Hermeneutics of Galatians and Its Doctrinal Engagement

ALEXIS K. YOON

WIPF & STOCK · Eugene, Oregon

HERMENEUTICS OF GALATIANS AND ITS DOCTRINAL ENGAGEMENT

Copyright © 2025 Alexis K. Yoon. All rights reserved. Except for brief quotations in critical publications or reviews, no part of this book may be reproduced in any manner without prior written permission from the publisher. Write: Permissions, Wipf and Stock Publishers, 199 W. 8th Ave., Suite 3, Eugene, OR 97401.

Wipf & Stock
An Imprint of Wipf and Stock Publishers
199 W. 8th Ave., Suite 3
Eugene, OR 97401

www.wipfandstock.com

PAPERBACK ISBN: 979-8-3852-6297-7
HARDCOVER ISBN: 979-8-3852-6298-4
EBOOK ISBN: 979-8-3852-6299-1

VERSION NUMBER 12/16/25

Scripture quotations, unless otherwise noted, are taken from the New Revised Standard Version Bible, copyright © 1989, Division of Christian Education of the National Council of Churches of Christ in the U.S.A. Used by permission. All rights reserved.

Scripture quotations marked NIV are taken from The Holy Bible, New International Version®, NIV®. Copyright © 1973, 1978, 1984, 2011 by Biblica, Inc. Used with permission of Zondervan. All rights reserved worldwide. www.zondervan.com.

For

Koh Moon-Ja

Contents

Acknowledgments | ix
Abbreviations | xi
Prologue | xiii

Introduction | 1
Chapter 1: The Twofold Typology of the Elected Community | 9
Chapter 2: The Church as a Third Way of Her Existence | 49
Chapter 3: The Word of God in Its Threefold Form | 83
Conclusion | 124

Appendix: The Prophecy of Habakkuk and the Covenant of Grace | 133
Bibliography | 151

Acknowledgments

I OWE THE GREATEST degree of gratitude to the theologians at Candler School of Theology, Emory University. It was fascinating to read the literature and comments suggested by the theologians Drs. Theodore Brelsford, Anthony Briggman, and Walter Wilson, among others I was not able to meet in person. Their insights were not only valuable but also guided me to a deeper theology, which has formed my research interests in the hermeneutics and its interconnected doctrinal understanding as well as pedagogical approaches to the use of Scripture and pure doctrines attesting the communal life of the church. Their open, excellent scholarship encouraged me to think freely, even utilizing my physics background. One comment, encouraging me to "write my own theology," has been lingering in my mind ever since. I have not stopped pondering it.

Wrapping up my time at Candler, I was occupied with a thought about a third way of the church's existence, neither as a community of sin nor a community of revelation. Ever since, reading with Galatians, I have tried to systematically explore the third way and its relationship to the threefold form of the word. So, this book was born of Candler, a special place in a delightful time in my life.

Along the way, there are times I have found myself perplexed. In all these moments, I would remember the insights and encouragement that I received from the scholars at Candler. Also, the memorable encounters were supportive, including encounters with Drs. Paul Nimmo and Mark Elliott, who gave me constructive comments, and Drs. Stephen Plant and David Fergusson, whose responses and encouragement advanced me. I appreciated these encounters, which have kept me working on this book.

Acknowledgments

Moreover, I would like to express my appreciation to Dr. Ann Belford Ulanov, as her teachings appeared in my mind and guided me to shape the interpretation on Søren Kierkegaard.

I am, first and foremost, grateful to the late Dr. Donald Capps, the teacher who most invested in me.

—Alexis K. Yoon

Abbreviations

ASCE	*Annual of the Society of Christian Ethics*
BI	*Biblical Interpretation*
BTB	*Biblical Theology Bulletin*
CBQ	*Catholic Biblical Quarterly*
CD	Karl Barth, *Church Dogmatics* (referenced in-line using *CD*, volume, part-volume, and page number)
CH	*Church History*
CTQ	*Concordia Theological Quarterly*
ELJ	*Ecclesiastical Law Journal*
ET	*Expository Times*
HTR	*Harvard Theological Review*
IJST	*International Journal of Systematic Theology*
JBL	*Journal of Biblical Literature*
JBR	*Journal of Bible and Religion*
JBT	*Journal of Bible and Theology*
JJE	*Journal of Jewish Ethics*
JQR	*Jewish Quarterly Review*
JRE	*Journal of Religious Ethics*
JSNT	*Journal for the Study of the New Testament*
JSOT	*Journal for the Study of the Old Testament*
JTS	*Journal of Theological Studies*
MT	*Modern Theology*
NTS	*New Testament Studies*

OTE	Old Testament Essays
RE	Religious Education
SCJR	Studies in Christian-Jewish Relations
SJT	Scottish Journal of Theology
TB	Tyndale Bulletin
TrinJ	Trinity Journal
TT	Theology Today
ZAW	Zeitschrift Für Die Alttestamentliche Wissenschaft

Prologue

GALATIANS 4:9A DESCRIBES HOW the Galatians came to know God and received justification from death to being risen in Jesus Christ (2:20). However, despite these encounters with the living Lord, the Galatians went on to engage not only in "basic principles of the world" (4:3), but also in the battlefield (5:17). Taking this into account, the book presented here discusses the ontological characteristics of the church's existence, exploring encounters and antagonisms. What causes the church to be estranged from the Spirit-led life? What does it mean for the church to be under two opposing forces of the Spirit and the flesh? Galatians and baptized believers in general tend to think of this in terms of a binary opposition rather than allowing for a "third way," viewed as neither a community of sin nor a community of the living Jesus Christ. Can this particular way of the church's existence be investigated by both exegetical and theological accounts? Karl Barth's doctrines offer a critical framework for exploring these issues. In his doctrine of creation, Barth utters that nothingness is a third way, which is also captured in terms of his doctrines of election and providence. Theologians discuss Barth's doctrine of nothingness with respect to sin and evil, while acknowledging that Barth did not complete this work.[1] Alongside the existing approaches, my book aims, first of all, to further develop Barth's theology with respect to the doctrine of the word, and second, discuss naming the church as a third way of her existence.

We explore whether the ontological characteristics are influenced by teachings of Scripture, doctrines, and ethical agency. Also, the consequences of the word are given attention, both when the word is in

1. See Hans Urs von Balthasar, Sung-Sup Kim, Wolf Krötke, Paul T. Nimmo, and Gunter Thomas.

harmony with the gospel and law and when it is in tension with them. There are two possible ways to approach this issue. One approach uses the law to fulfill a gospel function, by earning salvation through the works of the law. However, this implies a view of Judaism simply as legalism, characterizing it as primarily law observance for the sake of salvation, and this is not a view I am willing to adopt. Indeed, the primary concern Paul raised in Galatians was that his opponents misrepresented the covenant of grace by prioritizing the law over the gospel. A second approach uses the gospel to fulfill a legal function, deriving ethical norms from the gospel, as Jesus Christ fulfilled the law and replaced it with himself. This approach appears to make the law both unnecessary and irrelevant, but it would be a mistake to assume that it means we no longer need to follow the law. We acknowledge that, while an overemphasis on the law can distort the gospel's purpose, the gospel itself is incomplete without the law. In our discussions throughout the book, therefore, we seek to understand the doctrine of justification achieved by the accord of gospel and law.

Moreover, we assess the discord that deviates from the authentic covenant of grace and how it fosters estrangement, a third way (or the battlefield), and a life guided by the flesh. Specifically, we evaluate the covenant based on the works of the law, which not only misdirects the genuineness of the covenant between God and the elect but is also entangled with the fear of punishment in response to disobedience and the expectation of reward for obedience. Fear and expectation are both used to caution the Galatians and pressurize them into obeying the law ordinance. A discussion of this requires us to analyze the four Old Testament texts in Gal 3:10–13, which illustrate two antithetical concepts: law versus faith and curse versus blessing. By drawing our attention to the texts, we can therefore appraise Paul's intentions and pose the critical questions for investigation. For example, who are "the righteous" in Galatians and Habakkuk? How did Habakkuk describe the righteous as well as the wicked? What did the wicked priest do or not do in the prophecy? Are there parallel deeds between the wicked and the opponents? What were Paul's implication regarding the wicked priest in the prophecy? Who are the wicked pastors in Galatians? Does the passage convey deeper meanings beyond the way we read it? Are there substantial messages we might have missed? These questions must be studied and addressed as they are useful to disclose the doctrine of justification within the covenant of grace. Paying close attention to the meaning of the terms "curse" and "blessing" within the covenant, this study examines traditional views on the antithesis of law and faith, incorporating the prophecy of Hab 2:4b to illuminate the meaning of the law in Galatians. Through this process, we reevaluate Paul's theological claims on righteousness, offering new insights alongside the traditional perspective on justification. We then proceed to review erroneous doctrines, leading the church not only to a third way (or the battleground) but to drift from the Spirit-led life. This gives rise to more questions: Are there any differences between Paul's uses of Scripture and that of his opponents? Did the prophecy of Habakkuk affirm the authenticity of scriptural teachings? A further exploration, resulting from pondering these questions, will determine the modern-day relevance of these declarations by delving into Gal 3:11 and Hab 2:4b and examining the potential hindrances stemming from false doctrines.

This calls for a closer analysis of Barth's claim of *Deus dixit* (God has spoken)—the reality of the word takes place by divine possibility. In the event of *Deus dixit*, we are summoned to the word to agree with it. The *concursus Dei* (divine concurrence) is on one side, and the covenant partner (the Galatians and all others) on the other. There is also the Spirit walking with the church while God accompanies our free and contingent activities and confirms divine activity. The analysis indeed substantiates that the church is to align with the divine commands of God, which are perceived as permission and prohibition. In this alignment, we are not only to discover the specific meaning and purpose of God's will and acts for the church in Jesus Christ but to witness a collaboration between divine freedom and our freedom. This takes us to first examine the relationship between human freedom and the characteristics of the church, particularly as they relate to the word commanding. Second, we review the church's tendency toward passivity when responding to God's commands, which does not imply that the church is incapable of hearing Jesus Christ. We then explore how estrangement and a third way contribute to this passivity. The following points will be covered: What will inspire the church to align her freedom with the freedom of the Trinity? What motivates her to walk in the freedom of the Spirit rather than unfreedom? Can the church, in estrangement and the third way, witness *concursus Dei*? To field these questions, we scrutinize the notion of *concursus Dei* to resolve the dichotomy between human acts vs. acts of God.

Alongside, we acknowledge that the word is commanding and arose from a particular history involving temporary expression and demands. This intrigues us, and we are moved to investigate whether that same divine purpose for the Galatians, and us, can live on in the present. What makes the church hear this continuity? What prohibits her from this hearing? Drawing on Barth's doctrinal insights, we assess how God's original commands to Abraham are still relevant and what the core purpose is for believers today and in the future. The next logical step seeks to recapture the history of a single covenant and its divine purpose for all, thereby preserving the church by divine grace through a lineage that stretches from Abraham to Galatians and to us today. This portion of the book, therefore, focuses on a critical exploration of 4:9a (self-revealing God) and 4:4–6 (God sending the Son), appraised through the threefold form of the word that engages with the pre-existent Jesus, the God of Israel, the Trinity, and the *concursus Dei*. Reading Galatians as part of this investigation is particularly fascinating because it allows us to view the relationship between divine speech and its revelatory co-occurrence of past, present, and future: we witness more history of the covenant of grace as declared to the Galatians. We thus highlight the teachings of Galatians that are relevant to us today, even if the challenges we face are quite different. In view of these challenges, this book evaluates the theological shifts in the I–Thou relationship and offers constructive suggestions for modifying these shifts through the centrality of Scripture and the restoration of pure doctrines, based on a new orientation presented within its pages.

In short, Galatians provides a highly influential framework from Paul that has reshaped our perspective on the essential nature of the Christian community. Galatians accordingly constitutes a solid theological resource for investigating the characteristics of the church's existence, examined through Barth's doctrines and exegetical accounts. We explore this with reference to a third way, i.e., describing the church as a particular way of her existence—neither a community of sin nor a community of revelation. We also reevaluate Paul's theological claims on righteousness and the word as both divine command and the unity of gospel and law; this approach sets out to unveil new insights into the meaning of law in the prophecy and Galatians. The book furthermore demonstrates the interconnected explanations between elements of revelation and Scripture, doctrines, and the word. This interconnection formulates theological insights relating to a through line of arguments and, in doing so, connects all the disparate elements of revelation. The arguments naturally join in a conversation about systematic theology, biblical exegesis, and the life of the covenant community to disclose the foundations of a concrete life and speech for the church. My book therefore offers profound theological explorations of exegetical accounts that connect with Barth's doctrines, providing original contributions and potential implications for the church as hearers.

Introduction

SYNOPSIS

BAPTIZED BELIEVERS NOT ONLY live by a new "I" (Gal 2:20) after receiving the resurrected Christ (1:1[1]) but also live under two opposing forces—the Spirit and the flesh—each pushing against the other (5:17). On the one hand, flesh-led life mutes the new "I" by pulling away from Spirit-led life and renounces the promise of baptism.[2] On the other hand, we repel the powers of the flesh and live life in the Spirit who dwells in us. In the speech and life of the church, put another way, these two opposing forces are observed in moments of the church's life. Living under this new "I," the church hears the word in the Spirit of God and encounters a momentary revelation: our lives are led by the Spirit, urging us to pray directly to God and confirming that we belong to God. These moments are evident in the lives of Galatian Christians when they have come to know God (4:9a) and are enlightened by the knowledge of Jesus Christ. The Abba cry (4:6b) is confirmation of "children of God," the extraordinarily high status requiring covenantal obligations. This signifies that the Galatians are not merely in reception of "the Spirit bearing witness" but also pursuing a life of the fruit of the Spirit (5:22–23). In contrast, some other moments arise when we are estranged from the word. These moments in the life of the church are apparent when the "I" (2:20) is disordered and pulls away from Spirit-led life, engaging in pagan activities, the deadly sins, and the basic principles of the world (4:3). These estrangements,

---

1. The resurrected Christ (Gal 1:1) is identical to the "Spirit" (2 Cor 3:17a) who is given to believers and dwells in them. See Betz, *Galatians*, 124.

2. Betz, *Galatians*, 277–90.

caused by the flesh-led life (5:19–21), constantly disrupt the peace of the communal life of the church.

In addition to the dualistic characteristics, there is also a battleground of the Spirit and the flesh, as outlined by Gal 5:17. This third way of the church's existence is paralleled by Karl Barth's doctrine of nothingness.[3] Specifically, nothingness belongs to a negative side of creation, although it is harmless and innocent. It is "an unavoidable by-product of divine activity: insofar as God in eternity wills positively to elect humanity in Jesus Christ as the purpose and goal of creation, there is something which God does not will."[4] Nothingness is what God rejects, and what God rejects is divine non-willing. Peculiarly, God grants "impossible possibility"[5] in nothingness, and through this, we recognize Jesus Christ, who is "the objective ground of knowledge of sin and nothingness."[6] This recognition brings us to an awareness of our sin and the acceptance of Jesus Christ as our savior, without whom we would be eternally lost. Nothingness is then paradoxical, contradicting God's self-manifestation in the incarnate Word and deepening the knowledge of Jesus Christ. God allows this paradox and gives us freedom to exercise impossible possibility under divine grace. Nothingness is therefore associated with limitless freedom and yet may or may not escort us to sin because the actuality of sin only exists when breaking God's law (while we are never truly sinless). As such, nothingness is impossible possibility, and the new "I" is subdued in certain moments of the church's life. In other words, the church in nothingness—i.e., a third way of the church's existence—is neither a community of sin nor a community of encountered revelation because the "I" has not yet fallen into sin or entered into the experience of the word.

An important question to consider is thus what changes the church in estrangement and a third way of her existence, and what it must do to become attuned to the word in the Spirit of God. The truth is that the church exists and continues when in dialogue with God's self-revealing nature. Simply put, God speaks, and the church hears. John Webster states that the church "is brought into being and carried by the Word; it *is* (as Reformers often put it) *solo verbo*. The 'Word' from which the church has its being is thus the lordly creativity of the one who, as Father, Son,

---

3. See *CD* III/3, 289–368.
4. Nimmo, "Karl Barth," 292.
5. *CD* III/3, 351.
6. *CD* III/3, 309.

and Holy Spirit, *calls* into being the things that are not."[7] The word as revelation gives us an irresistible view of God's will, and drives us beyond ourselves: the church as hearers, in faith and obedience, integrates herself into the gospel of salvation proclaimed in the risen Jesus Christ.

Using this groundwork, chapter 1 explores the hermeneutical approaches of Gal 2:15–21 with Paul's claim that "Christ lives in me" (2:20). This "I" died and rose in Christ, an expression as the first-person singular, is shifted from the first-person plural (vv. 15–17) and remains through verse 21. This change signifies Paul's intention to declare justification for all that was achieved by Jesus Christ. In this context, first, the biblical exegesis reveals the two characteristics of the Galatian churches that are evident when the Galatians align themselves with the Spirit or counter the work of the Spirit in them. This polarity of the church is also appraised through the doctrine of election. In particular, the elected community of God, according to Barth, is described as a twofold typology elected together in unity, whereby Jesus Christ is both the crucified Messiah of Israel and the risen Lord of the church. Second, the typology of the elected community is assessed using biblical exegesis and its doctrinal engagement. Third, Paul's opponents pressure the Galatians with their teaching on "the works of the law" as a means of justification. This teaching misguides the eschatological judgment of God, which can be met through faith in Jesus Christ, although this does not imply that the law should be disregarded. Looking into the conflicts of the Galatians, the section assesses two doctrines (one taught by Paul and the other by the opponents) and the unity of the word in gospel and law.

This sets up arguments on the covenant of works recognized by federal theology with the illogical nature of the law, causing the ambiguous distinction between the law and grace in addition to hearing the command of God's judgment as the fear of punishment and the expectation of reward. This disingenuousness escalates the law with its promise and threats, for the covenant of works promises eternal life to those who obey but threatens eternal punishment to those who disobey. The covenant is derailed from the covenant of grace, and some of the main derailments are discussed, including Paul's defense of the gospel, particularly the way in which Gal 3:10–14 speaks of curse and blessing as associated with the punishments and rewards of the works-based covenant. On the contrary, the covenantal righteousness of God's elect is attained through faith in

---

7. Webster, *Holy Scripture*, 44. Italics his.

Christ, including obligation of the law as a means of justification. Approaching the passage with both biblical exegesis and its doctrinal understanding, I argue that it is necessary to comprehend the command as God's judgment via the doctrines of justification and sanctification, leading us to eschatological blessing in our temporal consecration. The word commanding is also appraised with respect to the church hearing the word of God in both gospel and law within the covenant of grace.

Chapter 2 introduces "a third way" of the church's existence, with neither the elected community encountering revelation nor estranged from it. Namely, this particular way of the church's existence is viewed neither as a community of sin nor a community of those who encounter the living Christ.

First, with respect to the "I" (2:20) in the context of Gal 5:17, various interpretations help to understand the tension in the overlap of the Spirit and the flesh (5:17). One common way to read the verse is grounded in the superiority of the Spirit.[8] The power and efficacy of the Spirit influence the flesh while, under the guidance of the Spirit, believers in their powers—to some extent—live by the Spirit. As the work of the Spirit is stronger than that of the flesh, it transforms flesh-led desire, will, and feeling. After all, believers desire to do good even when the flesh is opposed to the Spirit. We really desire virtues for the church and for Christian lives even when the communal life led by the flesh is opposed to the life guided by the Spirit. Besides, the flesh struggles against the Spirit, not directly against believers. Since the advent of the Spirit, the Spirit itself is opposed to the flesh and inspires the fruit-bearing living by drawing believers into God's presence. This does not mean that believers do not have to participate in the battleground between the Spirit and the flesh. Rather, we strive to obey the truth as the Spirit directs us to the goodness of God, and our actions, with the help of the Spirit, are to concur with divine activity. On this basis, our discussion advances the overlap of the Spirit and the flesh and its relationship to the word of God commanding as appraised with both systematic expositions of Barth's doctrines and exegetical accounts.

Paralleling the overlap of the Spirit/flesh (5:17), second, Barth's doctrine of nothingness articulates a third way, and I expand his doctrine within the context of the word in its threefold form (detailed in chapter 3). First of all, this third way is assessed by means of Barth's doctrines

---

8. See Zahl, "Drama of Agency," 335–52.

of election and justification, which speak of *opus alienum Dei* and *opus proprium Dei*. I argue that the third way can be described as the overlap between the threat of nothingness and God's providence, whereby we are under the influences of two opposites, where human sin (a concrete form of nothingness) is not actualized and our freedom corresponding to the word is unmotivated. This discussion leads us to scrutinize the third way (or the battleground) through the notions of freedom and unfreedom, explicated by Karl Barth and Søren Kierkegaard respectively. They claim the theological overlap in their own distinctive approaches and share a mutual understanding regarding the nature of freedom and unfreedom. Subsequently, we discuss the purpose of the command of God: hearing the command, we must align ourselves with the word in our freedom, for our choice determines the outcome—the fruit of the Spirit or the lusts of the flesh. Freedom, indeed, comes only from walking in the Spirit (5:16); the Spirit not only opposes the flesh but also guides us to living in the form of becoming a new being in Christ—"walk by the word" so we align ourselves with God. Put another way, hearing and receiving the word of God—"walk by the Spirit"—is emphasized. The last section of this chapter thus discusses that our freedom in Jesus Christ, corresponding to the word of God, is avowed in the covenant of grace.

Chapter 3 declares the church to freely experience the word, opening with a discussion of Gal 4:4–6, God sending the Son who preexists. Jesus Christ, the mediator of the covenant between God and all, preexists both creation and his eschatological manifestation. Engaging in exegetical expositions of the preexistent Jesus Christ, first, we assess the tradition of preexistent Wisdom, which is perceived as a personified being before creation. Rabbis and Hellenistic Jews respectively further developed the tradition, and Wisdom became Torah amongst the Tannaim and Logos for the Alexandrian Jews, especially Philo.[9] It is critical to recognize that the significance of the Torah became clear through the conflicts between the opponents' teachings and Paul's declaration of Jesus Christ, because the early church had a firm grasp of it.

Second, Barth's preexistent Jesus Christ is the one to be incarnated, hovering the dimension of transcendence over time and space in the context of the Christian proclamation. The church is to understand continuity within the context of the biblical notion of time and space, which involves, in the two Testaments, connecting our time to consummation.

---

9. Hamerton-Kelly, *Pre-Existence, Wisdom, and the Son*, 19–20.

This follows the systematic exposition of the threefold form of the word: proclamation, Scripture, and revelation. Namely, the church's preaching, Scripture, and the revelation of Jesus Christ are thus one and the same word of God. Entailing God's pretemporal decision on the election in Jesus Christ prior to creation, Barth's doctrine of the word in its threefold form is investigated via the biblical perception of time and space. The word is denoted as fulfilled time, articulated by the time of expectation and recollection of both the Old and New Testaments and by the time of both witnessing and anticipating revelation. This fulfilled time continues to the present and into the future, taking us to engage with the God of Israel in the Old Testament and the Trinity in the New Testament.

The next discussion involves the grasp of double agency (divine and human agencies), in the event of the word, in which the coexistence of the agency on the same plane is theoretically impossible but only possible by God's grace.[10] With this grasp, the doctrines of the *concursus Dei* and the I-Thou encounter are considered. Also, the revelation of the word attested in Scripture is appraised with the church's participation, sharing the knowledge of God. This considers Gal 4:9a, particularly the way the Galatians "have come to know God" (rather than "to be known by God"). They (and we) have come to know God only because God made Godself known to them (and us). God's self-disclosure—divine initiative in the Spirit—therefore involves their (and our) knowledge of God. The Galatians acquired the knowledge when they heard the gospel that Paul preached (1:8–9, 11–12).[11] This leads to the discussion of the church testifying about the word of God spoken from eternity—bringing time into God's own time as the word proclaims—and we in return confess the *concursus Dei* within the I-Thou relation.

In conclusion, I emphasize the significance of hermeneutics with doctrinal interconnectedness, which can restore a coherent theology of Scripture. Also, the declaration "Christ lives in us" is reassured within the covenant of grace. The pressure of the law ordinance that the Galatians faced might be irrelevant to some modern readers, as the challenge we face is quite different from those the early church encountered. Of these challenges, we confront theological shifts in the I-Thou relationship caused by commodity. We live in an era of a consumer culture related to God, theology, and church. Those shifts misconstrue the word as God's command

---

10. *CD* I/2, 790–91.

11. de Boer, *Galatians*, 273.

in Scripture, resulting in fluctuation between God and the elect. Some theologians indicate that theological education has moved away from the centrality of Scripture and its critical biblical interpretations with teaching of doctrines.[12] Learning from our investigations on biblical exegesis of Galatians and its interrelated doctrinal approaches, I argue that the reorientation of the shifts is achieved through our scrupulous examinations, restoring pure doctrines and the centrality of Scripture.

The Prophecy of Habakkuk and the Covenant of Grace

This auxiliary chapter first explores the prophecy of Habakkuk in order to see the purpose of Paul citing Hab 2:4b as we read the prophecy with traditional hermeneutics and the commentary of Pesher Habakkuk (1QpHab). Second, we investigate the function of Hab 2:4b in its wider context of the pesher and its immediate context of Galatians. With this knowledge, Paul's theological claim on righteousness is appraised, and this assessment appreciates new insights of the meaning of law in the prophecy, which furthers traditional views. Third, we scrutinize the wicked priest and the opponents, showing similarities in their deeds and teachings as well as their use of Scripture. The chapter then considers the history of God's covenanting with Abraham, based on the covenant of grace and salvation. This discussion leads us not only to instill the one covenant of both the Old and New Testaments but also to deliberate the covenant and its relationship to the word of God.

METHODOLOGY: HERMENEUTICS AND ITS INTERCONNECTED DOCTRINAL ENGAGEMENT

My methodology is comparable to that of Richard B. Hays, particularly the way in which Hays evaluates specific texts that convey what lies under Paul's arguments—the texts function as "a 'mode of recapitulation,' restating and defending the basic content of [Paul's] message"[13] in the letter of Galatians. In his analysis of narrative christological formulation, Hays examines Gal 4:3–6 and 3:13–14 to find their differences and commonalities as they can assist in developing understandings of the texts and their relationship with the substructure. Hays argues that 4:4–5 and

12. E.g., Webster, *Holy Scripture*.
13. Hays, *Faith of Jesus Christ*, 73.

3:13 come together in the narrative structure: "They are united, *at the level of Paul's usage of them*, in a single-story structure."[14] Paul's message in 4:4–5, an integral story about Jesus, should be read within 4:3–6, since Paul's teaching and messages are shaped by the story of God's redemptive act through the faithfulness of Jesus Christ.

In a similar fashion but different from Hays's analysis, I employ in this study systematic, exegetical narratives that integrate interpretation of Galatians into doctrinal approaches. The core of my argument lies in the notion that Jesus Christ lives in us, living, acting, and speaking, and we, the covenant partners of God, hear the word addressed to us. Centered on "Christ lives in [us] . . . [and we] live by faith in the Son of God" (2:20 NIV), I therefore explore two dynamic characteristics of the church—estrangement and encountering—and their doctrinal engagements with the passages in 2:15–21 and 3:10–14. A third way of the church's existence, defined neither as encountering nor estrangement, is examined with Barth's doctrines, and its interconnected exegetical approaches are appraised with respect to 5:17 within an immediate context of 5:16–18. Furthermore, I highlight God sending the Son (4:4–6) and the revelation (4:9a), scrutinizing this through the doctrine of the word in its threefold form, which involves the biblical notion of time–space, the God of Israel and the Trinity, the *concursus Dei*, and the I–Thou encounter.

Within a broader context of Galatians, 4:1–11 and other passages are integrated into the arguments in each chapter. In addition, the four cited texts from the Old Testament in 3:10–13 are investigated by means of traditional views as well as the prophecy of Habakkuk, which is assessed in depth from the pesherist's perspective, revealing Paul's arguments against the opponents.

The discussions in the book are primarily interwoven with the hermeneutics of the Galatians and their interrelated doctrinal engagement but are also presented with the doctrine of the word, specifically considering the coherence of the word as both gospel and law.

---

14. Hays, *Faith of Jesus Christ*, 111. Italics his.

Chapter 1

The Twofold Typology of the Elected Community

THIS CHAPTER EXPLORES FIRST various hermeneutic approaches of "I" died and rose in Christ (Gal 2:20) within the immediate context (2:19–21), and its two dynamic characteristics corresponding to the work of the Spirit. Second, the same characteristics are dealt with in considering the election of the community and its relationship to the word as the unity of gospel and law. The third section of the chapter also examines hermeneutic understandings of 3:10–14 and interconnected doctrinal engagements. In particular, the nature of a works-based covenant and the way the covenant perceives the command as God's judgment are assessed. This assessment exposes the doctrines of justification and sanctification from their temporality to eternity, with respect to the covenant of grace.

THE POLARITY OF THE CHURCH

Galatians 2:20 first and foremost teaches that we have a new "I,"[1] which is compared with the inner concept of "our old self" (Rom 6:6), identical

---

1. We identify the "I" (Gal 2:19–21) as a collective of baptized individuals. See Best, *One Body in Christ*; according to Best, "the individual Christian is in Christ; but it is not only the individual, as individual, who is in Christ; groups of Christians are regarded as in him; thus the Churches of Judaea are in Christ (Gal. 1. 22; cf. 1 Thess. 2. 14; 1.

to the "flesh" and the "sinful body." "Our old self," which previously led us to live against what God demands of us, dies and rises with Christ in baptism—that is, the old "I" is dead, but the resurrected Christ (Gal 1:1) and the self-sacrifice of the Son of God as an act of love lives in the "I." The risen Christ is, in fact, identical to the "Spirit" (2 Cor 3:17a) given to believers and dwelling in them.[2] The gospel of "Christ in me" is therefore actualized by the work of the Spirit uniting the "I" with Christ. In this event (the baptism of the Spirit), the new "I" not only witnesses but also corresponds—freely and obediently—to the divine work of Jesus Christ, through which all people are reconciled to God. In the righteousness of Jesus Christ, put differently, the baptism of the Spirit connects to the union with the believer in whom Christ lives. We confess that we have been crucified with Jesus Christ; we do not live in the flesh but live by faith in the Son of God, who rose from the dead and took over our lives of the flesh, previously leading us to live against what Scripture teaches. After all, our sins vanished in the baptism of the Spirit so that we may be raised up with a new self. We died with Jesus Christ so that we might also live with him. Verse 20 is therefore crucial in demonstrating the justification achieved from the salvific event of the cross, as the conflict between law-obedience and faith is resolved in understanding the significant meaning of the righteousness that Jesus Christ accomplished.

Commentators offer various interpretations to grasp the assurance of "I" on justification coming through Jesus Christ. In general, they agree with the theme of dying to the law in Gal 2:19–21, signifying the invalidation of the law. In addition, verse 20 is treated as Paul's own confession to support his claim on justification, as Paul notably shifts from the first-person plural (vv. 15–17) to the first-person singular (v. 18), and "I" remains through verse 21. The first-person singular emphasizes that Paul's ethnic background demands crucifixion with Christ, expressing his personal relationship between God and himself as "Christ in me," including "the Spirit dwelling in me." Further, many view this shift as Paul's intention to include all, corresponding to verse 15—he intends to remove the barrier between gentiles and Jews escalated in the Antioch

---

1). A congregation can be said to be in Christ just as easily as an individual" (25). Best also writes that "Christ, the whole Christ, dwells in each believer; but it is the corporate whole of believers who dwell in Christ. It is Christ who lives in Paul (Gal. 2. 20); but it is Paul and his fellow-believers together who live in Christ . . . all [members] can be said to be 'in him,' and he can be said to be in each of them" (9–10).

2. Betz, *Galatians*, 123–26.

incident. In other words, the union is not limited to his ethnicity as Paul makes his argument relevant to the situation of the Galatians and to the biased view of the Antioch incident. Verse 20 thereby settles the doctrine of justification for believers who participate in divine righteousness on the basis of Christ's work of salvation through the Spirit. As a result of the faithfulness of Jesus Christ, we are freed from the law and justified before God, which resonates with Paul's declaration in the rest of the letter.

Many scholars, moreover, delve into the union to signify spiritual rebirth through the death of Jesus Christ on the cross, with the believer participating with him in his crucifixion. Albert Schweitzer interprets the union with Jesus Christ—"Christ lives in me" and "I live by faith of the Son of God"—as Christian mysticism. As such, the sacraments of baptism and of the Lord's Supper are means of mystical participation—i.e., "the mysticism of the being-in-Christ."[3] Alternatively, dying and rising with Christ as a mythical participation in the coming kingdom of God is perceived by "the concept of the pre-Messianic tribulation"[4] as the first Christians bring their sufferings into relation with that of Jesus. Distinct from a subjective mystical experience, according to Lewis B. Smedes, the unity of persons "in Christ," whereby we are members of the new, forgiven people, is analogous to their unity "in Adam," whereby we are members of the old, sinful people. The union represents the beginning of a new history with all who are incorporated in Christ as we not only die "in Adam" by his act, giving the history of destiny, but also are alive "in Christ" by his act, giving the history of a new destiny—both Christ and Adam were decisive on the history of humanity on account of each event.[5] Martin Luther and John Calvin are both attentive to Christ's righteousness, which connects to the believer in whom Christ lives. For Luther, first, we by nature cannot join Christ as the "I" is bound to the law, which always falls short in justifying one before God. However, the law functions to evoke the sinfulness in human nature and, at the same time, drives us closer to Christ: justification cannot be carried out by the law if the law is not of faith. We are justified through Jesus Christ, who exchanged himself with sin for the believer, and we in return receive his righteousness. Luther regards this union as a "joyous duel":

---

3. Schweitzer, *Mysticism of Paul*, 20.
4. Schweitzer, *Mysticism of Paul*, 144.
5. Smedes, "Being in Christ," 149–50.

> Paul would like to draw us away completely from looking at the Law, sin, death, and other evil things, and to transfer us to Christ, in order that there we might see this very joyous duel: the Law battling against the Law, in order to become liberty to me; sin battling against sin, in order to become righteousness to me; death battling against death, in order that I might have life. For Christ is my devil against the devil, that I might be a son of God; He destroys hell, that I might have the kingdom of heaven.[6]

In this joyous duel, we are one body in the Spirit, signifying that righteousness, life, grace, and eternal salvation are present, but the Law, sin, and death are absent. Paul, for Luther, directs us to see the justification through faith in Christ, which is far from the works of the flesh.[7] Second, Calvin recognizes that "'I' living in Christ" can be accomplished by holding real and actual communication with Jesus Christ.[8] This denotes that the life of "I" is governed by the Spirit of Christ who makes "I" a partaker of his righteousness, for we are justified by free grace. That is to say, Christ grants us participation in his righteousness "so that, while we can do nothing of ourselves, we are accepted in the sight of God."[9] For Calvin, the works of the Spirit in sanctification and justification are inseparably joined together, and our union with Jesus Christ thus has the double benefits of being justified and sanctified.[10] The benefits make apparent that Jesus Christ truly lives in the believer, in finding "a fluid way"[11] of justification and sanctification in union with Christ. In light of this, verse 20 aligns well with the eschatological passage of 5:22–25, for "Christ in me" guides all our actions and reveals their connection with Christian life through those who participate in achieving expectations of the eschatological promise.[12]

In addition, Roy Ciampa interprets the verse with respect to the two ages—the passing of the "present evil age" (1:4) and the commencement of a new post-resurrection age in Jesus Christ.[13] The "present evil age" from which Jesus Christ has redeemed us ended the old community as

---

6. Luther, *Lectures on Galatians*, 164.
7. Luther, *Lectures on Galatians*, 168; See Luther, *Galatians*, 112–32.
8. Calvin, *Galatians and Ephesians*, 57.
9. Calvin, *Galatians and Ephesians*, 57.
10. Chester, "When the Old Was New," 326–27.
11. Chester, "When the Old Was New," 326.
12. My emphasis on 2:20 and its close relation to 5:22–25.
13. Ciampa, *Presence and Function of Scripture*, 203–15.

The Twofold Typology of the Elected Community

the death (2:20) to the law took place: "Israel's death (exile)," writes Ciampa, "occurred through the execution of the curses of the Mosaic covenant and law upon the sinful people of God."[14] This indicates that God's restoration establishes the newly created community in terms of the death and resurrection of Jesus Christ. Specifically, Ciampa and other scholars have shown that God builds an eschatological community by employing Jeremiah's metaphor (Jer 1:10); God plants a new covenant community after uprooting the exiled one because of its disobedience to the law. Namely, the Mosaic covenant pertaining to the old pre-resurrection community, on the one hand, is thus uprooted. God, on the other hand, inaugurates "a new beloved Jerusalem"[15] in a post-resurrection context.

Enhancing these interpretations, Karl Barth offers a refined dogmatic approach to the notion that "Christ in me/I in Christ" is the divine presupposition of our existence as it is founded in the Elector and Elected Christ who fulfills the objective status of "I" in the election of a community. Through the event, the "I"—facilitated by the election of the church—is delivered in Jesus Christ and called to live as a covenant partner with God. This union is, for Barth, described as a covenantal partnership, which entails the election of a community in the Elector and Elected Christ. That is, the election of individuals is truly born out of the hearing church elected in Elector Jesus Christ, who is also elected. The baptized "I"—elected in and with the church—witnesses the living Christ as the church corresponds to God, who "in His Son or Word elects Himself, and in and with Himself elects His people."[16]

We attain the event of the union by the faithfulness of God, who sent the Son, for we—sinful and yet baptized—are judged and justified. In the history of every believer, the event of coupling[17]—"Christ in us" and "we in Christ"—thus creates the beginning of our new history[18] as we

---

14. Ciampa, *Presence and Function of Scripture*, 209.

15. Brueggemann, *To Pluck Up*, 24.

16. *CD* II/2, 76.

17. We will discuss in depth what I call "the experience of coupling" with respect to the word of God in its threefold form in chapter 3. Briefly, I will argue: because of the Christ who lives in us, our soul encounters the word, and we are thus to be coupled with the word via the indwelling of the Spirit as a mode of divine action operating in us. That is, we receive God's revelation through the Spirit of God, who is also the Spirit of the word. This argument is comparable to Barth's claims of "the experience of the Word" and "*Deus dixit*," which will be also appraised in the chapter.

18. This phrase "Christ in us and we in Christ" signifies not only an individual election but also the elected community. See also *CD* IV/4, 19–100.

grasp the event of Jesus Christ emerging into our own salvific history. For Barth, "*Christ in us* is never the process by which 'we' apprehend the divine word addressed to us, and therefore that it must never be identified with 'our' perception."[19] Achieved by the power of the Spirit, Jesus Christ effects the union, and we become aware of our very existence through participation, not just passively but actively, in God's grace.[20] This participation entails that we in freedom and obedience correspond to what God demands of us. It does not lie within our own capacity, even though this partnership places the emphasis on the "I"'s partaking in faith and obedience, corresponding to God's freedom—the authentic freedom of the Trinity. This means, on the one hand, that God freely wills us to associate Godself with all of us that we—in our freedom in Jesus Christ—will to be the companion. What God wills and determines is thus demonstrated via the interwoven essence of the partnership and freedom of the church. On the other hand, for the participation is associated with the event of reconciliation, God is benevolent to the faith of the "I" with the capacity for seeing God at reconciliation: "Christ in the I" is the word of God addressed to us, and thus the church—a collective group of individual "Christ in me and I in Christ"—hears the word in faith and obedience.

The "Christ in us and we in Christ" thus embodies particular essences, reflecting that the presence of the Spirit of Christ in us governs the communal life of the church, and this is evident in the lives of the Galatians. Precisely, first, the Galatians were raised in Jesus Christ, and the Spirit of Christ dwelled in them. By the work of the Spirit, they received the Spirit of adoption. A correlation consequently exists between receiving adoptions and receiving the Spirit, engaging in a new relationship with God. As the status of believers is changed by the grace of God, the Spirit draws them to God the Father, and they evidently call "Abba Father" (4:6b) because of their indwelling in the Spirit of Christ, who cries out to God the Father on behalf of the believer.[21] The Abba declaration is not only the firmness and confirmation of "children of God" but also sets out that enslavement and being God's children are mutually

---

19. Barth, *Romans*, 286. Italics his. Additionally, Barth writes that "this is the condition of that liberty which is ours beyond the law; this is the solution of the riddle which religion sets before us with such intolerable precision" (285).

20. *CD* IV/4, 6.

21. Betz, *Galatians*. Betz notes that "Gentiles and Jews do indeed call God 'Father' in different languages, but the cry of both is the same, since both cry 'Father.' The doubling of the invocation 'Father' seems to reflect the bilingual character of the early church" (211).

exclusive. Put differently, the Galatians were truly adopted as children of God through the Spirit of Christ by God's law and justice. Receiving the extraordinarily high status of God's children, their status was changed from unrighteous to "becoming right with God." Becoming right with God was required and punishment of sin demanded, with the life, death, and resurrection of God's Son Jesus Christ satisfied and fulfilled God's justice and law. Second, the Galatians "have come to know God" (4:9a) and gained the knowledge of God because God in divine grace revealed Godself to them. The Galatians are, as Paul urges, to remember the illumined knowledge of God (i.e., "the experience of coupling"). Indeed, "to know" (v. 9a) means "to experience" in the biblical sense—"in being sons of God" (3:26) and "having the Spirit of [God's] Son" (4:6), rather than "to perceive" or "to acquire knowledge about."[22] This "knowing" originates with God, who is the source of the relationship. The encounter through God's self-revealing motivates them, as children of God, to disengage in the elemental spirits—e.g., "the basic principles of the world" (4:3). Third, a fruit-bearing communal life of the Spirit (5:22–23) validates the "divine life" that is empowered by the indwelling Jesus Christ and faith in him. Namely, the Galatians are justified in Christ through having died and been raised in Christ and called to live a sanctified life to become *imago Dei*. By the gift of the Holy Spirit, they are to grow in goodness and live in good acts, speech, and minds.

Unlike these encounters, nevertheless, we read some passages where the Galatian Christians show a tendency to resist the work of the Spirit in them. In these passages, they are estranged, and the baptized "I" is disordered and pulls away from life in the Spirit, accordingly falling under the influence of the flesh. That is to say, justification is affected by law-observance, meaning that the Galatians consequently become enslaved to the law, which is employed as a means of making them righteous. This estrangement is evident in Paul's concern that the Galatians would return to the slavery of the flesh, allowing themselves to be subjected to "the basic principles of the world" (*Stoicheia*; 4:3).[23] Paul figuratively

22. Longenecker, *Galatians*, 180.

23. *Stoicheia* is a difficult term with several meanings, such as the code of behavior set forth in Jewish law or quasi-demonic powers that oppress humans. "Either way, Paul's *we* includes Jews and Gentiles in a common state of slavery before Christ" (Attridge, *HarperCollins Study Bible*, 1978); Longenecker, *Galatians*, 165–66. According to Longenecker, "the meaning of τὰ στοιχεῖα has to do with 'elements that make up a series,' 'inherent components,' or members of a row'" (165). He also cites Gerhard Delling's definitions of στοιχεῖα, which is composed of the four elements (earth, water, air, and

describes the two concepts of legal adoption and enslavement (4:1–3)[24] as "under the law," for the law contains "basic principles of the world" (τὰ στοιχεῖα), which is synonymous with "under the law" (3:23). Another estrangement is apparent in 4:8–11 when Paul warns the Galatians, reminding them of what they were "formerly." Before coming to Christ, the Galatians were "enslaved to beings that by nature are not gods" (v. 8), implying their past involvement in the service of idolatry, although Paul does not mention the details of their former religion. Nevertheless, they took up "the weak and beggarly elemental principles" (v. 9b) and fell back under the estrangement. They are consequently alienated from God who first revealed Godself to them, recognizing God with their worship. Other moments of estrangement are portrayed in 5:19–21, where such life lived as the flesh constantly disrupts the peace of the communal life as it is directly opposed to the life in the Spirit, the virtues of which are depicted in 5:22–23, permitting inheritance of the kingdom of God.

The two characteristics of the church, encountering and estrangement, are revealed in Barth's doctrine of the election of the community. In particular, the elected community of God witnesses the election of Jesus Christ, corresponding to the double predestination of Jesus Christ. The elected community has the twofold feature that Jesus Christ is both the crucified Messiah of Israel and the risen Lord of the church. The first characteristic relates to our inclination to turn away from God, and

---

fire), refers to the fundamental principles or rudimentary teachings of subjects (such as music, mathematics, and child care), and implies the stars and other heavenly bodies because they are composed of the chief and finest of the elements—fire—incorporating the stellar spirits, gods, demons, and angels. Also, he argues "Paul takes κόσμος in an ethical sense to mean 'worldly' with its synonym being 'fleshly,' as opposed to 'spiritual' (cf. *Comment* on 'flesh' and 'spirit' in 5:13–26). Thus Jews under the law were 'under the basic principles of the world,' with τοῦ κόσμου used here in much the same way as it appears later in Heb 9:2 with reference to the tabernacle, which is called τὸ ἅγιον κοσμικόν ('a worldly sanctuary')" (166). According to Betz, a large number of scholars conclude that "these 'elements of the world' represent demonic forces which constitute and control 'this evil aeon' (1: 4)" (Betz, *Galatians*, 204). See de Boer, *Galatians*, 252–61.

24. Many scholars agree that the legal system derives from Greco-Roman society, but others believe that Paul's illustration does not conform to the specifics of any of these laws—i.e., Roman, Greek, Semitic, or other ancient inheritance laws. In fact, a father-son relationship employs a legal practice made up of guardians and trustees. The son (minor: νήπιος) is bound by rules and regulations and holds legal ownership of his father's inheritance until a time his father has set. This relationship of minors and servants is associated with enslavement to "the basic principles of the world." The term νήπιος (minor) signifies immaturity in the Christian life as Philo explains that it refers to a beginner or pilgrim on the journey from sense perception to virtue. See Longenecker, *Galatians*, 162–64.

accordingly, the determination of God necessitates the rejection and judgment of what God chooses for Godself in Jesus Christ. The second speaks of the determined God turning towards us, and this determination entails fellowship and mercy in God's compassion in Christ. That is, the church exists in its twofold biblical typology—Israel and the church. Israel, the first form of the typology,[25] is appointed with hearing and prearranged the promise of God. The first form recalls the stubbornness of disobedient people and represents people who are unresponsive to Jesus Christ. As a result of this unresponsiveness, the community reflects the divine judgment whereby God elects for Godself in Jesus Christ. At the same time, our election in Jesus Christ attests to the divine judgment that God elects for Godself in Jesus Christ, the crucified Messiah. In him, what God has chosen for us is revealed and determined. This first element of the typology thus represents the elected Jesus being rejected and judged for our disobedience and serves the eschatological *telos* of God. The community in this fold portrays Jesus Christ, who bears judgment and is elected to serve divine judgment. In the second element of the typology, the elected community demonstrates the electing God turning towards the church by virtue of communion in Jesus Christ. They witness God's determined act in Jesus Christ, who is elected for mercy and glory. In other words, the church is responsive to Jesus Christ as the risen Lord. We recognize the divine mercy of God in Jesus Christ, in which God elects humanity in the risen Lord Jesus Christ. As with the first typology, the church hears and receives the promise. At the same time, the church is capable of responding to God in her faithful obedience to the word and therefore grasps the divine election and eternal life in the kingdom of God. On the one hand, therefore, the community in its typology as Israel not only represents divine judgment but also witnesses divine mercy as it remains irrevocably elect in Jesus Christ. On the other hand, the church takes the first form, arising from the history of Israel and witnessing the fulfillment of the election of Israel, whereby God elects people to make a covenant with Godself. The church preexists in the hidden form of Israel from the beginning and thus represents the election of Israel.[26]

25. According to Barth, "[God] elects the people of Israel for the purpose of assuming its flesh and blood. What is really meant by the humanity of the whole elected community of God, what it costs God to make Himself one with it, to be its God, emerges in its Israelite form" (*CD* II/2, 207).

26. Calvin explicitly grasps the dual typology reading of Gal 4:1–7, which narrates the double predestination of the community where Paul allegorically introduces a metaphor of two relationships—father/son and owner/servant—both requiring

The elected community of God—portrayed as the twofold biblical typology—is therefore essentially different but inseparably related to realize the one covenant of grace in Jesus Christ, for differentiation and unity can be known within the election of Jesus Christ as Israel represents the hidden life of the church. The elected community thus has distinctive features, but these are not separate entities as they are together in their unity through the election of Jesus Christ. The community is elected in and together with Jesus Christ—the electing God and elected man—just as individuals are elected in and with Christ. The typology as one entity is identified with an eschatological community, in which Jesus Christ redeems and promises our communion and everlasting covenant. In brief, one church in a twofold typology is elected together in unity. First, the community turns away from the electing God, since she, corresponding to Jesus Christ as the crucified Messiah, portrays our disobedience, which resists our election and therefore attests to the divine judgment. Second, the community evidences the electing God turning towards the church because she, corresponding to Jesus Christ as the risen Lord, represents the Christian community of all who recognize and confess the mercy of God in Jesus Christ. The twofold typology cannot be separated but constitutes a unity in distinction as each accomplishes a role within the divine election. For each typology as God's covenant partner serving the divine *telos*, the typology is designated as the community in Jesus Christ, incorporating both the crucified Messiah of Israel and the resurrected Lord of the church. Both Israel and the church therefore represent a typology of Christ, who is both Elector and Elected. Together, they are also God's elect people as they are God's covenant partners, constituting an accord in a community. The typology of the elected community parallels

---

guardians and trustees. Calvin sees this relationship with the Old Testament, in which God's children are free and yet under the law, lasting until the coming of Jesus Christ. The children of God are the elect, even in the womb, but remain like slaves under the law until, by faith, they come to freedom. For Calvin, thus, the former predestined community existed under the Old Testament and the latter predestined community exists by the New Testament. In other words, those under the Old Testament were divinely elected and kept the obligation to the law, which was regarded as "the everlasting rule of a good and holy life" (Calvin, *Galatians and Ephesians*, 95). Moses, kings, priests, prophets, and believers became subject to the law although they were heirs through Jesus Christ, and their freedom was not yet revealed. They (as the elect) purposefully prefigured God's people, enjoying God's blessings through the Son, who existed before he was sent by the eternal God. With Christ's coming, the double predestined community appoints the elect, who have known Christ and thus no longer require this guardianship or are under enslavement to the basic principles in their lives—to the Torah or to religious practices.

The Twofold Typology of the Elected Community 19

her two characteristics—estrangement and encountering—observed in the life of the Galatian churches. These characteristics are also apparent in the communal life of the church today in which we are raised and in which we die with Jesus Christ.

With our understanding of the polarity of the church, we now turn to discussion of the elected community of the Galatians and the discord between gospel and law, primarily caused by the works-based covenant.

THE ONE WORD OF GOD IN GOSPEL AND LAW

One main crisis that the Galatian churches faced involved perfect obedience, which Paul's opponents[27] pushed. Their message, which Paul calls "another gospel" (1:6–7), centered on the need to observe the law and circumcision (including cultural rites and calendrical customs) so that the Galatian Christians could reach perfection and fully inherit the blessings of Abraham.[28] With the spread of false teaching in Galatia, Paul

---

27. They were Judaizers from the Jerusalem church, who were a higher authority than Paul; Nanos identifies the opponents as outsiders who are not Galatians (Nanos, *Irony of Galatians*, 159–83). For Dunn, the opponents are Christian-Jewish missionaries who came to Galatia to refute Paul's teaching so that his converts become the heirs of Abraham through circumcision and thus are under the law (Dunn, *Galatians*, 9–11); some scholars argue that they were gentiles. Of these, Segal writes, "[Paul's] opponents in Galatia are a circumcising party (*peritemnomenoi*), Christians who accepted circumcision when they converted to Christianity and proselytes of a conservative Christianity in which conversion to Judaism was a necessary prerequisite" (Segal, *Paul the Convert*, 208). See Segal, *Paul the Convert*, 209–18.

28. Perfect obedience has been widely debated by numerous scholars, who have offered slightly different views on the concept of this law-observance. In general, they agree that no human can perfectly fulfill the law and that justification is possible only through faith in Christ. Paul's opponents also agreed that the law cannot be perfectly fulfilled by human effort alone, yet they asserted that perfect obedience is possible with the help of the Spirit. In the view of some scholars, "the law" encompasses not just the Torah and its interpretation but the whole law. For instance, Martin Luther and John Calvin both argue that their opponents' focus on law-keeping extends to the entire law, including its moral, ceremonial, and Torah components; see Lavender, "*Nomos* and the Dispute," 1–19; Lambrecht, "Paul's Reasoning," 53–74. According to Chester, all human works are inadequate before God if we want to be justified by law-observance—that is, "if all parts of the law are equally worthy in their own nature, then one part cannot have been removed from a role in justification while another remains relevant" (Chester, "When the Old Was New," 322). Utilizing his narrative logic in Gal 3:1—4:11, Hays recognizes that Paul's concern does not lie in whether it is possible to fulfill the law; Hays, *Faith of Jesus Christ*, 163–207. For Hays, "Paul rejects the Law not because of an empirical observation that no one can do what it requires but because its claim to give life, explicitly articulated in [Lev 18:5/Gal 3:12] is incompatible with the gospel story, which

responded to a report concerning his opponents who had troubled the Galatian churches and set out his theological claim on justification by faith in Gal 2:15–21. This passage takes up at the end of Paul's dispute with Peter at Antioch (2:11–14), which regarded unqualified gentiles for the table fellowship. The fellowship—which signifies the presence of God—came by way of circumcision, one of the distinguishing features of the identity of Israel as God's people.[29] Accordingly, the people at the table belong to the community, which earned their salvation through the particular regulations of the Mosaic covenant and law. These requirements are employed to define God's people, whom God has chosen for Godself and made covenant with. As the Torah demanded circumcision of all who would enter the people of God, the opponents demanded circumcision of gentiles as the entrance requirement of the covenant. Justification is hence assured by living according to the standards of the law, and in return, redemption and forgiveness of sins are received. Commentators generally agree that Paul's rivals also believed that faith in Jesus Christ was necessary for the eschatological promise and the gentiles were to be incorporated into the people of God. In addition, Paul holds that the Torah was given to Israel as God's gracious gift and considered as a fundamental principle guiding God's elect for both Jews and Gentiles.[30] The law therefore functions as the standard of righteousness that assists believers in grasping the responsibility of being God's people. The ordinance of law itself is, however, inadequate as a means of justification as this misguides the eschatological judgment of God, which can be met through faith in Jesus Christ. At the same time, this does not imply that the law should be disregarded since this law-free gospel has no authority but its own. This suggests that Paul declares the harmony of gospel and law, which must be construed, for justification achieved from the salvific action of Christ

---

says that Christ had to die in order to give life to us (3:13–14; cf. 2:21)" (Hays, *Faith of Jesus Christ*, 179). Sanders affirms "covenantal nomism" by discussing the works of the law and the divine grace in the election; Sanders, *Paul and Palestinian Judaism*, 419–556. See also Lambrecht, "Transgressor by Nullifying God's Grace," 217–36.

29. Garlington writes, "In virtue of the distinction of their peculiar customs [Israelites] do not mix with others to depart from the way of their fathers" (Garlington, *Obedience of Faith*, 262n62). Also, he notes, according to H. Conzelmann, that "since the time of the exile Jews had come to learn that they could survive times in a foreign land with no political independence or temple without losing their identity" (Garlington, *Obedience of Faith*, 262n60). The main reason for excluding the gentiles is because Israelites would engage with idolatry and adultery from nations; so this sense of separateness was reinforced in their exile.

30. See 2 Cor 3:7–18 and chapter 3.

resolves the conflict between faith and the works of the law. Further, the covenantal righteousness of God's elect is attained through faith in Jesus Christ, including the obligation of the law and other practices as means of justification.

The teachings of the opponents, therefore, lack the unity of gospel and law as the law is prioritized, which parallels, according to Barth, the so-called "covenant of works" endorsed by federal theology.[31] This theology focuses on the arbitrary nature of the law, causing the ambiguous distinction between the law and grace: the law became prioritized as it is independent of grace. Ulrich Zwingli first introduced the concept to defend infant baptism by way of analogy with the Abrahamic covenant of circumcision in the Old Testament, as part of which he contributed to the establishment of the covenant of grace between God and humanity.[32] Among federal theologians who have followed the theology, John Coccejus asserts that the first principle of the covenant based on the law was set between God and Adam. The word of God comes to Adam as the law "with its promise and threats,"[33] communicated by God through the prohibition to eat from the tree of the knowledge of good and evil. With this, the tree of life signifies the reward of eternal life promised to those who are in perfect obedience. Adam is given wisdom, free will, innocent spirit, and competence to keep God's command and receive the eternal blessing. Regardless of God's prohibition, Adam freely chooses to do what is forbidden by God, resulting in the loss of his genuine relationship with God. Thus, Adam did not establish his will in obedience and failed to obey. Sin entered, and consequently, Adam and humanity fell under the divine curse and judgment. On this basis, Coccejus focuses on the covenant of works in terms of God's relationship with the human covenant partner, in which divine grace comes subsequently.

First, Coccejus's ruling principle for the covenant is the law. We are preserved by God as we keep the command (the law), but we are incapable of fulfilling our obligation. He writes that "bondage still rules, and with it the fear of death. But all the same the Law, with its demand for righteousness and its types and shadows, is a witness to the promise. Circumcision and the passover already point to the atoning death of Christ."[34] Coccejus argues that the redemption of Jesus Christ demonstrated perfect

---

31. *CD* IV/1, 54–66.
32. *CD* IV/1, 55–59.
33. *CD* IV/1, 59.
34. *CD* IV/1, 60.

righteousness as the obedience of the Son, fulfilling the whole law, and is written on the hearts of every believer by the Holy Spirit. The cross of Jesus Christ frees us from the fear of death, and the redemptive work of Christ extends to building the church among the gentiles. The covenant of works is in agreement that God determines to be merciful and sends a mediator to fallen human partners to make peace between God and humanity. God also promises us eternal life through the works-based covenant when we are obedient and faithful. When we are fallen, though, God redeems us through the covenant of grace.[35] There are thus positive aspects of Coccejus's argument, as William Klempa points out: Coccejus rightly observes human dependence on God as

> the human partner is taken up into communion with God by means of the covenant and is enabled to respond to God's demand only by God's grace. In this respect, Coccejus is faithful to the fundamental idea in Reformation theology that the individual is dependent on God in all things.[36]

However, the works-based covenant offers salvation on the condition of obedience, and, when this condition fails, the covenant of grace is offered freely to those who believe.[37] This covenant, then, for Coccejus, makes the work of Christ secondary, coming after dealing with the performance of the law. Put another way, the death and resurrection of Jesus Christ constitute a condition to meet the demands of the covenant of works or to agree the demands based on a contract term. With respect to sanctification and justification of believers, moreover, Coccejus exhorts us to see that "the Law is now a weapon in the warfare of the spirit against the flesh."[38] By means of law-observance, believers are thus regenerated through taming the sin conflicts we face. According to Barth, for Coccejus, "the regenerate will not commit wilful sin, and from those that remain he will always seek refuge in the grace of God, earnest self-examination, and prayer for a pure heart,"[39] affirming that eschatological redemption is validated by the covenant of works. This method of validation, however, ceases to grasp the authenticity of righteousness before God—the covenant of grace declared by the cross of Jesus Christ. In Jesus Christ, we

---

35. Klempa, "Concept of the Covenant," 101–2.
36. Klempa, "Concept of the Covenant," 104–5.
37. Klempa, "Concept of the Covenant," 103.
38. *CD* IV/1, 60.
39. *CD* IV/1, 60.

are bestowed "eternal life and salvation by the resurrection from the dead in virtue of His merit, in which the souls of the pious participate directly at death,"[40] as Barth emphasizes.

In support of this federal theology, Davis Dickson holds that "the Father has made a covenant (contract) with the Son that *if* the Son fulfills the conditions of the Covenant (contract) of Works for the elect, God will be gracious to the elect. Correspondingly, [God] makes a covenant (contract) for the elect that on the *condition* of faith and repentance they will receive the benefits of Christ's redemptive work."[41] James Torrance, on the other hand, argues that the original *telos* of God's covenanting with us lies in God, who has loved us and redeemed us. He underlines divine love, which brings its obligations; while the obligations of love are not the conditions of love, we are unconditionally loved by free grace.[42] This essence is altered by the covenant of works (like a contract), which demands that we live by the law and stay within the covenantal terms. In line with this, Torrance states,

> The covenant has been turned into a contract, and God's grace made conditional on [human] obedience. It is precisely against this inversion of the order of grace that Paul protests in Galatians 3.17–22. God made a covenant with Abraham, and although the law came four hundred and thirty years later (to spell out the obligations of grace) it did not suddenly introduce conditions of grace. It did not turn the covenant into a contract. To introduce conditions would be to break a promise.[43]

Further, Torrance observes the ambiguity of the gospel when the covenant of grace is subordinated to the preaching of the law and the alteration of atonement, which confusingly declare that "Christ died for you." That is, we are flawed. We are under the law and under judgment. When we repent, however, our repentance brings us the comforts of the gospel, becoming evidence of election and grace. The significance of Jesus Christ here moves away from "what Christ has done for us" to "what we have to do to stay in covenant with God." In the context of preaching, as Torrance

---

40. *CD* IV/1, 60.
41. Torrance, "Covenant or Contract?," 62–63. Italics his.
42. Torrance, "Covenant or Contract?," 56.
43. Torrance, "Covenant or Contract?," 56.

argues, "this means that the emphasis falls less on the indicatives of grace and more on the imperatives of repentance, obedience and faith."[44]

Just as Barth notes the positive aspects of federal theology, Klempa agrees with its positivity. Yet, they both point out that the federal theology misrepresents the fundamentals of the covenant of grace, and the works-based covenant disrupts the event of Christ.[45] This works-based covenant adjusts the event, which can be replaced with the work of humans, and thus increases the ambiguities of the salvific history of God. In the covenant of grace, distinguishingly, the covenant is a mutual relationship between God (initiates our freedom) and all of the covenant partners (in our freedom corresponding to divine freedom) as it is founded on God's own self-sacrifice. Only in this divine grace are we capable of a covenant with God. Barth asserts that

> the first covenant and its Law loses its relevance only in that *eschaton* which is the fifth and final stage of the whole development. In spite of all assurances to the contrary, this side of the *eschaton*, in time, there is no effective abrogation of the covenant of nature and works, either in the Old Testament economy or consequently in the New. For the New Testament freedom is only freedom from the Law of the Old Testament—impressively maintained by Coccejus, e.g., in relation to the Sabbath—but the validity of the Law of that first covenant is the guiding thread which runs through the whole development, indeed it controls that development. Grace itself, whether as justification or sanctification, is always the fulfilling of that Law (perfect in Christ, imperfect in us). There is no escape from the relationship of *do ut des*, no liberation from the insecurity of the whole connexion between [human] and God, the fear of punishment and the expectation of reward, no radical cessation of the unfortunate preoccupation of [one] with [oneself] and [one's] works and of the even more unfortunate control of God to which this inevitably gives rise. This is impossible even in the covenant of grace connected with the covenant of works and orientated by it. This covenant of grace could not be clearly and convincingly portrayed as such.[46]

---

44. Torrance, "Covenant or Contract?," 69.

45. *CD* IV/1, 60. According to Barth, Coccejus describes "a pre-temporal occurrence, an eternal and free contract (*pactum*) made between God the Father and God the Son, in which the Father represents the righteousness and the Son the mercy of God, the latter adopting the function of a Mediator and pledge in the place of [humanity]."

46. *CD* IV/1, 63. Italics his. In brief, Coccejus speaks of five abrogations, the first

Federal theology therefore recognizes a historical understanding of God's relationship with humanity but misses the significance of the covenantal history with Israel that lies in God's grace. This theology does not see canonical unity, causing the concept of the covenant to be derailed from events attested in Scripture. The covenant of works as a system prioritizes the fulfillment of certain requirements so that our salvation can be assured. The consequences are fear of punishment and expectation of reward, as God's interactions with humanity relate to our own performance. The works-based covenant is hence described as a relationship of "*do ut des.*"[47] Based on law-ordinance, on the one hand, we are qualified to be loved by God and are promised eternal blessing. On the other hand, punishment comes if we are unqualified. The law with its promise and threats rules that the covenant of works promises eternal life to those who obey but threatens eternal punishment to those who disobey. Here, the goodness of the covenant shifts to the human side: this covenant excludes God's unconditional love for us, which reveals the unique nature of divine grace.[48] As a result, the core proclamation in the covenant of grace, which relates to what God wills for us in eternity, is considered less significant. Also, since the works-based covenant emphasizes the perfection of the human side, the covenant alters the genuine relationship between God and humans as well as the divine work of Jesus Christ that was accomplished on the cross, ceasing to be the history of the covenant. For Barth, this covenant therefore does not recognize the authentic history of

---

of which occurs through sin when Adam freely chooses to do what is forbidden by God. By choosing to disobey, Adam's offspring (all of humanity) inherited a marred state of being, resulting in a loss of our unblemished divine likeness, a separation from God, and subjection to divine curse and judgment. The second is the covenant of grace. God, in his mercy, determines to send a Mediator to humanity, which has fallen. The Mediator forges peace between God and humanity, and the promise of salvation is a gift from God, not a reward we have to earn. The third abrogation is the promulgation of the covenant of grace. This covenant, which is hidden and occasionally revealed in the Old Testament, prefigured a form of the relationship between God and humanity. In this form, we are justified sinners (as discussed in Rom 3) and the righteous are found among the wicked. As the obedient Son, Jesus Christ demonstrated perfect righteousness and fulfilled the whole Law, and he then, through the Holy Spirit, wrote God's law on the hearts of believers, thereby planting the Church among the gentiles. The mortification of the sinful flesh, as for the fourth abrogation, is understood as the believer's progressive sanctification, a process enabled by the covenant of works. The fifth abrogation concerns the restoration of believers who will receive eschatological redemption and consummation through God's grace (*CD* IV/1, 59–61).

47. *CD* IV/1, 63.
48. *CD* IV/1, 12.

Jesus Christ. The revelation is misconceived, and Scripture is accordingly misunderstood in connection with the witness to the event of the cross. For this reason, the God who commands us and God's intention in commanding are incomprehensible to us. In contrast, the covenant of grace continues for the elect to witnesses God the Creator: the living Lord who preserves, accompanies, and governs us all. This is God, who initiates the communion with us and keeps the asymmetric relationship as it underlies God's commands to us (the covenant partner), who are free in Jesus Christ. This covenant is possible only through Jesus Christ, who atones for sin for us and satisfies the demands of the law. Only in this way are we admitted into fellowship with God by virtue of the reconciliation of Jesus Christ, which Coccejus seemingly places as a subordinate substance, as Barth argues.

Significantly, the covenant of grace is achieved by Jesus Christ who fulfills the law, and we are restored by God's Spirit and promised the gift of eternal life as we put our trust in Jesus Christ. It is thus important that we seek unity in gospel and law so that the covenant of grace is proclaimed as it is attested in Scripture. Keep in mind that the covenant and its law apparently unparallels the covenant of grace, and the gospel and law can be easily treated as separate articles. The gospel and law are indeed dissimilar and infinitely different, but this does not represent the difference between good and bad. Rather, the way they function in being heard as the command of God is distinct. The word of God is "first Gospel and then Law,"[49] for the command of God begins with the gospel and not with the law. Gospel is not law as the law is not gospel, but gospel and law bring coherence in their peculiarity as they are interrelated. The word of God is therefore both gospel and law, although the gospel is not the word of God, and the law is not the word of God. The one word of God is thus differentiated into gospel and law respectively. It is not the law by itself, independent of the gospel, and it is also not the gospel without the law. The law is in the gospel, for it is "the necessary form of the Gospel, whose content is grace."[50] The content of the gospel declares the work of Jesus Christ, who has fulfilled the law and kept all the commands. Accordingly, law and gospel are distinctive but joined. In the covenant of grace, God not only elects us to establish the covenant in Jesus Christ but also commands us in God's grace. The electing God is the commanding God, addressing to the elect

---

49. *CD* II/2, 511.
50. Barth, *Community, State, and Church*, 24.

The Twofold Typology of the Elected Community

within the covenantal history from all eternity. The law comes to us in the form of the gospel, in which the elect not only witness God's grace but are also involved with permission and obligation. This means that the law of God was revealed as the law of grace in Jesus Christ, in whom we have both the gospel and the law; namely, for he not only replaced himself with all law (including misused, desecrated, and malformed) but reconciles us with God, illumines us through word, and consoles us.[51] In the light of Jesus Christ, the unity of gospel and law is accomplished inasmuch as the covenant between God and the elect is established.

Put another way, hearing the command—which comes to us as the unity of gospel and law—is sanctioned in the covenantal relationship, and we obey the command in our freedom. Divine election for all people is the good news of the gospel, as well as the command of the law: "In its content, it is Gospel; in its form and fashion, it is Law."[52] The one word of God is both gospel and law and thus one cannot exist without the other. As the Galatians deal with the whole law, including the Torah and religious and civil laws, the law must be rightly grasped—it must be filled with its content—the gospel—so that the one word of God as gospel and law is preserved. Hearing the word as God's command is to witness that the word lives, acts, and speaks in Scripture by the grace of God. God is the subject of the command, and we are commanded, hearing with "the person of God, with the action and revelation of this person, with God Himself."[53] The command of God attested by Scripture thus encounters us in a personal way, constituted in a relationship between God and us hearers in the person of Jesus within the elected community, as Barth posits: "I am myself the subject of responsibility to the command of God. . . . But I am this only as included in the 'we.'"[54] Our hearing is therefore both individual and communal. Further, God's command gives Godself to be known. God is to be heard, and the covenant partners are made responsible for accordance as we are brought into hearing and fellowship with Jesus Christ.[55] In this, again, the command arrives in the dual form of gospel/law. It comes to us as gospel, and we hear it in the faithfulness

---

51. *CD* II/2, 539. Also, Barth indicates that "the elect man is chosen in order to respond to the gracious God, to be His creaturely image, His imitator" (*CD* II/2, 413).

52. *CD* II/2, 511.

53. *CD* II/2, 676.

54. *CD* II/2, 655.

55. *CD* II/2, 548.

of Jesus Christ. It also comes to us as law, and we respond to it in free obedience.

In particular, when we hear the command in either way, gospel or law, God confronts us with a specific meaning and purpose. We hear the command as "an explosive encounter, contradiction and reconciliation, in which it is the part of the divine will to precede and the human to follow, of the former to control and the latter to submit."[56] In the event of the divine command, then, the Spirit reveals and makes known the will of God; the command not only meets us "purely in the form of concrete, historical, unique and singular orders, prohibitions and directions"[57] but also demands our obedience in a covenantal relationship. We may disregard the command but cannot alter the fact that God "speaks with us so truly and continuously in His Word, [and] we are in a position [not only] to hear Him with the same truth and exactitude [but also] to obey Him accordingly."[58] Truly, our obedience is born out of freedom that corresponds to the eternal election of humanity in Jesus Christ. We, by faith, understand our own free will, revealed to us in Jesus Christ, in which "God's foreordination [governs] our self-determination."[59] Our freedom, attained by understanding of the free will, chooses to align with "the God who at all times precedes us all in Holy Scripture, and in adherence to the action which He takes by Scripture."[60] We are harmoniously obedient to the word, whereby "faith is altogether the work of God, and it is altogether the work of [human]."[61] This interrelated freedom, faith, and obedience is important to understand that the law—in the form of the word of God—is the command to utilize our freedom appropriately, while the gospel—the content of the Word of God—is the good news of the gift of our freedom.[62] For the gospel is the primary message of Scripture, and the primacy of gospel over law must be kept in the covenant of grace while seeking unity of gospel and law.

In the command, moreover, there are only concrete divine claims, for God's will expressed can be recognized "in all times and places, nations and spheres of life, by the fact that it is good in the full sense of the

56. CD II/2, 644.
57. CD III/4, 12.
58. CD II/2, 745.
59. CD II/1, 586.
60. CD I/2, 673.
61. CD III/3, 247.
62. Nimmo, *Being in Action*, 115.

term."[63] At the same time, the divine command is indefinite and indeterminate to us and thus cannot be understood as "a rigid prescription inscribed, as it were, on a stone tablet, which the church and its members have to read off mechanically and translate into their own mode of thought and speech."[64] We are to be attentive to hear the command with careful, meticulous exegesis as particular texts must be "understood historically and concretely and not in a general, non-spatial and non-temporal sense."[65] As the decrees of Scripture absolutely concern themselves with their historical concreteness and singularity, "nothing can be made of [the divine command in the Bible] if we try to generalise and transform them into universally valid principles (unless, of course, we artificially distort them)."[66] Particular texts are thus interpreted in light of their historical context, in which what "God requires from the individual is proclaimed in [the concrete divine command] as His will for His people or Church, and therefore for the individual members of this people or Church."[67] Importantly, there is a continuity of the divine command because the word of God in Scripture "produces the same effect in continually new forms"[68] via the power of the Holy Spirit. The command of God is therefore the same and not the same in different times and circumstances. This also means that the divine command heard by both the Galatians and ourselves cannot either formally or materially differ from that given to the witness of Scripture (e.g., Abraham); thus, we claim it is our realization that matters are still the same here and now.

This comprehension therefore connects with Barth's claim to seek the unity in distinction of the divine command, a continuity from the divine command in Abraham's day to Paul's day to even the present, while admitting that the command given to biblical characters in Scripture is from a very different time and situation. That is, the Galatians observe the law to disclose veiled meanings for them at their "definite time, in a definite place and in a definite way to the history of the covenant and salvation controlled by [God]."[69] When the divine command in Scripture

---

63. *CD* II/2, 712.

64. *CD* I/2, 672.

65. *CD* II/2, 681. Some biblical texts—such as the Ten Commandments and the Sermon on the Mount—offer a more timeless ethical instruction.

66. *CD* II/2, 672.

67. *CD* II/2, 682.

68. *CD* I/2, 684.

69. *CD* III/4, 12.

for Abraham's day encounters the Galatians and us across spatial, cultural, and temporal distances, the historical context delineates the specific circumstances in which the context of Abraham has the concrete and particular commands of God in Scripture. In other words, the command of a concrete, historical reality "has eternal and valid content for [the Galatians and us] precisely in its temporary expression, and demands that we should hear and respect it in our very different time and situation."[70] This means that the command for Abraham is relevant and meaningful to the Galatians (and to us today), for the very particular commands of God "tell us, not only that God does demand and how, but also what He demands."[71]

YHWH desires the covenantal relationship. Willingness to engage in subordinate obligation is a free choice on the part of Israel to be God's people. As for Abrahamic faith, circumcision is not only an acknowledgment between YHWH and Abraham but also denotes a legal ritual in which two partners together accept mutual obligations. The one and only significant difference between Abraham and the Galatians (and us) is the unbreakable covenant achieved by Jesus Christ, in whom we died and were raised. Whether the hearer of the command of God is Abraham, the Galatians, or even us, the command is not only given within the context of this unity of "the history and sequel of the covenant of grace"[72] but also to be heard within a concrete relationship between God and the Galatians/us in the covenant of grace. The relationship between divine action and Abraham's corresponding conduct represents the real history taking place between God and Abraham, which is given a definite specific content, relating the command of God to Abraham's particular community in his certain time and circumstances. Within a particular context, whether for Abraham, the Galatians, or us, the one word of God in gospel and law entails "the existence of God as the Lord who rules over us, but who discloses this divine existence in the act of His lordship and work, and His work as that of establishing, maintaining and confirming the covenant of grace."[73]

In light of this, hearing the one word of God in gospel and law stipulates that we can joyously participate in this covenantal term, in which we witness the goodness of God's command. For God permits and

---

70. *CD* II/2, 707.
71. *CD* II/2, 704.
72. *CD* II/2, 706.
73. *CD* II/2, 704–5.

liberates us to fulfill the divine command, and the command mutually anticipates the decisive act of the elect in relation to Jesus Christ as we hear the command and correspond to it in our decision on the right use of freedom. That is, the elect desire "the apostolic formulation [which we] can only will to be what we are in Jesus Christ."[74] The elect in freedom, for Barth, joyously obey the command because of the love of the cross—we are analogous to God who has given Godself to us, rather than because of human reasoning to submit to the command of God.[75] Accordingly, divine love toward the elect (who are sinful, flawed, and disobedient) is to be witnessed, for "God and His command are good in the full sense of the term—genuinely and truly good":[76] the goodness of the command climaxes the elect's eternal destiny in the Elector and Elected Jesus Christ. On the basis of divine love, the command is "the good of the divinely controlled history of the covenant of peace and its subsequent developments, the good of God's eternal election of grace, [and] the good which bears the name of Jesus Christ."[77] This goodness of God's command is inseparable from the will of God, founded in the history of God in which God elects Godself for humanity. This goodness includes a particular content and a specific meaning and purpose in certain circumstances; for the goodness entails the will of God, it comes to us as "a specific command of God in each specific form of his dealings with [the human partner], in each specific time, in relation to the presuppositions and consequences of each specific existence of each [partner]."[78] On account of this particular meticulousness, the goodness of God—reflected in the command of God—remains within covenantal grace as it is disclosed in the person of Jesus Christ, in whom almighty God determines the eternal decision for all and comes as goodness in person. This goodness is, for Barth, thus primarily founded by the work of Jesus Christ, which Godself has predicated. That is, the purpose of God's command relates to the goodness of God in which the will of God mutually joins the decisions of the elect and the community. Insofar as our hearing of the word is both individual and communal, this goodness of the command comes to us exclusively and personally and, at the same time, is reciprocally communal, aligning with

74. *CD* II/2, 610.
75. For Barth, "freedom is given to us, and we are always grasping after empty possibilities, acting as though we were still prisoners" (*CD* IV/2, 364).
76. *CD* II/2, 708.
77. *CD* II/2, 703.
78. Barth, *Christian Life*, 60–61.

the nature of the covenant relationship between God, the elect, and the church. As Barth asserts, "I am myself the covenant-partner of God, but my God is our God. I may and must hear [God's] command, but [God's] command applies to us all."[79] In addition, the will of God expressed in God's law and the criterion of the good of our conduct, for Barth, are associated. Necessitating our discernment, the will[80] is to be discovered by the elect who hear the command, see the goodness of God, and mutually agree with the work of Jesus Christ. The command is therefore cohesive with God's will and goodness, for it demands particular permissions and obligations relating to what we ought to do or not do as we practice our freedom at will. According to John Webster, both Luther and Barth advocate that our good actions are "described through the language of desire, projection, judging. For both, a Christian theory of the good takes its rise in the doctrine of God" as they characterize the good as beyond the choice of Christian ethics.[81] This clarifies that, at the heart of the command of God, the will and the goodness of God are grasped by the elect, for the command attested in Scripture conveys its goodness, "which is integrally connected with the establishment and proclamation of [God's] covenant."[82]

79. *CD* II/2, 655.

80. See Werpehowski, *Karl Barth and Christian Ethics*. Werpehowski writes, "God's eternal will is for humanity in Jesus Christ; the normative criterion is identical to God's will and the history it accomplishes. On the other hand, and because of the concrete, determinate character of God's self-determining will, we are not talking about an arbitrary 'rightness' which accrues to God's will as a mere result of [God's] power. Yet we are not then required to say that God commands what [God] does (both proximately, to individual creatures, and ultimately, with respect to [God's] self-determination to be for persons) because it is right independently of [God's] will. Barth wishes to deny this proposition unequivocally" (7–8); According to Barth, "power as power does not have any divine claim, no matter how imposing or effective it might be. To maintain [oneself] against power as power, even to [one's] own undoing, is not merely a possibility for [one]. It is not merely the assertion of [one's] right and dignity. It is the duty which [one] has to fulfill with [one's] existence as [human]. The very [individual] who is claimed, for whom God has become too strong, who is overcome by God, is distinguished from the falling stone by the fact that it is in [one's] own most proper freedom that [one] has been determined for God, in [one's] own most proper freedom that [one] has decided for God. By deciding for God [one] has definitely decided not to be obedient to power as power. It is in this way and this way alone that [one] is subdued and subject to the power of Almighty God. The [one] who comes from this decision knows freedom. [One] will 'maintain [one's] right against all might.' And it is in so doing that [one] fulfils [one's] foreordination. Power as power cannot possibly be the basis for [one's] obedience" (*CD* II/2, 553).

81. Webster, *Barth's Moral Theology*, 178.

82. *CD* II/2, 703.

The Twofold Typology of the Elected Community

Within our context of Galatians, specifically, the will and the goodness of God are understood in relation to hearing the command as God's judgment. Put differently, God's judgment comes to us as unity of gospel and law. However, when it comes as fear of punishment and expectation of reward, we stray from the authenticity of the covenant in grace. In the Old Testament, the covenantal history of Israel is indeed viewed from the perspective of reward and punishment. Reward, in the form of God's blessings, comes by way of obeying the law, while punishment follows curses from God as a result of disobeying God's command. The verdict of God's judgment is either blessings that God rewards when we obey or curses that God punishes when we disobey the command. Perceiving the terms curse and blessing within the context of fear of punishment and expectation of reward would prevent us from seeing the God of Israel, who is the Creator and Redeemer in the covenant of grace. The command should therefore not be perceived merely as a tyranny representing degradation of our will and freedom. The command primarily arrives with the divine *telos* and its meaningfulness as it appeals to us, connecting with our heart and thus consent, rather than dominating. This indicates that the sovereign God exercises authority without any coerced reciprocal responsibility toward humanity but with anticipation that we willingly keep the two great commandments. This sets up our discussion of divine judgment as justification and sanctification.

DIVINE JUDGMENT AS JUSTIFICATION AND SANCTIFICATION

We now turn to Gal 3:10–14. Paul brings the four scriptural texts (Deut 21:23, 27:26; Lev 18:5; Hab 2:4b) to preserve the accord in the gospel and law for the Galatian churches. Fully integrating into the family line of Abraham, the opponents caution the Galatians with a curse of uncircumcision as they appeal to the benefits of embracing circumcision, such as inheritance, blessing, and covenant.[83] The duality of blessing and curse is contingent upon the Galatians' conformity to the law as the opponents advocate complete law-observance by focusing principally on Abrahamic and Deuteronomic traditions. The story of Abraham is well

---

83. Wilson, *Curse of the Law*. As Wilson cites Justin, *Dial.* 8.3, where Trypho admonishes Justin, "first be circumcised, then observe the precepts concerning the Sabbath, the feasts, and God's new moons; in brief, fulfil the whole written law, and then, probably, you will experience the mercy of God" (49n12).

suited to promote circumcision. It persuades the Galatians with blessings of Abraham[84] while a warning of "cursing" comes from failure to take on the covenant of circumcision, which would bring the person falling under the curse of the law. Indeed, the story of Abraham, embedded in the code of Deuteronomy, states that God will curse those who curse Abraham (Gen 12:3) and that those who neglect the covenantal obligation of circumcision will be cut off from their people (Gen 17:14). This teaching of the opponents troubled the Galatians (Gal 1:7), as J. Louis Martyn accentuates that "in their instruction of the Galatians the [opponents] are certain to have balanced their comments about God's blessing of Abraham with references to the threat of God's curse."[85] The opponents are "frightening the Galatians out of their wits, intimidating them with the threat of damnation if they do not follow the path prescribed in the [opponents'] message!"[86] A number of scholars also agree that the opponents used the curse of the law as part of their polemical strategy to support their teachings, meaning that the curse falls upon those who fail to embrace the law and its works. L. Ann Jervis affirms that "it is easy to see how at least three of the four Scriptural quotations (Deut. 27:26; Lev. 18:5; Deut. 21:23) could have been put to good use by rival evangelists."[87] The opponents promoted the curses of Deuteronomy as a means of warning for the Galatians, who feared the serious consequences of failing to comply with the demands of the law. John Barclay also argues that "if the Galatians took their Scriptures seriously they were doubtless urged to do what [the opponents] say in this matter" because Scripture clearly "declares a blessing on those who keep the law and a curse on those who neglect to do so."[88] In his defense,[89] accordingly, Paul responded to the

84. See Martyn, *Galatians*. Martyn writes that "we can be confident that [Paul's opponents] made much of Genesis 17, emphasizing the definition of God's covenant as circumcision" (423n94); see also Wilson, *Curse of the Law*, 58–64.

85. Martyn, *Galatians*, 324. Martyn also comments about the teaching of the opponents: "Walk in the way of Law observance, and, as the Law declares, God will bless you within the corpus of Abraham's descendants. Walk in the way of nonobservance, and, as the Law also declares, God will place [God's] curse on you, excluding you from his people. God's holy Law speaks of these two ways, blessing and curse" (325).

86. Martyn, *Galatians*, 112.

87. Jervis, *Galatians*, 96.

88. Barclay, *Obeying the Truth*, 67.

89. Sanders, *Paul: The Apostle's Life*. Sanders argues that "in Galatians 3 Paul is not laying out a theology that is good for all times and conditions, and he is not distinguishing between laws that should be discarded and those that should be kept. He is, rather, fighting desperately against people who would destroy his entire mission by forcing

Galatians by citing the scriptural texts that the opponents used to reinforce the ordinance of the law and its consequence of curse or blessing based on Deuteronomic and Abrahamic traditions. As most scholars indicate, Paul thus alluded to the same texts to dissuade his opponents' teaching and elucidate the authenticity of righteousness, which dealt with the terms curse and blessing in the covenant of grace.[90]

Taking this into account, Gal 3:10–14 comes after Paul's emphasis on the faith of Abraham. Through him, God justifies the gentiles by faith, and they are called men of faith because they are heirs of Abraham. Setting this prelude of faith, Gal 3:10–13 cites three texts from the Torah (Deut 27:26 and 21:23; Lev 18:5) and one from the Prophets (Hab 2:4b). The passage is constructed as a statement and citation pair—"all who rely on the works of the law are under a curse" (v. 10) with its proof-text from Deut 27:26, uttering that "no one is justified before God by the law" (v. 11) with Hab 2:4b, noting "the law does not rest on faith" (v. 12) with Lev 18:5, and accentuating "Christ redeemed us from the curse of the law by becoming a curse for us" (v. 13) with Deut 21:23. Verse 14 assures us that "in Christ Jesus the blessing of Abraham might come to the Gentiles so that we might receive the promise of the Spirit through faith."

In verse 10, some scholars place importance on the word "all" and interpret this as meaning that anyone not keeping the entire law falls under a curse.[91] The opponents advocate that obedience to the law is demanded as proof of faith to inherit the blessing of Abraham. Perfect obedience is, however, impractical—in truth, merely human endeavor in law-obedience will fail, and, as a result, all fall under a curse. Desiderius Erasmus argues that the law does not offer righteousness but has pedagogical aspects to regulate the conduct of believers to yield a virtuous life because "the fear of punishment might restrain them from great

---

his gentiles to obey one of the 'works of law,' the requirement of circumcision. In this polemical situation, he wishes to force a complete separation between obeying the laws of the Bible and having faith in Christ" (526).

90. Barclay suggests a mirror reading, using "the text which answers the opponents as a *mirror* in which we can see reflected the people and the arguments under attack" (73–74). Italics his. This reading interprets what the text reflects rather than what it explicitly states. Focusing on specific words or phrases can yield insight into the text's historical context. Furthermore, elements like allusions, affirmations, dominant themes, and points of emphasis may indicate areas of contention between Paul and his opponents. See John Barclay, "Mirror-Reading a Polemical Letter," 73–93.

91. See footnotes 28 and 104.

outrages."[92] Through law ordinance, they can gradually make progress, which will lead to Jesus Christ. As part of this teaching, obedience to the law causes serious conflicts for the Galatians, whose religious societies view the law as sacred. The Galatians might consider the law as a system of conduct in favor of Christ's teachings and guidance from the Spirit. Law-obedience is then a matter of life or death to the Galatians and its relationship to curses and blessing brings them religious legal conflict.[93] Calvin exhorts, however, to "notice these words very carefully: they do not say 'Cursed is the one who has rejected the law and has altogether disobeyed it,' but rather, cursed is [one] who fails to observe every jot and tittle of it."[94] For Calvin, Paul's use of the antithesis between the entire law and faith is to evoke the consequences of disobeying the law. Paul's citation of Deut 27:26 (v. 10) thus clarifies that those who disobey the law are under a curse because they did not keep God's law.

Galatians 3:11–12 takes the antithetical relationship between the law and faith, citing the two texts, Hab 2:4b and Lev 18:5. In verse 11, Paul introduces Hab 2:4b ("the one who is righteous will live by faith") to support his claim that no one is justified before God by the law. To be "justified before God" is the precise opposite of being condemned by God; put differently, it means "being right with God." With this assertion, verse 12 states "whoever does the works of the law will live by them," citing Lev 18:5.[95] Commentators typically read the two texts as indicating that no one is justified by the works of the law because justification comes only by faith (Hab 2:4b), while obeying the law (Lev 18:5) is unworkable because no one fulfills it perfectly. The two texts are therefore seemingly incompatible because Hab 2:4b articulates the faith of the righteous as Lev 18:5 promises the covenantal blessing for obeying the law.[96]

According to James Dunn, Lev 18:5 asserts that people who observe the law are justified by God, and also refers to how this righteousness

---

92. Erasmus, *Paraphrases on Romans and Galatians*, 113–14.

93. Betz, *Galatians*, 50.

94. Chester, "When the Old Was New," 324.

95. "You shall keep my statutes and my ordinances; by doing so one shall live: I am the Lord" (Lev 18:5). The verse is seen as a succinct covenantal term, indicating that the righteous continue to live by doing the law or keeping the commandments, which entail Israel's obligations and its corresponding consequences. The verse thus represents Israel's covenantal communal life with YHWH and expresses how first-century Jews would have understood righteousness.

96. We will further investigate this view in the appendix section "The Prophecy of Habakkuk and the Covenant of Grace."

should be lived out. The opponents have thus put too much emphasis on law-observance, as justification should be rooted in faith learned with its aid (i.e., the law). Dunn points out that "[the law and faith] have different functions within the divine dispensation of grace. The two have been brought into confrontation, but the implication of Lev. 18.5 rightly understood is that their roles should properly be regarded as complementary."[97] Comparing this verse with Hab 2:4b, accordingly, the Galatian Christians could see the distinction between the old and new covenants. Rudolph Bultmann reads the two verses with respect to sin, writing that "*the Law brings to light that [the human] is sinful*"[98] and "[*our*] *effort to achieve* [*our*] *salvation by keeping the Law* only leads [us] into sin, indeed this effort itself in the end *is already sin*."[99] E. P. Sanders agrees that fulfilling the law is simply beyond human capability, and thus Lev 18:5 is inadequate in righteousness before God. However, he argues that the view of Bultmann—relating to human endeavor in law-observance leading to sin, which is itself sinning—is not evident in the Galatian passage.[100] Paul, for Sanders, uses the antithesis of law and faith as they are both necessary for a covenantal relationship—law-observance is essential to faith.[101] Works undertaken outside faith do not fulfill the law, for the law, as included in the Deuteronomy and Leviticus passages, is unable to be isolated from God. The law also serves to reveal ourselves as sinners—we have broken the laws of God and brought ourselves under the curse of the law, which is the curse of God. Nonetheless, because God's salvific plan is achieved through Jesus Christ, we become righteous before God through faith, although we never become sin-free.

This reading leads to verses 13 to 14 on the covenantal tenet, which engage with the connection of curse and blessing through the Christ event. The curse here recalls the curse pronounced in verse 10 upon all who fail to satisfy the law. A curse is marked not only on all who depend on the works of the law but also on those who do not obey it. This reappearance of "the curse" is no longer valid because Christ redeemed the curse for us. The word "redeemed" indicates the historical event of Christ's death on the cross, in which God undeniably reversed the curse for Paul

---

97. Dunn, *Theology of Paul the Apostle*, 153.

98. Bultmann, *Theology of the New Testament*, 265. Italics his.

99. Bultmann, *Theology of the New Testament*, 264. Italics his.

100. Sanders, *Paul and Palestinian Judaism*, 482.

101. We will discuss this in depth in "The Prophecy of Habakkuk and the Covenant of Grace."

and the Galatian Christians (and all). This accursed death is underlined as Paul connects the phrase "hang on a tree" (Deut 21:23),[102] alluding to God's redemptive work in Christ. Specifically, the curse (denounced on the breakers of God's law) was invalidated by the death of Christ, who was hanged on a tree as the consequence of Christ becoming a curse for us. Bearing the curse on behalf of us is required to prove that the work of the law is inadequate to receive the covenantal blessing—the other side of the curse. The Torah accurately sets forth the curse, and Christ's bearing of the curse results in blessing for the gentiles and all. In fact, Paul's intention of employing "the hanged man" from Deuteronomy lies in the emphasis on "the 'curse' or 'repudiation' of God, whose severity of punishment was reserved for individuals who had cursed God and in turn must incur his curse."[103] Therefore, it was God who took the curse for all. The antithesis of curse-blessing speaks of the true purpose of giving the law to God's people, and the Galatians thus need to hear the covenantal blessings of Abraham, which are available to the gentiles through Christ.

This interpretation of the passage, however, does not settle for the Galatians whose religious societies are strictly legalized, or fully deliver Paul's intention to take our readers back to certain times of Scripture. Moreover, many leave out delving into the curse in this passage, which might have to do with contemporary readers who find it uneasy. The curse[104] is nonethe-

---

102. See von Rad, *Deuteronomy*. The body is removed "from the tree" on the day of the execution and buried as "the land must be protected against ritual pollution" (138). This hanging execution is evident in the Dead Sea Scrolls, indicating that crucifixion was also practiced by both Judaism and the Romans. Philo of Alexandria referred to this Jewish practice (25 BCE–50 CE).

103. Garlington, "Role Reversal," 105.

104. Scholarly views on the curse are divided between an individual and a collective interpretation. Some scholars contend that the curse afflicts all of Israel, while others maintain it resulted from an individual sin. The curse (v. 10b) is the concluding verse of the curses list in Deut 27, which corresponds to individual transgressions; Cowan, "Curse of the Law," 211–29. According to Cowan in his research on the Dead Sea Scrolls, the LXX, the targumic tradition, and the MT, there is no direct evidence in reading Deut 27:26 as a collective rather than an individual curse. This finding includes his exegesis on Jer 11:3–5, which speaks of "the punishments that individuals have brought on themselves throughout Israel's history" (222). Jeremiah's treatment of Deut 27:26 does not therefore indicate a collective curse, or a curse on the people of Israel as a whole. Cowan thus argues that "the first-century interpreters would less likely read the text as a reference to a collective curse on the nation of Israel" (229). Israel as a whole fails to keep the Torah, and thus, Deut 27:26 is regarded as a collective curse upon Israel; Wright, *Climax of the Covenant*, 140–56. For Wright, this signifies that Israel fails "in her task of being the light to the nations" (155), while emphasizing a different point: "[Christ] *is* Israel, going down to death under the curse of the law,

The Twofold Typology of the Elected Community 39

less related to blessing. With this in mind, we move to engage in more in-depth readings of the passage (3:10–14) in its wider contexts of the scriptural texts to see Paul's counterclaims against the opponents.

In verse 10, Paul cited Deut 27:26 to evoke the connections between law and curse, which works well with Paul's retold story of Abraham (vv. 6–9). In addition, this sets up a connection between faith and blessing (v. 14). Deuteronomy 27:15–26 lists twelve curses on individuals who commit sins, which are recited as a part of a ceremony. The ceremony begins with writing the law on stones and giving burnt offerings. The six tribes who are blessed stand on Mount Gerizim and the other six who are cursed stand on Mount Ebal. The people respond to each curse with the word "Amen." Verse 26 serves as a summary curse, concluding the consequences on anyone who commits sin.[105] The ceremony is therefore intended to remind the people of their responsibility to God's law and to remove the responsibility of community from the committed sin with individuals, even in secret. The following chapter of Deut 28 furthermore involves blessings of obedience and curses resulting from disobedience. With respect to covenantal rewards based on obedience and disobedience, the terms blessing and curse are commonly understood in the Old Testament and the early church. In Paul's day, some Jews thought that they had been exiled as they were under Roman government after their return from Babylon. The curse pronounced in Deut 27 fell upon the unfaithful, just as the Deuteronomist in his day saw that God's people were cursed because of their failure to keep the covenant and the political decline of the southern kingdom. As a result, they were exiled and under the curse. In the first century, also, the Jews understood that they were under the curse in their exile and that the prophecies of Israel's restoration were unfulfilled. Paul's citation of Hab 2:4b is then grasped as the fulfillment of God's deliverance for the righteous at the appointed time. From this perspective, the opposition between Lev 18:5 and Hab 2:4b is well balanced to portray the promise of eschatological life, which is indeed accomplished in the death and resurrection of Christ. In fact, this interpretation of Habakkuk's text is common to some scholars, indicating

---

and going through that curse to the new covenant life beyond" (152). See Caneday, "Redeemed from the Curse," 185–209; "The deuteronomical conception of the curse of the law," writes Caneday, "[does] not atomize the curse to individuals distinct from identity with the covenant nation" (194–95).

105. Cowan, "Curse of the Law," 211–29. As Cowan emphasizes, "there is little evidence in ancient Jewish literature that Deut. 27:26 was interpreted as a reference to a curse on the people of Israel as a whole" (222).

Hab 2:4b as a familiar text of a prophecy of God's judgment in the early church. Namely, Paul cites Hab 2:4b not only as a prophetic eschatology speaking of the appointed time that has arrived with Jesus Christ but also as a supporting text for Gal 3:23–26, where he speaks of faith coming and being revealed.[106]

The purposes of the two covenants are, then, enhanced as the antithesis of the law and faith concerns the contrast between the old covenant represented by the Torah and the new covenant of the Messiah.[107] In addition, Paul tries to convey hidden layers of meaning, using four proof texts to support his claims, as Gal 3:10–14 is placed between the inheritors of Abraham (3:6–9) and the covenant and its promise (3:15–18). Verses 11–13 attract the attention of the audience, and verse 14 gives a succinct climax and connects to the story of Abraham from verse 15.

Looking into the background, it is critically important for the Galatians (and we) to comprehend the authentic nature of the covenant of grace. The law in the Old Testament is the centerpiece of the everlasting covenant that the God of Israel makes with the elect. Indeed, the covenant and the law go together as the whole life of ancient Israel was connected with the law and obedience to it. Obedience to the law is thus what gave Israel a right to stand before God. Yet, the law, rather than being defined solely by its principles, also embodies spiritual truths; these truths are intended to serve as lessons for spiritual understanding, not as literal rules for practice.[108] For Israel, to be a covenant people was to live within the boundary set by the law of God, with their salvation assured. The way in which the people of Israel become God's own people is by taking upon themselves the sacred obligations of the covenant. The Torah as the primary expression of God's voice is not only God's gracious gift to the

---

106. See also Willitts, "Context Matters," 105–22.

107. In 2 Cor 3:7–18, Paul contrasts his ministry with that of Moses, addressing the concerns of his opponents regarding the Torah. The Torah, though it offered ways to become righteous for salvation, lost all salvific significance after Jesus Christ fulfilled it in his death and resurrection. Alongside his discussion of Exod 34:29–35, Paul recalls that God's glory was revealed to Israel on Mount Sinai when the Law was given. After speaking with God, divine glory was made known through Moses, whose face radiated with this reflected divine glory; the glory of the Law radiated from Moses' face, showing that he had been filled with God's own glory. Moses thus served as the minister of that set-aside glory until God revealed eschatological glory in Jesus Christ. The super-apostles, as Paul argues, misperceived the ministry of Moses because they were oblivious to its set-aside glory, which foreshadowed the eschatological glory (detailed in the appendix section "The Prophecy of Habakkuk and the Covenant of Grace").

108. Graves, *Inspiration and Interpretation of Scripture*, 66.

community but also represents fundamental principles (with spiritual truths) to govern the life of God's elect. The law guides the people of Israel to be God's own people as they conduct their lives, living in covenant with YHWH. The law and the covenant are thus inseparably intertwined, indicating the seriousness of Israel taking the covenant. The covenant agreement between YHWH and the people comprises both what YHWH has done and Israel's appropriate response to the divine redemptive activity of YHWH—the one believed to be both Creator and Redeemer. Vowing to YHWH, the covenant created new dimensions of responsibility in the ongoing life of the Israelite community. The covenant is therefore regarded as a vehicle for faithfulness, but Israel is not forced to agree to it. Israel freely chose to accept or reject YHWH's overture. On the basis of an act of gratitude and faith, the covenant ties the elect with YHWH, entailing obligation and obedience of the elect, representing their loyalty to what the God of Israel had already done. When the Israelites were in captivity and exiled from their homes, Abraham—the patriarchal father of the Israelite nation—represents Israel and God's people as he becomes the central character, both giving hope to the community and keeping their identity and purpose with the God of Israel. The community can identify with Abraham, and, just as the God of Israel promises Abraham, the same God promises Israelites in the early church. Namely, YHWH promises that there will be a future and hope for them. Their name, their way of life, and their relationship with YHWH serve as blessings to others and all nations.

In light of this, first, the term "works in righteousness" as a form of keeping law is differentiated from the covenantal agreement that is understood between YHWH and Israel. Israelites become God's people by virtue of being elected, but not by virtue of obedience to the law. It is by the covenant that the people are constituted as a community and given the task of conducting their lives as a community marked by its belonging to God. Israel is to be faithful, keeping the covenant and the law. Accordingly, the law-observance that Paul's opponents push to the Galatians is distinguished from the original intention of the law, declared by the covenantal term. Second, hearing is obedience—that is, hearing God's voice—which is equated with obedience to God's law and command. Hearing God's voice (i.e., the command) is related to obeying or disobeying the God of Israel. Hearing God's command and law is regarded as one and the same activity.[109] Obedience and disobedience are connected to hearing God or not hearing God's voice. Obedience is correlated with keeping the covenant while disobedience is said to be covenant-breaking; to remain faithful to the covenant requires obeying the truth, which entails the law and command of God. Hearing God, we stand in the covenantal relationship, in which we acknowledge that we belong to God. The Galatians (and we), like Israel, are summoned to hear God. Obedience is required of us in our relationship with God as it was in the Old Testament. The notion of righteousness thus signifies a comprehensive assessment of the elect's faith to God's covenant. Faith and obedience are a twofold action as faith speaks of obedience, proven by obedience as it speaks of faith. Put differently, hearing God involves people with Jesus Christ—the Word that has been with God—via the obedience of faith. Those who listen to the Word put their trust in God, and thus their hearing and faith of obedience come together while disobedience is the consequence of unhearing. As "faith is right hearing,"[110] obeying God's law and trust in God is a twofold action as they are indivisibly coherent when responding to God's word. In the history of Israel, the elect continuously fail to obey God's voice and the consequences of unbelief are divine judgment and curse—the opposite of blessing. With respect to divine judgment, curse or blessing, Abraham is an essential representation of the people of God as he was a channel of God's judgment (Gen 12:3). Failure in law-observance (i.e., disobedience) results in sin and curses. As part of God's curses, consequently, the Galatians are prevented from entering the family line of Abrahamic faith. The curse terminology perplexes the Galatians, who hear a different doctrine from Paul. According to Paul's teaching, God (who is Creator and Redeemer) continues the salvific history through Jesus Christ, who ultimately secures the righteousness of the covenant for all people. As a result, this faith, along with God's blessing, is to be incorporated into heavenly Jerusalem (4:26). The history of this covenant, indeed, stands separate from the teaching of the opponents as the opponents misconstrue the truthfulness of keeping the law (God's command) between God and the elect.

Moreover, Paul declares the meaning of "descent" as part of the covenant. Belonging to the family line of Abraham, a new corporate identity is achieved by dying and rising with Christ, which becomes a mark of being

---

109. Garlington, *Obedience of Faith*, 10–13.
110. Käsemann, *New Testament Questions of Today*, 177.

one of God's elect. Paul focuses on the notion that all people become the heirs of Abraham and thus receive eschatological blessings through Jesus Christ, by whom we are justified and sanctified. Also, salvation, which is open to all, is brought about by the proclamation of Christ, which unifies the gospel and law. Nevertheless, the opponents are unwilling to perceive the covenantal boundaries extended to the gentiles by the cross of Jesus Christ, revealing the covenant of grace. Counteracting the opponents, Paul not only uses the same scriptural texts that his opponents refer to the Galatians but also sets up the contrast between the original intention of the law and its actual function. God's grace was revealed originally in the law but was twisted because the law was misunderstood as a demand for achievement. Certainly, there are both positive and negative aspects of the law. Law-observance (for the purpose of covenant keeping) sets apart God's people, and the function of the law leads to experience of sin while the law in its truth does not belong with sin. Confronted by the law, then, sin reveals its force, and law can lead us to do good—in and by the law, light is shed on what sin is. Misuse of the law, however, distorts the goodness of God's will and the significance of the righteous; because the misuse insists that we learn forgiveness of our sin based primarily on law-keeping. In this sense, Paul's statement climaxes in verse 13—Christ, hanging on a tree, became curse for all. This assures us that the covenant's obligation, intertwined with the laws, must be understood through the work of Jesus Christ, and that the identity of God's people is described solely by faith in the risen Christ. When God's judgment—as either a blessing or a curse—comes to the Galatians and us, we, as a new creation in Christ, can hear it differently. Through Jesus Christ and by the Spirit, we, in our faith and obedience, hear the command as an eschatological blessing that incorporates us into heavenly Jerusalem (4:26).

With this knowledge, the command of God's judgment is correspondingly to be heard by us in the covenant of grace, as Barth posits that we belong to God and are subject to be judged by God's command. It is in the covenantal tenets God bounds Godself to us—i.e., God ties with us in the divine command, particularly the way in which we are subjected to the command as God's judgment. We are summoned by God's judgment. Divine judgment takes place as God gives us the command, which reflects God's truth, righteousness, and the law of the covenant of grace. God judges us as God fulfills the judgment in Jesus Christ, the Son who is God's Elector and Elected. The very condemnation of him embodies the reconciliation that Jesus Christ has completed from all eternity and in time. In the doctrine of God, divine judgment brings us to the reverse side of the election of grace as, in our election, Jesus is chosen for God's judgment of wrath. Those who are elected in Jesus Christ are sinners but justified on the basis of the righteousness of Christ. We therefore receive the righteousness of God in Jesus Christ, in whom God's condemnation and rejection were exchanged with our transgression. At the same time, our election is accomplished by the justification and adoption of God in Jesus Christ. This judgment thus lies in "the form of God's eternal predestination"[111] and entails the reconciliation of all. Specifically, God has pronounced and executed the sentence on the beloved Son in our place. Divine judgment for us was already predecided in Jesus Christ, in whom the command of God is revealed and actualized as it is established and fulfilled: this Jesus Christ is the holy God and sanctified man whom God summons to obey. The curse, in the first instance, has therefore fallen on Jesus Christ on behalf of all, including the Galatians and us. Barth indicates that we "submit to the judgment that has fallen on [Jesus Christ], so that in virtue of His rejection we may be the elect and sanctified, consenting to hear and accept the curse which is pronounced on us as it was pronounced on [Jesus Christ], but also to hear and accept the promise of love."[112] It is in Jesus Christ that God judges us, and yet the judgment passed us as Christ not only gave us himself but also directed fellowship with God. In Jesus Christ, on the one hand, we experience "God's command as God's judgment, and God's judgment as [our] own condemnation and execution."[113] On the other hand, the resurrection of Jesus Christ, as the Son persisting in the judgment, is the revelation of his faithfulness for us. Thus, we, hearing the command, are justified in the judgment: even in the midst of the condemnation pronounced upon the Son, we are "already placed on the way of forgiveness and obedience which is the intention of the command."[114] In light of this, Jesus Christ not only establishes the legitimate basis for our sanctification but also actualizes eschatological blessings for the righteous through divine judgment. This also signifies that our true sanctification for God is already irrevocably accomplished through the work of Jesus Christ.

Furthermore, confronting the command as divine judgment, "we are totally evil when we enter [God's] judgment and totally cleansed

---

111. *CD* II/2, 739.
112. *CD* II/2, 741.
113. *CD* II/2, 739.
114. *CD* II/2, 735.

The Twofold Typology of the Elected Community

when we leave it,"[115] according to Barth. Even though our sin is acquitted and justified by God, God judges us in Jesus Christ as God judges the Son, in whom God establishes our relationship with us. "We cannot and we will not escape the real judgment of God which is executed in the death of Jesus Christ, for it is our actual meeting with God."[116] What is noteworthy is that, for Barth, "faith corresponds exactly to the judgment and grace of God."[117] We take God's judgment into account in all our actions. In God's judgment, "we attest [faith] in our action (because God has Himself attested it to us in this judgment); [magnify] it (because God willed to magnify Himself in us in this judgment); [and display] it in our action before God and [humanity] and all angels."[118] We are to acknowledge the purpose of judgment and sanctification as the command of God's judgment directs us to live by God's grace. We hear the Lord Jesus—"for the Word is true and actual"[119]—whereas our disobedience repudiates hearing the divine judgment. By the command of God, we therefore come afresh into the judgment of God and keep its purpose of the divine command. This hearing, as seen earlier, is obeying. It is thus our faith that we not only obey the command but also grasp the purpose of divine judgment, primarily lying in our sanctification. For Barth, it is faith that awakens us as it confirms and accepts the election and sanctification of God in Jesus Christ. In this faith, we recognize that we are justified sinners, living the life of those who are forgiven by God and acknowledging the purpose of divine judgment. "In this faith, we are holy: we are sanctified for God and eternal life"[120]—in this very faith, Jesus Christ lives in us, and we in him. By the Holy Spirit, God accomplishes our participation with the Son, and in the same Holy Spirit, divine conversation is conducted.[121] This participation involves our sanctification as what God blesses us is determined in Jesus Christ, the only begotten Son of the Father, loved from all eternity. That is, conforming like Jesus Christ, whose divine characteristics are presented, our sanctification takes place as we participate in the begotten Son.

115. *CD* II/2, 757.
116. *CD* II/2, 749.
117. *CD* II/2, 766.
118. *CD* II/2, 767.
119. *CD* I/1, 182.
120. *CD* II/2, 780.
121. *CD* II/2, 750–51.

By the command as the divine judgment, as Barth deems, we have to recognize "the act of love in which God has turned Himself, to [everyone], from all eternity and in time."[122] We live with repetition of the death of the old "I"—a restoring baptized "I." We "die and rise in Christ" every moment as we correspond to the divine command in our faith and obedience. Entering each new day, we live in the judgment to which we are condemned, but through which we are also forgiven and justified. Our effort to align ourselves with the judgment necessitates that we hear the command of God. After all, we must be the kind of elect who walk with the Lord. We may disbelieve, but God, without ceasing, speaks to us in the everlasting word, willing us to be our sanctification for eternal life. On each new day we enter, our faith responds to the divine judgment, resulting in the act of repentance. When we repent the sinfulness of our being and action, this repentance engages with the course of obedience. For Barth, good works please God as our sin is recognized in our repentance. Each repentance turns "from disobedience to obedience. And this is what God wills of those who are judged by Him."[123] Moreover, Barth confesses that it is God's voice through which we are summoned to repent:

> No other voice ever can or will call us to repentance. No other voice ever can or will make us able and willing to believe. No other voice ever can or will transpose us from a state of disobedience to one of obedience. No other voice ever can or will win our hearts. And in God's command it is a matter of accepting from the heart the sanctification which has taken place for us. The voice of Jesus Christ is the voice of God Himself, who wills to have us for Himself, to make us free and ready for eternal life.[124]

The command as God's judgment therefore involves the sanctification in us so that we can prepare the eternal life that is promised and openly revealed to covenant partners. Anticipating eternity in God, we are prepared: Jesus Christ, to whom we conform ourselves according to the judgment, is sanctification. We are judged by God: the command of God concerns us, for the divine command does convey particular meanings of

---

122. *CD* II/2, 737.

123. *CD* II/2, 768. Barth asserts that "it is the Gospel, and not a Law abstracted from the Gospel, that compels us to recognise our transgression, to take our guilt seriously, to accept the consequent distress as a just punishment rather than refusing it as an injustice. . . . Just because we are forgiven, as those who need forgiveness—this is the one vital thing in the faith which is demanded from us by the divine judgment from which we come" (*CD* II/2, 769).

124. *CD* II/2, 779.

God's will, treating us as God's own. It is our unbreakable covenant with God in which we joyfully participate here and now as we become ready for the eternal blessing. Therefore, we must take ourselves seriously when we hear the command as God's judgment. This is because our sanctified life is cultivated from this hearing, signifying that the sanctification of our conformity can only be furthered by our faith. This faith, in turn, is a gift that allows us to see divine justification as a vehicle of conformity. We stand under the purpose of divine judgment as we keep living the life of "Christ lives in us and we in him"—we are those who are judged by Jesus Christ and, accordingly, ought to live as the "I" died and rose in Christ. By God's grace, obedience (growing out of faith) has to be apparent in those who have died and risen with Christ, whom God has determined for God's own image. As our sanctification by God's command surely takes place in the covenant relationship, we become what we are only in relation to Jesus: "We owe the reality and essence and continuance of our human life to [Jesus Christ], because He is the life of our life."[125]

For Barth, therefore, those who grasp the divine *telos* of the command as God's judgment live the eternal life in its temporal form, and it is through faith and obedience we perceive the *telos*. Put differently, the faith of the "I" who died and rose in Christ is "our temporal orientation, preparation and exercise, and therefore our sanctification for eternal life,"[126] while eternity is present in its concealment. In this concealment, we are sanctified by the command, entailing indivisible goodness of God and what God wills for us, even before creation and for eternity and in time, as Barth underlines that

> we do not yet live eternal life here and now. But we are here and now made free for eternal life. Each act of divine judgment from which we come is the offer and work of this freedom. And each act of faith in which we give ourselves to live as those who are judged by God is the acceptance of this offer, the consequence of this work, our real entry into this freedom, a provisional form of the great final step into eternal glory and clarity and harmony, into the eternal service for which we are selected.[127]

---

125. *CD* II/2, 778.

126. *CD* II/2, 773.

127. *CD* II/2, 773–74. Barth also emphasizes that "all transformation or renewal of our life has its basis and mysterious essence in the fact that our life is ready to be lived in this true and natural surrender to the death of all self-centred dignity and power—true and natural to the extent that we always come from the judgment of God, and on the basis of this judgment are always given up to this death in order that we may really live

The eternal covenantal blessing is "conformity," which we meaningfully perceive as what this blessing in the present means for us both horizontally and vertically—i.e., a life of harmony with God and our neighbors in a temporal form of blessing. Our lives are truly indebted to divine righteousness via Jesus Christ, a fact we acknowledge. We also declare that the resolution of the divine judgment is associated with God's salvific activity. Above all, Christ, who lives in us, sanctifies us from then until now and beyond.

SUMMARY

In the context of Gal 2:15–21, the polarity (encountering and estrangement) of the elected community and its twofold typology are dealt with in the doctrine of the word, particularly the way in which the word of God is heard either through the unity of both gospel and law or by prioritizing law over gospel. The discord of the word in gospel and law, endorsed by the works-based covenant, misinforms the *telos* of the covenant of grace. In this view, the evident deviations of the works-based covenant are evaluated, looking through the claims that the covenant of works raised. In contrast, by recapitulating the history of the covenant of grace, this covenant is understood via the word of God—the preserver of the church—in the harmony of both gospel and law. Within the context of Gal 3:10–14, the last section of the chapter discusses the command of God as judgment by means of hearing and obeying as well as understanding with the doctrines of justification and sanctification.

---

beyond this death" (*CD* II/2, 770).

Chapter 2

The Church as a Third Way of Her Existence

THIS CHAPTER FIRST EXPLORES various scholars' views on the overlap of the Spirit and the flesh (Gal 5:17) within the context of 5:16–18. Second, a third way of the church's existence is appraised by means of Barth's doctrines of nothingness and providence. Third, the third way and the word of God commanding are examined through the lenses of freedom and unfreedom.

THE OVERLAP OF THE SPIRIT AND THE FLESH

Galatians 5:17 expresses a battlefield of the opposing forces of Spirit and flesh, and the Spirit is not the human spirit but the Spirit of Christ at war engaged in the tension of the flesh. From various commentators' descriptions of the word flesh (σάρξ: *sarx*[1]), Paul's use of flesh falls into two categories: flesh as human weakness to accept with humility and live in gratitude, and flesh as sin, living life outside of Christ.[2] Similarly, flesh denotes "[one's] essential nature in contrast with God or with 'Spirit,' to emphasize [one's] frailty, dependence or incapacity."[3] Not flesh but the sin

---

1. Longenecker, *Galatians*, 239–41.
2. Smedes, "Being in Christ," 142–54.
3. Davies, *Paul and Rabbinic Judaism*, 18.

of the flesh becomes the ultimate enemy of the Spirit of God, as W. D. Davies indicates that the antithesis of the flesh and the Spirit represents "the complex product of Paul's Old Testament background and his Rabbinic training."[4] According to Charles K. Barrett, flesh means "self-centred existence, egocentric existence; not specifically a proclivity to carnal sins (as we call them), but a concern focused upon oneself."[5] Because flesh as the opposite of love stands against the Spirit, it pulls us from obeying the law of God, and we consequently look away from the commandment of love for the neighbor (5:14). Flesh can also be understood as the outward aspect of life and human will, which chooses to do evil rather than good. In addition, this relates to humanity's fallen, corrupt, and sinful nature, which is distinguished from the image originally created by God, therefore suggesting that an essential aspect of the human condition is in opposition to the Spirit, for the pursuits of the flesh are distinct from the goodness of God. Hans Betz defines the flesh as a human agent of evil and the Spirit as the divine agent of good. The dualistic forces—Spirit and flesh—are impersonal forces agitating against each other, and believers are in warfare between these forces. There are three wills—human, Spirit, and flesh. In the overlap of the Spirit and the flesh, on the one hand, human (i.e., "I") will is unable to carry out its own intentions within these forces. On the other hand, when the human (the "I") wills to walk in the Spirit, "the Spirit takes the lead, overwhelms, and thus defeats evil."[6] This will, for Betz, evidences the genuine existence of believers (and the Galatians),[7] not only in the battlefield between the two forces but also in producing the fruit of the Spirit (5:22–23)—the works of the flesh (and the law) cannot do this.

According to Augustine, "the life of the believer is divided into four stages, corresponding to the four stages of the biblical history of salvation: 'prior to the law,' 'under the law,' 'under grace,' and 'in . . . eternal

---

4. Davies, *Paul and Rabbinic Judaism*, 17.

5. Barrett, *Freedom and Obligation*, 73; O'Donovan, "Flesh and Spirit," 271–84. According to O'Donovan, the Spirit/flesh is projected *"across the field of moral life,* for 'walking by the Spirit' is an enduring commitment to moral consistency through time, not a mere repetition of the pathos of a conversion moment" (284). Italics his. He emphasizes that "the life in the Spirit is known by the authority it commands to interpret moral law within a framework of mutual service, the love of neighbor as self" (284).

6. Betz, *Galatians*, 281.

7. Betz, *Galatians*. "This is true of Christian existence," writes Betz, "since only there we can assume the Spirit is present" (281).

The Church as a Third Way of Her Existence 51

peace' (*Exp. Gal.* 46. 4–9)."[8] The first stage of human life is prior to the law. Before the law is established, no malice is prohibited and thus there is no need to be against malice. The second stage is under the law prior to grace. When we are under the law, we tend to serve what the flesh desires and fail to resist sin because we do not yet love righteousness for the sake of God. In this stage, we see the love of righteousness on the one hand and temporal comfort (i.e., the lust of the flesh) on the other. We choose comfort over righteousness, however. The third stage is under grace, and we choose righteousness through spiritual love, "which the Lord taught by his example and gave by his grace."[9] Despite the Spirit/flesh conflict in this stage, our will resists consenting to sin, led by the lust of the flesh. As we are under the grace of God, for Augustine, we do what we want in the Spirit even though we cannot destroy the desires of the flesh. We are not yet in the fourth stage—"eternal peace made perfect in every part of us"—but no longer under the law where "the mind is held guilty of transgression since the lust of the flesh leads it captive into consenting to sin."[10] That is, those who are under grace are not condemned because "the penalty is visited not on the one engaged in battle but on the one defeated in battle."[11] Our will in the third stage is disordered by the flesh but overcomes the disorder by God's grace because we love righteousness, and this is true for the Galatians. They can accordingly carry out the love of righteousness and willfully choose to walk in the Spirit, not fulfilling the lust of the flesh. Augustine therefore highlights the second and third stages as they reflect Christian existential experience.[12]

J. Louis Martyn specifies "the six motifs"[13] with which Paul's opponents press the Galatians to become observant of the law so that the

---

8. Augustine, *Galatians*, 114.

9. Augustine, *Galatians*, 211.

10. Augustine, *Galatians*, 211.

11. Augustine, *Galatians*, 211.

12. For Augustine, the first and fourth stages thus do not reflect Christian existential experience in a way that the second and third stages do: "'under grace' does not mean to be free from sinful desires but to be free from their domination (*Exp. Gal.* 46–48)" (Augustine, *Galatians*, 114).

13. Martyn, *Galatians*. Martyn outlines the six motifs regarding the Impulsive Desire of the Flesh. The first motif is internal to the individual; "the Impulsive Flesh has the individual as its major locus of operations." The second describes that the Flesh is "to some extent an entity with a life of its own, but it remains within the individual." As for the third, the Flesh is "dangerous to the individual." The fourth explicates that "the individual can master the Impulsive Flesh by choosing to observe the Law." According to the fifth, based on the doctrine of the Two Ways, "the Impulsive Flesh presents the

Galatians will not fall prey to "the Impulsive Desire of the Flesh."[14] This desire is limited to the individual struggle and can be overcome by law-observance. Indeed, when 5:17 connects to the later verses on vices and virtues (5:19–23), the Spirit–flesh dualism relates to the ethical code of Galatians' daily life, guiding fundamental behaviors for the church. As the opponents suggest, the code is part of God-honoring solutions (e.g., observance, circumcision, and rites) to give clear guidance as to what is right and wrong so that the Galatians become righteous. Taking a different stance from the opponents, Paul acknowledges that the law reflects the love of God and is positively related to daily life in the church, so the church outside the law does not live. However, the law is disparate from God's commandments, and the opponents misinform the Galatians regarding the fundamental meanings of the flesh, the law, and the Spirit, respectively, and their relationship to one another. Belonging to the human sphere, the flesh is opposed by the law, but flesh and law are secret allies. As the Spirit is of the sphere of God, the Spirit and the flesh are mutually exclusive and engaged in warfare with each another. In this light, Martyn indicates that the significance of 5:17 for Paul closely connects with eschatological life, which is promised by God, who sends the Son and the Spirit of the Son and takes the battleground against the flesh. This struggle between the Spirit and the flesh is not only personal dimension but also communal, so the teaching of the opponents is a danger to the new community created by the Spirit. Caught between two extreme teachings, the Galatians need to discern what lies behind the opposition between the Spirit and the flesh, as it is the faith with which we—in Jesus Christ and by the help of the Spirit—walk out of the battlefield. In addition, Martyn affirms that the opposition between the Spirit and the flesh refers to the new creational struggle of an apocalyptic war, "declared by God when he sent his Son and the Spirit of this Son into the territory of the Flesh."[15] The weapons of war are described as the fruit of the Spirit, through which the church not only bears goodness but also overcomes the ruin of Christian communities driven by the flesh.

---

individual with the necessity of making a choice; the individual is competent to make that choice and is responsible for the effects of that choice." Finally, "to observe the Law is not only to master the Impulsive Flesh; it is also to achieve perfection of virtue" (526–27). Martyn uses the capital F to indicate that the desire of the flesh is related to an apocalyptic, cosmic, and supra-human power (see 485–86).

14. Martyn, *Galatians*, 483–86.
15. Martyn, *Galatians*, 530–31.

John Calvin also sees the tension in the overlap of the Spirit and the flesh as both individual and communal struggles, as false doctrines (taught by Paul's opponents) not only cause disagreement between members within the church but also lead to ruin and consumption of the whole body (v. 15). The word "flesh" fundamentally denotes, for Calvin, an old nature, which disobeys and is rebellious against the Spirit of God. Through the work of the Spirit, "regenerated nature" is renewed by God's grace and accordingly capable of producing the fruit of the Spirit. Calvin articulates that

> [Paul] condemned the whole nature of [humanity] as producing nothing but evil and worthless fruits. He now informs us that all virtues, all proper and well regulated affections, proceed from the Spirit, that is, from the grace of God, and the renewed nature which we derive from Christ. "[Nothing] but what is evil comes from [human]; nothing good comes but from the Holy Spirit."[16]

Just as Gal 5:17 informs us about difficulties arising from our natural opposition to the Spirit, so too does obedience to the Spirit demand our labor, fight, and utmost effort.[17] Resisting the rule of the flesh thus involves yielding ourselves to the guidance of the Spirit; the goodness in human free will, led by the Spirit, resists all fleshly thoughts that are contrary to the law of God. So, those who are under the burden of the flesh are subject to commit sin, for they do not walk according to the Spirit. Teaching of the true doctrine—i.e., "walk[ing] by the Spirit"—not only resolves the condemnation of the law but also yields freedom from "ceremonies [that] mark the condition of a slave."[18] Calvin thus asserts that the Galatians cannot live outside old and regenerated natures: in other words, old nature is uninterested in the righteousness of God, from which false teaching causes the Galatians to stray. On the contrary, regenerated nature, taught by Paul, walks according to the Spirit to be free from the dominion of the law and pursue the holy affections that God grants upon believers in divine grace. Only one or the other nature is possible, for it is impossible to follow both Paul and his opponents.

In a similar fashion, Martin Luther indicates that the tension the Galatians experience comes from two doctrines—one is taught by Paul and the other by the opponents. The doctrine of the opponents not only blinds

---

16. Calvin, *Galatians and Ephesians*, 137.
17. Calvin, *Galatians and Ephesians*, 132.
18. Calvin, *Galatians and Ephesians*, 133.

the Galatians to the authenticity of keeping God's commandments but also misleads them about being righteous before God. Pushed to live by law-ordinance, the Galatians became unable to see the life led by the Spirit, only life led by flesh. Specifically, Luther views flesh as pride, wrath, fear, impatience, and unbelief. The flesh is also identified with a sinful nature, which not only tempts us into sin but also rebels against the Spirit. Put another way, for Luther, the church experiences tension between the Spirit and the flesh (in sinful nature). Taking against the Spirit, a sinful nature "rob[s] the church of a unique consolation, abolishing the forgiveness of sins and making Christ of no value."[19] The struggle between the flesh and the Spirit can dishearten us because sinful nature triggers new battles against the Spirit and submits to the flesh. Luther recognizes that "it is impossible to follow the guiding of the Spirit without any hindrance by the sinful nature,"[20] because we are unable to shake off sinful nature. Nevertheless, we are given the Spirit and thus can live by the Spirit. For Luther, it is in the Spirit that good will facilitates us, even while sinful nature resists this good will. Because of Jesus Christ, who was "born under the law [redeems those] under the law" (4:4–5), we can be liberated from the yoke of the law and also truly righteous and not under the law, for the law is circumscribed to accuse the faithful. As Luther confesses in the battlefield,

> my sinful nature is fighting against the Spirit. Let it do so as long as it likes; I must just see that in any case I do not consent to it, to doing what it wants, but must rather live wisely and follow the leading of the Spirit. By doing so, I am free from the law. My sinful nature accuses and frightens me, but in vain.[21]

In addition, he wants believers to be attentive to the word. This attentiveness both reassures us in battle and enables us to lean on the help of the Spirit as he declares:

> When you feel this battle, do not be discouraged, but resist in the Spirit and say, "I am a sinner, and I feel sin in me, for I have not yet put off the sinful nature. But I will obey the Spirit and not my sinful nature. I will by faith and hope lay hold upon Christ, and by his Word I will raise myself up and will not do what my sinful nature desires."[22]

19. Luther, *Galatians*, 309.
20. Luther, *Galatians*, 310.
21. Luther, *Galatians*, 315.
22. Luther, *Galatians*, 310.

The Church as a Third Way of Her Existence

In this faithful confession, we become aware of ourselves in "part sinful nature and part Spirit"[23] and, consequently, keep sinful nature under the guidance of the Spirit. In the overlap of the Spirit and the flesh, put differently, faith comes humbly when we see sinful nature rebelling against the Spirit and falling into sin, and this faith keeps us witnessing the reign of righteousness in the battleground. For Luther, it is therefore positive to see the tension of our sinful nature (i.e., the flesh opposing the Spirit) because we seek forgiveness of our sins in Jesus Christ and grasp the righteousness of faith.

In this battleground of "part sinful nature and part Spirit," Luther accordingly claims to rise up by faith (which is his central belief and theology) as he offers profound understanding of Scripture based on the insightful experiences of his faith and church. Just as his confession is grounded in the word of God, in which he finds avowal, our faith in the word secures us in the battleground of the opposing forces of Spirit and flesh as the word, accompanying the Spirit, shields us from sinful nature and protects us from the flaming arrows of the devil (Eph 6:16). In other words, our faith is connected with the word of God. We rise up by faith when the experience of the word becomes a possibility, revealing in and with us; because, after all, "Christ lives in us and we in him." The experience of God's word is indeed promising as Luther declares the experience, going under and withstanding the trial of faith. We are brought up against our part-sinful nature as the word of God is not only heard by us through the gift of the Spirit but also inspires us by the power of the Spirit. In this view, Barth concurs that it is a divine possibility that we as sinful humans receive the word in faith. As the word of God is a matter of faith for the church, the possibility of experiencing the word in the Spirit becomes actualized and comes to us as the reality of the word attested in Scripture, in which we connect with "the right hearing of obedience or the wrong hearing of disobedience."[24] In line with this, Paul Nimmo affirms "it is by Word and Spirit that God works in the incarnation, posits Barth, and by the same Word and Spirit that God works in us."[25] Standing before God and living in Jesus Christ, we perceive "walk[ing] by the Spirit" as turning from the flesh to the Spirit: after all, God is the Truth

---

23. Luther, *Galatians*, 311.
24. *CD* I/1, 201.
25. Nimmo, *Barth*, 98.

that wills, and the Truth motivates us to hear Jesus Christ in us as we obey the Truth.[26]

Bearing this in mind, we now turn to a third way of the church's existence with respect to the collective "I" of Gal 2:20, which is described as neither a community of sin nor a community of encountered revelation, examined through the doctrines of nothingness and providence, as well as the relationship between the word and freedom.

A THIRD WAY OF THE CHURCH'S EXISTENCE

Karl Barth defines nothingness, *das Nichtige*,[27] as a third way of its own existence, which belongs to a shadow side of creation. The first creative work separates the primitiveness of the beginning in its formlessness, emptiness, darkness, and water, in which the Spirit presents.[28] Light proclaims the will of God, while darkness is what "God neither wills nor creates."[29] Accordingly, this shadow side of creation is what God rejects, and what God rejects is divine non-willing. On the one hand, what God wills belongs to a positive side of the creation, which is what God elected. On the other hand, what God does not will belongs to its negative side—it is what God rejected. Nothingness therefore belongs to what is rejected—God distinguished what God did will from nothingness, which is what God did not will. The ontological characteristics of nothingness oppose what God determines, particularly its hostile and aggressive power against the positive side of God's creation. It opposes God's lordship,

---

26. Barth, *Romans*, 315–16.

27. Thomas, "Sin and Evil," 354–72. According to Thomas, Barth uses the phrase nothingness—*das Nichtige*—as the neuter-gendered noun, which does not imply a person, or a devil, but rather "a living agency of active destruction" and "a power of its own" (364).

28. Chaos is, in fact, the uncreated reality that God rejected at the word even before the beginning of time. It differs from the shadow side of creation—which is merely night. Chaos is also distinct from light, as it represents a distortion that opposes both God and the creature. In creation, God's command brings it within divine order. Regarding Barth's doctrine of creation, von Balthasar clarifies that "the contrasting pairs of light and darkness, right and left, power and weakness, fullness and emptiness, which are inherent to the nature of God's creation, are not 'dialectical' in and of themselves. These pairs are meant to be. They do not impair creation but are part of its natural 'perfection'" (von Balthasar, *Theology of Karl Barth*, 251). Thus, for Barth, these pairs "do not signify contradiction or resistance to God's creative will." Rather, they are "its fulfillment and confirmation" (von Balthasar, *Theology of Karl Barth*, 251–52).

29. *CD* III/1, 117.

The Church as a Third Way of Her Existence

threatening and corrupting the goodness of God's creation. This peculiar way of nothingness is known through God's activities, segregated from what God elects for the purpose of God's creation, grounded in the covenant between Godself and humanity. It is thus construed as the frontier, venting what God wills, for the existence of nothingness relays the two aspects of God's judgment in terms of the binary act of election and rejection in creation.

From this perspective, Barth unfolds the divine justification, which is associated with God's alien work (*opus alienum Dei*) and God's proper work (*opus proprium Dei*). As Martin Luther notably influenced Barth, explicating the *opus alienum*—actions that are alien to God, such as wrath—and the *opus proprium*—actions that belong to God's nature, such as mercy. Nothingness is an object of *opus alienum Dei*, described as "the truth of falsehood, the power of impotence, the sense of non-sense."[30] By God's activities in *opus proprium*, on the other hand, nothingness exists only by the fact that God does not will, and the divine non-willing accepts nothingness as God's own cause. Nothingness then contradicts God's *opus proprium*, in which God (of grace, love, faithfulness, and glory) fulfills the divine work. God, though, actually engages in nothingness to act *opus proprium*, so nothingness can only serve the will of God. This dualism of the divine work denotes the opposite of each other but yields the purpose of God, as God's *opus alienum* takes place simultaneously with God's *opus proprium*. That is, God's activity on the left hand is as necessary as God's activity on the right. These dialectic works of God obviously stand to temporality (with the eternity of *opus proprium Dei*) as the essential determination and justification of God's sovereign action. The existence of nothingness thus does not imply that God creates nothingness and permits its existence in order to demonstrate God's decision and judgment against the hostility of nothingness. Rather, its existence substantiates God's No in light of God's eternal Yes. Just as creation has its being in the divine Yes, nothingness attains its reality on the basis of the divine No. Nothingness falls into all that God does not will, from the very first, which was part of creation and exists because God allows it to be. So, nothingness belongs to God, which was denied at once by God in creation. Barth states, "In all the power of its peculiar being, it is nothing but a receding frontier and fleeting shadow. It has no substance."[31]

---

30. *CD* III/3, 361.
31. *CD* III/3, 361.

Nothingness thus exists as something yielding and defeated, drawn upon the traditional teaching of God's permission of evil. God does not will evil but permits it in order to realize God's plan of salvation. This means that evil also belongs to the negative sides of life and has an endangering power of its own but is insignificant in its relationship to God, who has already been conquered in Jesus Christ.

Indeed, nothingness, for Barth, exists as a threat and becomes actualized as sin, evil, or death,[32] considered a form of nothingness—a hostile, negative power within God's creation. In his treatment of sin as a form of nothingness, Barth utters that "sin itself is only [human]'s irrational and inexplicable affirmation of the nothingness which God as Creator has negated."[33] Sin is a human act of resistance against God, with the human as a responsible agent. It is the product of human disobedience, rebellion, and ingratitude towards God, and the sinner has fallen victim through nothingness, exercising a power in relation to the creature.[34] Sin can thus be defined as an act and a state in which we are overwhelmed by the power of nothingness, and we can become a victim of this power, standing in need of liberation.[35] However, with a focus on the life, death, and resurrection of Jesus Christ, God took upon this challenge from nothingness, which God opposes and judges with divine wrath. Divine victory over nothingness was demonstrated in the events of the cross and resurrection, in which nothingness as a "sinister neighbour"[36] has already been judged and refuted. The reality of nothingness was therefore indeed invalidated by God's decision to defeat it since the beginning of all God's work. At the same time, this defeat remains hidden to us and its final annulment occurs in the return of Jesus Christ. In him, the peculiar nature of nothingness is thus explicated. Just as the reality of evil is a problem for every theological position, the reality of nothingness is at work and

---

32. Sin, evil, and death are, for Barth, forms of nothingness. As finite, mortal beings, our natural death is part of our good nature as creatures of God. Barth distinguishes this from the death of judgment—the radical negation of life we bring upon ourselves through sin—by noting that the judgment we deserved was already carried out when Jesus Christ exchanged his life for ours. As Barth affirms, "The necessity of death means, therefore, that our life is one which is bounded by the menace of this negation . . . our death into connexion with [God] as the One who summons us to account and judges our life according to its deserts" (*CD* III/2, 625–26).

33. *CD* III/2, 143.
34. *CD* III/3, 349–68.
35. Thomas, "Sin and Evil," 368.
36. *CD* III/3, 77.

the continuing menace of nothingness is in need of justification. Along this line of argumentation, John McDowell observes that Barth takes the problem of evil lightly and so fails to establish a firm understanding of evil and nothingness.[37] Nimmo also points out that Barth

> has been criticized both for taking evil too seriously and for not taking it seriously enough. On the one hand, [he] describes nothingness as definitely existing (albeit in a very particular way), thereby according it an ontic status denied it in accounts of evil which speak of evil simply as privation. On the other hand, [he] describes nothingness as utterly defeated (on the cross of Jesus Christ), therewith affirming that present-day manifestations of evil lack genuine power or substance and serve the divine will.[38]

However, the conflicting interpretations have more to do with comprehending dogmatic difficulties that theologians face and less to do with Barth's account of nothingness, as Nimmo argues.

For Barth, nothingness indeed exists, and we can know its existence through God's activities against nothingness, which is granted its temporal existence under the sovereign rejection. Nothingness does not have perpetuity, for nothingness is what God has not willed and thus said No to from all eternity. Engaging in negation, at the same time, God in divine providence alone resists and conquers this adversary in what has taken place in Jesus Christ. The judgment of God is pronounced and revealed in him. That is, he takes the resolution of nothingness, and justification brings together the dialectic works of God as God elects rejection, so that what God does will works for election in Jesus Christ. Barth thus suggests that nothingness can only be known from the work of Jesus Christ, for whom God has designed the salvific history of the covenant.[39] Put differently, nothingness becomes knowable to us as God pronounces its existence by virtue of *opus alienum*, through which God exercises the divine non-willing and judgment. Justification, derived from the history of Jesus Christ, bears wrath and judgment in order to restore the rejected. Indeed, there is no judgment apart from Jesus Christ, who is "the Rejected, as and because He is the Elect. In view of His election, there is no other rejected but Himself."[40] Justification not only reflects God's righteousness

---

37. McDowell, "Much Ado About Nothing," 319–35.
38. Nimmo, *Barth*, 103.
39. See *CD* III/3, 302–49.
40. *CD* II/2, 353.

in "the identity of His wrathful holiness and His absolving mercy"[41] but also draws God's judgment on the existence of nothingness from God's negation—"the shadow of His work which both arises and is at once dispelled by His wrath."[42] Justification under the sovereignty of God thus becomes actualized in Jesus Christ, who discloses both divine election and rejection. As a result of the work of Jesus Christ, nothingness has lost its perpetuity. The ontology of nothingness is therefore understood as absolutely conquered on the cross of Jesus Christ, although it remains hidden for now. Divine determination will thus again take place in the return of Jesus Christ, in which the threat of nothingness will be overcome in the final revelation for all. Again, Barth sees nothingness as definitely existing in a very certain way, but nothingness has no perpetuity. At the same time, the threat of nothingness remains obscured from us. On this basis, for Barth, nothingness *is* and "may be real, but it is so only in its futility, in its transitoriness and in its final overthrow by God in Jesus Christ."[43] Thus, its existence—which gives insights into the theological negative[44]—signifies the denial of what God has affirmed unelected and yet temporarily allowed by God.

In addition to its temporal existence, according to Barth, nothingness—hostile both to the Creator and the creature—does not belong to either God or the creature. It exists but is not real, as God is or as the creature is. God is superior to nothingness, and nothingness is superior to the creature. It does not inherit essential attributes of God or share characteristics of the creature. However, the creature adjoins nothingness. When the creature crosses the state of being adjacent (although the state of being is not nothingness), nothingness achieves actuality in the creaturely world but is not identified with the frontier between God

---

41. Gockel, *Barth and Schleiermacher*, 129; see Barth, *Romans*. In his exegesis of Rom 5:6, Barth utters that "we, who have rejected our Creator, return to His love; and in so far as in His death the paradox of the righteousness and the identity of His holy wrath and His forgiving mercy becomes *for us*—the Truth" (160). Italics his.

42. *CD* III/3, 77.

43. Nimmo, *Barth*, 106.

44. von Balthasar, *Theology of Karl Barth*. In terms of Hegelian dialectics, von Balthasar argues that "we can speak of the power of negation arising within certain determined boundaries. Barth's issue goes beyond Hegel's philosophy of being or even Kierkegaard's philosophy of the negative side of free will, with its temptations to rebellion. Barth's whole problematic arises from the absolute actuality of God's decision. The real issue is the theologically valid concept of truth, which must be delimited from a philosophical or neutral concept. Truth is now directly constituted by the divine Yes just as untruth is brought about by God's No" (252–53).

and the creature. Barth thus asserts that nothingness characterizes its existence, distinct from God, the creature, and frontiers.[45] Confronted by nothingness, we are plainly inaccessible to the nature of nothingness and unable to recognize its existence. We tend to misinterpret this confrontation as if nothingness is in a positive relationship with God, although it is deplorable and justifiable. Given this tendency, we dismiss this confrontation simply as non-existent. In addition, Barth argues that there is no capacity for humans to deal with nothingness: it is beyond all human capacities to unravel ourselves from the danger of *das Nichtige*. We would not only be "overwhelmed by chaos and fall into nothingness"[46] but also might become its victim and even make ourselves its agent, although nothingness has no true power and remains under God's sovereignty. Barth therefore emphasizes that nothingness is God's affair, as the privation of nothingness primarily affects God, who desires our "permanence and continuity."[47] In the face of nothingness threatening and corrupting the good creation of God, accordingly, it is God who exposes Godself to the threat and wills us to take part in this privation through prayer.[48] Gunter Thomas agrees that it is God's affair to keep humans from this danger of nothingness as we are unable to separate ourselves from the danger. We can only recognize the danger as God's own affair—we are not called to participate in the affair but can gratefully acknowledge the work of God.[49] Nothingness therefore exists as something that has been invalidated, which is, for Barth, significant in comprehending the perplexing ontology of nothingness.[50] Nothingness is surely unable to

45. *CD* III/3, 349–50.

46. *CD* III/3, 74.

47. *CD* III/3, 79.

48. Barth emphasizes that the prayer of believers resists the outworking power of nothingness; this Christian prayer is an assurance that God confronts nothingness on behalf of the believer, and nothingness, in turn, holds no final power of its own. See Barth, *Christian Life*, 185.

49. See Krötke, "Barth and Evil on Nothingness," 207–16. Krötke indicates that covenant partners resist nothingness by exercising our own possibilities, and for Christians, prayer is the first act of this resistance, through which we align ourselves with Jesus's prayer, e.g., "deliver us from evil." This prayer against nothingness makes Christians less resigned to the sphere from which it arises. It also charges Christians with the task of understanding the deleterious power that threatens God's creation, despite the reality that there are times and places where nothingness will assert its power.

50. Barth underlines that the ontic and noetic nature of nothingness is "never as a subject of systematic formulation, even though the system be dialectical" (*CD* III/3, 354). It is a phenomenon that we are unable to theologically systematize its metaphysical essence.

contest God and yet allowed to be in conflict with God. It has a particular way of existence (rejected and overcome), which has presented from the very beginning, but what God said No to represents perpetuity, excluded as the eternal past.

Unlike the circumscription of nothingness, God grants permanency to temporal covenant partners as it is God's will that we are given eternal fellowship with the Creator God. The reason why God wants "permanence and continuity" for the covenant partner is to preserve the church and have us participate in God's victory over chaos, evil, and nothingness. As Barth asserts, the church taking part in fellowship with the beloved Son of God is in fact the goal of divine preservation. Nothingness then points to the divine act of providence, which we can acknowledge: "God controls and conquers nothingness even in the form of human sin, not in any sense being arrested by it, but setting it to serve His own glory and the work of His free love,"[51] for nothingness is at the left hand of God and yet under God's providence.[52] As God wills us to live by the grace of God and to continue our existence and activity in the covenantal relationship, we are saved by Jesus Christ and partake of this salvation by him, and therefore are sustained and preserved by him. According to Sung-Sup Kim, we gain true knowledge of nothingness only in Jesus Christ: "Only in knowing Christ, then, do we become fully aware of the seriousness with which God opposes and pours his wrath on nothingness."[53] We grasp this knowledge of Jesus Christ and the covenantal history of God's redemptive work, which is the affair of God to preserve the church from a third way—we are "menaced by nothingness, menaced in such a way that [the church]

---

51. *CD* IV/2, 398.

52. *CD* III/3, 84–90; God is the sovereign Creator who creates *ex nihilo*, yet also confronts the chaos manifested in evil. Creation does not emerge from a battle; instead, it is an act characterized by a transition from non-being into being. Also, the distinction between creation and nothingness demands constant stabilization, as only divine preservation can shield us from the threat of annihilation; this work of preservation is God's alone, yet we participate in it through our acknowledgment and praise of his faithfulness. See Thomas, "Sin and Evil," 363–64. Fergusson argues that "Barth has little use for the distinction between divine permitting and willing that has been deployed by scholars in other traditions (for example, Lutheran, Orthodox, Jesuit, and Methodist theologians) to offset the threat of divine determinism. For Barth, this distinction compromises the lordship of God over all things. He concludes with the dubious claim that those who cannot subscribe to this reading of providence are in the grip of fear and sin, especially the fear of God's sovereignty as this confronts us in Christ and his resurrection. The only remedy for such deep-seated affliction, Barth contends, is prayer and fasting" (Fergusson, "Providence," 381).

53. Kim, *Deus Providebit*, 15.

needs the divine preservation and sustaining and indeed deliverance if it is not to fall victim to it and [perish]."[54] Put another way, divine providence represents constant activities of God upon the church, preserving us in our existence and activity. Just as our covenantal relationship is possible through Jesus Christ, who fulfilled the covenant of grace, so too our continuing existence is possible only by divine providence, overcoming nothingness. We are preserved to coexist in Jesus Christ, in whom we have died and risen, for God essentially wills us to continue our participation in eternal election in Jesus Christ. In light of the life, death, and resurrection of Jesus Christ, God takes up nothingness, which God opposes and judges so that divine providence sustains participation, overcoming nothingness from now until fruition. Indeed, this deliberation will again take place in the final revelation for all in the return of Jesus Christ, in which this threat will be overcome. Barth therefore focuses not only on the history of Jesus Christ, as part of which nothingness is once and for all destroyed on the cross,[55] but on divine providence, which continues without ceasing, for the judgment of God anticipates the eschatological reconciliation and redemption of the Son. Furthermore, Barth affirms that divine providence is to be recognized by our faith:

> During the time allotted to [biblical characters], and to the very goal and end of that time, their hearts, etc., and they themselves, are literally preserved. In and with that which is committed to them their existence is preserved. In and with their spiritual life, in virtue of its origin and with a view to its destiny, their life is preserved in itself and as such. In so far as they live for Christ in faith, [they] live in time and in the cosmos cannot be abstracted from the higher and more decisive fact that they are in Christ and that they stand in faith.[56]

David Fergusson supports the argument that, for Barth, divine providence is known only through faith and the Son, asserting that the Son also reveals God's sovereign rule, which does not exclude God's justice and mercy at work.[57] In a similar vein, divine providence, according to

---

54. *CD* III/3, 75–76.

55. Barth focuses on the work of Jesus Christ, so he "does not start his work with abstract conceptions of God, creation or evil, nor does he operate with abstract ideas of divine omnipotence and goodness or human incapacity and fallenness" (Nimmo, *Barth*, 102–3).

56. *CD* III/3, 83.

57. Fergusson, *Providence of God*, 273.

Wolfhart Pannenberg, is an expression of the fidelity of the Son and the Father, as he highlights Barth's doctrine of providence for the creature: "God's faithfulness, which proceeds from the mutual faithfulness of the Son to the Father and the Father to the Son, is the basis of the identity and continuation of [God's] creatures."[58] Faithfulness in providence has been persistent with the word of God, and it is through Jesus Christ, "whom alone we come to know with certainty God's care for and rule over the world."[59] Further, Calvin, drawing attention to the revelation of God in Jesus Christ, affirms that the doctrine of providence is equated with hearing and receiving the word of God. Established by the word—God's eternal Wisdom (the Son) and God's Power (the Holy Spirit), for Calvin, God "sustains [*sustinere*], nourishes [*fovere*], activates [*agere*], preserves [*conservare*], by his goodness and power [*bonitate ac virtute sua*], apart from which all things would immediately collapse and fall into nothingness."[60] It is thus important that we, in faith, grasp God's providence primarily delivered through the word of God, through which we come to know and see God's providence in the world as we "stand in need of correction by the Word of God."[61] In light of this, the word moves us—in genuine freedom under divine providence—by the power, wisdom, and goodness of the Spirit, as Nimmo emphasizes.[62]

In brief, nothingness has its own third way of being, existing unnaturally and illegitimately "as inherent contradiction, as impossible possibility."[63] Its existence primarily embodies a theological negative as

---

58. Pannenberg, *Systematic Theology*, 2:53. In his distinction between God's creation, preservation, and world government, Pannenberg writes that "creation cannot be an act in time. We have to view it as the constitution of the finite existence of creatures and therefore of time as the form of this existence. Preservation presupposes the existence of creatures and consequently the preceding act of creation. It is thus structured in time. The same is true of world government or providence in its orientation to a goal. Preservation and world government differ from creation, then, in that they are expressions of the participation of God in the life of creatures and therefore in their time-structures. But they differ from one another inasmuch as preservation relates to the origin of creatures in God's act of creation, and providence or world government has a forward reference to their future consummation. What ultimately underlies the participation of God in the life of creatures that works itself out as their preservation and governing is the self-differentiation of the Son from the Father" (2:57–58).

59. Kim, *Deus Providebit*, 7.

60. Kim, *Deus Providebit*, 47.

61. Kim, *Deus Providebit*, 154.

62. Nimmo, *Barth*, 98.

63. *CD* III/3, 351.

nothingness belongs to what "God neither wills nor creates."⁶⁴ Nothingness is what God rejects, and what God rejects is divine non-willing. For it is what God does not will, it is disavowed with regard to divine providence. It exists in the context of justification: God's Yes is accompanied by No—as *opus alienum Dei* connected with *opus proprium Dei*. Nothingness as a third way of being gives way to a form of sin and at the same time divine providence. In the overlapping spheres of sin and providence, Jesus Christ remains. Put differently, the third way is adjacent to the frontier, which can exhaust nothingness into sin. As the frontier, alternatively, the third way leads the way in divine providence, sustaining a covenant partnership, which the church engages in a form of freedom. This means that, on the one hand, the church freely corresponds to the word, signifying a covenant partnership in Jesus Christ, in which we can know what freedom really is. On the other hand, there is a shadowy side of freedom, negating the partnership as this negation can only be understood in light of impossible possibility, placing believers between possible obedience and impossible disobedience.

FREEDOM AND UNFREEDOM

The third way therefore infers the overlap of divine providence and the threat of nothingness. We are under the influences of two opposites: human sin (the concrete form of nothingness) is not actualized, and our freedom corresponding to the word is unmotivated. In this overlap, we first look into the relationship between freedom and a third way. Divine providence, for the church, is determined by the self-revelation of God in Jesus Christ, in whom we exist as covenant partners. That is, God preserves the church, granting this advance of a covenant partnership, and the covenant, for Barth, is the internal basis of creation and needs an external basis—i.e., the influence of divine providence.⁶⁵ Based on the

---

64. *CD* III/3, 117.

65. *CD* III/3, 7. According to Elliott, "One can only get to a belief in Providence through some awareness of Election.... 'Barth on Providence' has fallen. His doctrine of Providence has had the guts taken out of it, and remains as an interpreted 'doctrine of comfort.' In some ways the threefold division of the topic holds: 'The threefold rule over creation, history and the lives of individuals, directed especially to the overcoming of evil, constitutes the pattern of providence in Scripture. It is clear that it lies behind the later scholastic distinction between general, special and most special providence.' If for Aquinas both Providence and Predestination were related parts of God's knowledge, then Barth wants to separate them, seeing Providence as part of Predestination

covenant of grace, the church therefore accords with the self-revealing God so that she—unconditionally elected by God's grace—freely associates with Jesus Christ, not only the perfect manifestation of God's nature and characteristics but also the revelation of God's salvific plan. As obedient to the begotten Son of God, the church engages in her freedom given by divine freedom, in which she relates to the knowledge of Christ. Put another way, we are free in and with God, who creates our freedom. This freedom comes from God's own freedom,[66] which involves the reality that we become free. In revelation, we are made in accordance with the word attested in Scripture via "the Holy Spirit is the Spirit of God, because He is the Spirit of the Word."[67] Through the work of the Spirit, the freedom of God continues in Jesus Christ. In divine freedom, the word is revealed—the Spirit with the Word, and the word with the Spirit. This freedom in the word and the Spirit, for us and in us, is received and grasped. Accordingly, the church hears the word in her freedom revealed in Jesus Christ. Apart from when divine freedom binds her freedom, the word is thus unheard, and the church is unfree. This is exemplified as enslavement to the basic principles of the world in the context of the Galatians.

Second, this unfreedom refers to a shadowy side of freedom, negating the partnership. The church is unresponsive to the association that we are to be a covenant partner of God in Jesus Christ—thus, we are unfree. "To be free" means to partake in the event of Christ—his death and resurrection (Gal 2:20), in which we participate in divine redemption as a member of the church community. Those who died and rose in Jesus Christ learn the union of participation in the presence of the Spirit among and within members of the Christian community. As Betz indicates, Spirit and freedom, for Paul, are one and the same thing—where the Spirit of the Lord is, there is freedom.[68] The authentic existence of the church therefore lies "in freedom," which is identical to "in and by the Spirit." The Galatians are gifted with the Spirit of Christ, sent out by God (4:6), which made them (who have died and risen in Christ) join Christ's salvific act of liberation, freeing them from estrangement, from

---

(Election). Yet in doing that Barth holds the two very close, and does not (in Gorringe's view) anchor it sufficiently to the Incarnation's message of God's condescension" (Elliott, *Providence Perceived*, 246).

66. For Barth, "this freedom of [humans] can only be a freedom created by God in the act of [God's] revelation and given to [humans]. In the last resort, it can only be God's own freedom" (*CD* I/2, 204–5).

67. *CD* I/2, 248; we hear the word by communing with the Spirit of Christ.

68. See 2 Cor 3:17.

The Church as a Third Way of Her Existence

the law, from the flesh, from idolatry, from social oppression, and from the basic principles of the world.[69] In Jesus Christ, then, the third way of the church's existence distinguishes her freedom from unfreedom as she contradicts the revelation of the incarnate Word but, at the same time, belongs to divine providence. For God's providence shields the church in divine possibility, she engages in freedom, corresponding to the divine word that influences the impossible possibility of obedience. It is through the Word of God, Jesus Christ, that we come to know divine providence. When the word comes to us as the divine command, demanding our decision in relation to Jesus Christ, this command does not come to us through a form of tyranny as it is disparate from all other forms of command. The word commanding comes to us as the accord of permission, freedom, and obedience, particularly the way in which the goodness of God's will is to be testified in and from us. For God preserves the church—where the command of God is heard, divine freedom for us is revealed as our truthful obedience corresponds to the command by virtue of genuine freedom.[70] The third way is thus depicted as the impossible possibility that the church as hearers relates herself in impossible disobedience, even when she invalidates her freedom responding to the word: this also indicates that the church acknowledges the history of Jesus Christ with respect to both *opus alienum Dei* and *opus proprium Dei*.

Importantly, God's influence on the church is genuinely mutual as the church freely corresponds to the free love of God—the eternal covenant of the Father with the Son.[71] This freedom "includes the fact that God creates, limits and directs it,"[72] while Nimmo holds that God grants our genuine freedom, and in this freedom, we live as covenanted with Jesus Christ.[73] God "not merely leaves the activity of the creature free, but continually makes it free."[74] For this reason, there is no contradic-

---

69. See Betz, *Galatians*. As Betz asserts, "the 'new creation' which the Christian existence is called (cf. 6: 15) is certainly the recreation of the primordial freedom of [humans]—but it is more than that: it is that freedom which is the result of Christ's act of liberation, and the sharing in this act" (256–57).

70. See *CD* II/2, 583–741.

71. *CD* III/1, 97.

72. Nimmo, *Barth*, 106.

73. Nimmo, *Barth*, 98.

74. *CD* III/3, 150; See Smith, *Theology of the Third Article*. As Smith explicates, "God shows us his unique freedom as God in the exercise of that freedom. He is not constrained by notions of autonomy on the one side; he is not 'God' because he is free from all things, existing in perfect aseity. And he is not constrained by notions of

tion between the sovereignty of God and the freedom of the church.[75] Put differently, God associates with us, and we are to be free partners in the covenant with God as we are attentive to Scripture and Jesus Christ. This association puts emphasis on the church's participation in faith and obedience, corresponding to divine freedom—i.e., the authentic freedom of the Trinity. Simultaneously, God inspires the faith of the church, which is the capacity for seeing God at reconciliation, for God in truth wills the association of Godself with people, who are free in sovereign freedom. In this light, the church can grasp the authentic meaning of this freedom when she encounters the event of address, for the word as revealed materializes only in the event of the self-revealing God. It is precisely achieved through hearing God's gracious covenant in Jesus Christ, in whom we are inalienable to the presence of God. The church, existing as the hearer of the Word that Jesus came in the flesh, continues her existence through the Spirit's empowering presence of the word.

Indeed, the fundamental relationship between divine freedom and ours with respect to the word is evident in Galatians. The Galatian Christians died and rose in Christ. God is the Spirit of the One who raised Jesus from the dead, and the resurrection of Jesus from the dead is their (and our) justification. As a result, the Spirit dwells in them, who become the bearers of the Spirit of Christ and are free to obey the command of God in the covenant of grace. The command—"the law of the Spirit of life"[76]—wills our life to be guarded under the lordship of God. When the concrete command of God, "walk by the Spirit" (Gal 5:16 NIV), is spoken to the Galatians (and us all), God therefore reaches us through the word and the Spirit. For the spiritual truth of the word is "revealed and operative in the presence and the work of the Holy Spirit,"[77] the word as the divine command in the goodness of God's will not only demands our decision in relation to Jesus Christ but also guides our determination. For the command does not merely exist as an authoritative, Barth emphasizes that

---

human incapacity on the other side; he is not 'God' by making himself a datum that we can understand. His accommodation is not to our native capacities of experience and reason, but in remaking our capacities as he addresses them. God is God in a third kind of freedom, beholden neither to independence nor to human need, but living in moment-by-moment self-determination, exercising unlimited right to limit himself reigning in submission, remaining Lord in the form of a servant" (172).

75. *CD* III/3, 166.
76. *CD* II/2, 728.
77. *CD* II/2, 603.

> God is *Spirit*, and therefore He truly awakens [the covenant partner] to freedom. That He causes His divine power to come on [us] does not mean that he overtakes and overwhelms and crushes [us], forcing [us] to be what He would have [us] be. He does not dispose of [us] like a mere object. He treats [us], and indeed establishes [us], as a free subject. He sets [us] on [our] own feet as His partner. He wills that [we] should stand and walk on [our] own feet. He thus wills that [we] should believe and love and hope.[78]

Where the command of God is declared, divine freedom assists us in corresponding to the command. God's will directs us and orchestrates double (divine and human) actions simultaneously as a single action (enclosed by the *concursus Dei*[79]). For the goodness of God's word is revealed, and we are to understand the word of wisdom in its fullest meaning.[80] God's determination in self-giving acts accommodates our determination with truthful obedience. In other words, the word spoken, embodying God's will, is addressed to us in Jesus Christ. Through the power of the Spirit, we are summoned not only to the word but also to hear and recognize it. The God who determines Godself in the self-giving act accommodates us in our willing, reasoning, and understanding, for divine agency makes a commitment to human agency. The third way of the church's existence can therefore confess to God, who accompanies us (i.e., the *concursus Dei*) as "walk[ing] by the Spirit," if the church is to witness "'pneumatic actuality' in the sphere of experience."[81] Through this walking, we recognize that Jesus Christ, who lives within us, addresses us; and that obedience (on the other side of faith) is a necessity, which means we must align ourselves to the word, as it is God's command. Our disobedience is accordingly excluded as "disobedience is not a choice, but the incapacity of the [covenant partner] who is no longer or not yet able to choose in real freedom."[82] Disobedience does not relate to the act of faith, and we can be disobedient but are unfree. As the command of God is dissimilar from all other forms of commands, it comes to us as the accord of permission, obedience, and freedom so that our obedience is initiated in genuine freedom, concurring with Jesus Christ: in him, "we

---

78. *CD* IV/3, 941–42. Italics his.
79. This will be explored in chapter 3.
80. *CD* III/2, 173.
81. *CD* II/2, 775–76.
82. *CD* II/2, 779.

see what it means for divine action to take place in, with and over [our] action without jeopardizing human integrity."[83] Nimmo therefore emphasizes that "a non-competitive construal of the relationship between God and humanity [celebrates] rather than fears creaturely life under the lordship of God. [The construal] affirms yet circumscribes the freedom of human action under divine providence."[84] We hear the command as God's word despite the state of our inner conflict, for we are bearers of the Spirit of Christ. This hearing also entails obedience, which is indeed possible via our freedom, gifted by God. When the command "walk by the Spirit" is declared, we, in our freedom, obey and follow the Spirit in the battleground, passing the frontier of the third way.

With this knowledge, we now appraise the nature of our freedom in relation to God, looking through the theological and anthropological perspectives of Søren Kierkegaard and the doctrinal approaches of Karl Barth.

Søren Kierkegaard claims that we comprehend the possibility of freedom, awakened by God-perceptivity. In his exegesis of the original sin, Kierkegaard argues that Adam was in his innocent state—i.e., a synthesis of body and soul united in a spirit—and discovered his limitless freedom as the "possibility of being able" when the judgment "you shall die" is followed by the prohibition, "You shall not eat of the fruit of the tree that is in the middle of the garden, nor shall you touch it." Adam ironically becomes more aware of his own limitless freedom at this point, as he recognizes that this freedom actualizes as "the possibility of possibility," plunging him into a state of conflict, which not only contradicts his state of innocence but also establishes the condition risking disobedience. Adam exposes himself to experience his freedom by taking the forbidden fruit. Though he desired to eat it, he had no conception of what God meant. Nor did he know the distinction between good and evil. He did not know the consequences of his action. Kierkegaard therefore rejects that sin came into the world by necessity or that we sin by virtue of our freedom. Between necessity and freedom, he indicates that the third factor relates to dizziness.[85] Dizziness is neither a determinant of

---

83. Nimmo, *Barth*, 100. Also, Barth asserts that "[God] is free for us and in us. That is the central content of the doctrine of Christ and of the doctrine of the Holy Spirit. Christology and Pneumatology are one in being the knowledge and praise of the grace of God. But the grace of God is just His freedom, unhindered either by Himself or by us" (*CD* I/2, 2–3).

84. Nimmo, *Barth*, 100. For Nimmo, this construal models Barth's essential understanding of our existence in the covenant of grace.

85. "If sin has come into the world by necessity (which is a self-contradiction),"

necessity nor of freedom but "an intermediate determinant."[86] It is the midway point between necessity and freedom. In other words, Adam was in a state of innocence and exposed himself to experience the possibility of freedom by taking the forbidden fruit, whether or not he desired to eat it. When Adam found his possibility of freedom, he may have likened dread to dizziness and became aware of his dizziness of freedom. In his transitional state with an intermediate determinant, his possibility of freedom might or might not escort him to sin. At the same time, he could actualize the infinite possibility of freedom to obey the word as God's command. Therefore, this possibility of freedom, for Kierkegaard, leads us to obedience or disobedience. This possibility also establishes itself in relation to unfreedom, which is a determinant oriented towards freedom. Such acknowledgment involves unlimited perceptions of our being, living freely by virtue of either freedom or unfreedom.

In the essence of his argument, Kierkegaard highlights the dizziness of good or evil. In dizziness, we arrive at the limits of language as we are muted, closing ourselves inwardly. Kierkegaard calls this "shut-up-ness" and sees this state as "demoniacal" as the "*shut-upness* [is] *unfreely revealed.*"[87] In this state, freedom is posited as unfreedom, for freedom is not only lost but also driven by unfreedom as the possibility of freedom manifests itself in relation to unfreedom. This is exactly the opposite of the innocent state, with freedom not suggested but appearing in dizziness. In the demoniacal state, put differently, we lose freedom. In this unfreedom, we become more and more shut up and want no communication: our unfreedom shuts ourselves.[88] We are then in an opposing relationship with good and unwilling to open up to communication. In our shut-upness, we become lazy returning to freedom. Kierkegaard, nevertheless, sees this state as good, for dizziness in this state "manifests itself at once in the instant of contact with the good."[89] The state is too demoniacal to shut up, but simultaneously, we become aware of our possibility to be free from the shut-up via the dizziness of the good (i.e., God-perceptivity). We

writes Kierkegaard, "then there is no dread. If sin has come into the world by an act of abstract *liberum arbitrium* (which no more existed at the beginning than it does at a later period of the world, for it is a non-sense to thought), neither in this case is there dread" (Kierkegaard, *Concept of Dread*, 45).

86. Kierkegaard, *Concept of Dread*, 44.

87. Kierkegaard, *Concept of Dread*, 110. Italics his.

88. Kierkegaard, *Concept of Dread*, 110.

89. For Kierkegaard, our God-perceptivity yields a clear distinction between necessity and freedom (Kierkegaard, *Concept of Dread*, 110).

experience the good, through which we can return to freedom, possibility, cheerfulness, productivity, and salvation. This shut-upness is an opportunity to expose ourselves to freedom as a possibility, which will lead us to relate with God, for the dizziness is affiliated with engendering faith. Kierkegaard therefore considers this paradoxical quality of dizziness to be both "*a sympathetic antipathy and an antipathetic sympathy.*"[90] Dizziness can function for good: it directs us to God and reminds us of our need for Jesus Christ. This state can be depicted as estrangement, meaning that we leave a certain state of experiencing everything whole—i.e., a synthesis of body and soul, of the infinite and the finite, of the temporal and the eternal, and of freedom and necessity. We are alienated from the whole and fall into an "intermediate state" where Adam experiences the possibility of *being able*. That is, the possibility of freedom comes through perceptivity, recognizing that we are separated from a primal unity and driven to one side as opposed to incorporating both sides. We become cognizant that we are not in relation with God: God's revelation is inaccessible, and we are muted. By means of the perceptivity of dizziness, we actualize the possibility of freedom leading us either to the possibility of limitless sinful acts or to the moment of contact with the good. This signifies that, in an intermediate state, we are competent to take a qualitative leap of faith on the basis of the possibility of freedom. In this state, we have the possibility of freedom and the power to reflect on estrangement from God, which can be accomplished by faith and the existential acceptance of something transcending—i.e., accepting God through faith.

This perceptivity, however, does not automatically lead to a leap of faith. Instead, it can educate us about a faith that saves us. That is, it can point us to God, remind us of our need for Jesus Christ, and thus guide us to finally relate to God. It further reveals that we tend to thin our guilt before God and, at the same time, can teach us that we are infinitely guilty before God. This recognition and acceptance of infinite guilt represent acknowledgment for us of the abundance of God's grace corresponding to guilt. Faith is then deepened through this understanding of God's grace in relation to infinite guilt, which elevates sin-perceptivity. This perceptivity of both sin and God is therefore educative to faith.

Significantly, the life of the church falls into an intermediate state (i.e., a third way), where the possibility of freedom is conceived by a qualitative leap, namely by the possibility of both freedom and unfreedom. In

---

90. Kierkegaard, *Concept of Dread*, 38. Italics his.

each fall, we experience the possibility of unfreedom and place ourselves in jeopardizing situations in which we are driven to the possibility of more and more sin. In the same fall, on the contrary, we pursue unity in the Spirit, in whom we choose the possibility of freedom rather than the possibility of unfreedom. As such, the fall is not only a historical event in the origin of humanity but also a constant theological question that is recurrent in the church. In the perceptivity of dizziness, we obey the word to be in contact with the good or disobey God to remain subdued.[91] It is therefore significant that we leap out of the intermediate state so that our body, mind, and spirit are integrated—we live in relation to God, which means that we live in relation to the self, to others, and to our environments, as Kierkegaard accentuates.[92]

In a different vein, Barth begins to explore the freedom of God and the nature of our freedom. Divine freedom, for Barth, lies in the freedom of the Trinity—i.e., the freedom of the Father and the Son in the unity of the Spirit.[93] God alone is free, and divine freedom is primarily recognized in Jesus Christ, in whom God has shown Godself.[94] We cannot acquire our own freedom for ourselves as it can be given only by God;[95] our freedom is not an inherent quality we can find in ourselves but a gift of God. Put differently, "to be free, [we] must be born again by God's Word and Spirit"[96] as we gratefully correspond to the eternal election of Jesus Christ, in whom our freedom is revealed and constituted. In light of this, we are free only in Jesus Christ. By the power of the Holy Spirit, we are awakened to our freedom, which was accomplished in the freedom of Jesus Christ. This means that we are free in him and thus obey God in our freedom because our persuasion in disobedience can be altered by

---

91. See Bretall, *Kierkegaard Anthology*. In Kierkegaard's journal entry for 14 April 1838, Bretall notes that "the fact that God could create free beings *vis-a-vis* of himself is the cross which philosophy could not carry, but remained hanging from" (10). Italics his.

92. As Barth also affirms, we exist only in our relationship with God (see *CD* III/2, 123).

93. Besides, Barth describes the love of the Trinity as the eternal love in which God as the Father loves the Son, and in which the Son loves the Father, and which is also the love addressed by God to us all (see *CD* III/2, 220); in a similar fashion, Webster argues that the concept of divine freedom and love is importantly Trinitarian and is self-giving. See Webster, *Barth's Moral Theology*, 106–8.

94. See *CD* II/1, 297–321.

95. *CD* III/2, 194.

96. *CD* IV/3, 447.

the Son of God, who has humbled himself to be obedient in our place.[97] From disobedience to obedience, our freedom takes place in Jesus Christ. Through faith, in Barth's account, we understand "the freedom of the confession of Jesus Christ as the one and only Prophet, light of life, and Word of God,"[98] and thus, the right use of our freedom is revealed to us in God's grace as we live out and exercise freedom in the act of responsibility, corresponding to the work of Jesus Christ. Otherwise, it is not freedom. God in divine freedom "will accomplish His personal life-act only together with us, and we can accomplish ours only together with God."[99] In this sense, our freedom does not mean that we have freedom to sin but the freedom in action to make a right choice.[100] This signifies that, apart from Jesus Christ, we are not truly free at all but slaves to sin.

Moreover, our freedom relates to God's decision as we belong to God, whom "demands of us that we finally act on our own decision—our very own, the one which corresponds to our determination."[101] This engagement sets ourselves against the domination of all other commands, such as our own desires, pride, and self-will, to which we subject ourselves. Our determination should therefore not be led by these types of commands as they can trick us, reducing us to unfreedom, which Barth distinguishes from the evil freedom that we in our pride have made for ourselves.[102] In unfreedom, we are unused to freedom, which is equivalent to renouncing our freedom. We do not make use of our freedom. Rather, we misuse it. In addition, we act as if we are not free despite the truth that we are already free in Christ. Sin and death would thus result for us if we claim this unfreedom,[103] leading us to "the accusation of sin, the curse of guilt, and consequent bondage and death."[104] Accordingly, for

---

97. *CD* IV/2, 311–12

98. *CD* IV/3, 90.

99. *CD* IV/3, 41.

100. *CD* III/2, 196–97.

101. *CD* II/2, 595; Webster, *Barth's Moral Theology*. Webster observes that freedom is, for Barth, "a way of describing certain acts as acts in which we are truly ourselves as we correspond to what we have been made in Christ" (114). Gunton notes that "according to Barth one must be determined in order to be free. But unless it is God who determines us, we are under the power of a demon, not the truth. His determination, because it is the work of the personal God, is a determination that liberates for true self-determination" (Gunton, "Triune God," 52–53).

102. *CD* IV/1, 745.

103. *CD* III /3, 166.

104. Nimmo, *Being in Action*, 114. The flip side of this freedom, for Nimmo, is "a

The Church as a Third Way of Her Existence

Barth, "what we do as sinners is not done in freedom, but in the greatest unfreedom,"[105] in which we are not grounded in Jesus Christ. In unfreedom, consequently, we will to sin and do sin. We follow the lust of flesh and choose evil, which results in "an alienation not only from God and our neighbor but also from ourselves. We do not act freely."[106] In this sense, unfreedom "can be described only as a freedom not to be free—which is nonsense."[107] Further, the sinful use of freedom—"the (sinful) free will of the ethical agent—is, for Barth, not true human freedom at all, but only an apparent freedom,"[108] as Nimmo accentuates. When our freedom is bounded by divine freedom in the covenant of grace, we "will no longer be a sinner or the slave of any fate."[109]

Indeed, the command of God sets against our free will, demands the renunciation that we oppose what God wills, and orders us to return to our true freedom.[110] Hearing the word as God's command, we are confronted by a decision that we have to either obey or disobey. The command of God grants permission for a very definite freedom, so we make our own decisions within the sovereignty of the divine decision. We—in the act of responsibility—correspond to the concrete meaning and content of God's command. Significantly, the command of God does not approach in the form of a tyranny because God does not take away our free will and decision, nor are we God's marionette.[111] Rather, God maintains the divine command to judge us so that God establishes a capacity of cooperation as we—in our freedom—obey to be governed by what God wills for us. This means that the command of God "imposes freedom on [us], just because it sets [us] free with the obedience which it requires of [us], just because it is the command of the grace of God."[112] It is therefore important to grasp that not only our genuine freedom is determined in

---

freedom for thankfulness, service and joy" (114).

105. *CD* II/2, 589. This is based on Barth's exegetical notes of Rom 6:17, 20.

106. *CD* IV/2, 93.

107. *CD* IV/2, 495.

108. Nimmo, *Being in Action*, 115.

109. *CD* II/1, 627.

110. See *CD* II/2, 594–97.

111. Webster, *Barth's Moral Theology*. Webster supports Barth's view that our freedom "characterizes and validates the unique dignity of the human person" (112); concerning the relation between God and the covenant-partner, for Barth, "it is absolutely the will of God alone which is executed in all creaturely activity and creaturely occurrence" (*CD* III/3, 115).

112. *CD* II/2, 596.

the freedom of Jesus Christ but the word of God also involves removing our unfreedom and elevating the right use of freedom as the children of God.[113] For we are free subjects hearing the word, we are permitted and commanded to make our own freedom in divine freedom, in which we align ourselves with the faithfulness of Jesus Christ within the covenant of grace. In reality, God in divine freedom meets us—who died and rose in Christ—in our freedom. Free God and free human meet and are one in Jesus Christ.[114] By the power of the Spirit, thus, freedom is the obedience of the free human to the free God;[115] we are therefore in this true human freedom of Jesus—the freedom for obedience.[116] Further, our freedom is genuine under the word when it corresponds to God, who at all times precedes us in Holy Scripture, revealing God takes divine action.[117] We are free when we are in the Spirit—that is, when we are free, we can exercise an authentic freedom as the eternal God gives us concrete direction to proceed. Guided by the Holy Spirit, our freedom is cultivated as it is aligned with divine freedom, and the church truthfully exists to conform through divine guidance to using freedom. Indeed, the church, free in divine freedom, makes trustworthy determinations as she experiences the word. Barth declares that

> [the experience of God's Word] is itself decision, decision concerning [humans] which is manifested as the characterising of [our] decision as a decision for faith or unbelief, for obedience or disobedience. In the first instance, then, the conformity to God's Word to which we have just referred might mean either obedience or disobedience. Even in disobedience there is an acknowledgment of God's Word, though against [our] will and to [our] perdition. Even in [our] disobedience, [we] characterise [ourselves] as the [covenant partner we are] before God's Word. Even disobedience is in its own way a confirmation or approval of God's Word to the degree that it is disobedience against God's Word and to the degree that even in disobedience [our] self-determination is a fulfillment of [our] determination by the

---

113. *CD* I/2, 260.

114. *CD* IV/3, 383. Barth also indicates that "the conjunction or unity of true God free for [humans] and true [humans] free for God constitutes the existence of the One who is the true Witness" (383).

115. *CD* II/2, 561.

116. *CD* IV/2, 93.

117. See *CD* I/2, 672–81. "As God co-operates with [our activity]," writes Barth, "[God's] own activity precedes, accompanies and follows that activity, and nothing can be done except the will of God" (*CD* III/3, 113).

The Church as a Third Way of Her Existence

Word of God. The same may naturally be said of the decision for obedience. Just because experience of God's Word is such decision, [we] can and must be summoned in the Church to ever new experience and therefore to decision.[118]

The relationship between the word of God and our decision of utilizing freedom is thus advanced, for Barth, as we are guided by and determined by Jesus Christ, the origin of our freedom and its authority. Some question whether our freedom is framed by God as we are compelled to be obedient by the word of God commanding. The debate between freedom and obedience is, nonetheless, irresoluble and inexplicable because it takes faith to witness our freedom, participating in the Son with the Father by the Spirit. This faith acknowledges not only the word as divine command, distinct from all other imperatives, but also as the eternal love of God the Father who loves the Son, engrossed by the Spirit. Truly, our freedom in the divine freedom revealed by Jesus Christ is genuine freedom, and any other decisions outside him represent unfreedom.[119] This unfreedom includes the church as a third way of her existence.

Alongside the notions of freedom and unfreedom, we now interpret the overlap of the Spirit and the flesh (5:17) with respect to the concrete command—"walk by the Spirit" (5:16 NIV)—and assess the word commanding in the overlap and a third way.

Paul claims that the divine providence is promised in the command of the word: "Walk by the Spirit." In this walk, we live by the Spirit and thus shall not fulfill the lust of the flesh as the command of God "always opposes the error and folly of [our] own attempts at living the fact that God is for [us], and that [God] demands only—but with sovereign power—that [we] should and must direct [our] life accordingly. It always advises [us] that all [our] attempts at self-justification and self-sanctification are futile."[120] For God preserves and protects us all from overthrow by what God has denied, and this walk transcends the flesh-led life (5:19–21), which is never compatible with walking by the Spirit. According to Martyn, the Spirit opposes "the desire of the flesh" under cosmic power arrayed against God, which "can take up residence in a human community, leading that community into patterns of behavior that

---

118. *CD* I/1, 206.
119. Barth, *Christian Life*, 45.
120. *CD* II/2, 728.

destroy it as a corporate entity."[121] Similarly, Betz indicates that no flesh-led life can be in force where the Spirit is present, and there is freedom in the Spirit. Walking by the Spirit—i.e., hearing and obeying the command—therefore engages with the freedom that Jesus Christ has brought for us. In this walking, it is notable that true fellowship takes place in the freedom of the Spirit, in which we are in fellowship with one another. Barth affirms that "the command of God will never allow [us] any other freedom but a freedom in fellowship. It will never permit [one] to break off [one's] unity with others, no matter what may be the circumstances of [one's] relation to [others]."[122] The command of God is good for the life of the church and thereby unifies each individual member in Jesus Christ by the Spirit.[123] We therefore trust the goodness of God's will that brings unity in the church under the divine command. In addition, we continue to live in this freedom by the gift of the Spirit, which makes the event of Christ be manifested in the life of the church. Paul calls this manifestation of divine redemption "the fruit of the Spirit" (5:20), which is another term for freedom,[124] as Betz emphasizes:

> [The manifestations of divine redemption] occur in the Christian community as manifestations of Christ's presence in the church by means of the Spirit. The individual Christians participate in them as members of the "body of Christ" and "[people of the Spirit]." Having been given the Spirit and having been seized by it, they become agents through whom the "[fruit of the Spirit]" manifests itself. The set of three times three manifestations of the Spirit, with "[love]" at the beginning and "[self-control]" at the end, represents perfection and completeness. Where all these manifestations occur, they "fill out" the life of the church as well as of the individual Christian. There is no room left for the opposite, the manifestations of evil ("the works of the flesh").[125]

The Spirit-led life thus validates that Christian life takes place "in the flesh" and involves "divine life" empowered by the indwelling Christ. As a result, the nine manifestations (or virtues) of love, joy, peace, patience,

---

121. Martyn, *Galatians*, 493.
122. *CD* II/2, 717.
123. See *CD* II/2, 726–32.
124. Betz, *Galatians*, 257.
125. Betz, *Galatians*, 33. Betz argues that "the fruit of the Spirit" do not represent "virtues" in the traditional sense but "manifestations" of divine redemption.

kindness, goodness, faithfulness, gentleness, and self-control are expected to influence us, who died and rose in Jesus Christ. Before we act, the indwelling Christ enables, empowers, and motivates the virtues in us. The virtues are not laws to obey. Rather, they are refined by our freedom as the unity of permission and obligation, revealed and fulfilled in Jesus Christ. They materialize in the church because the indwelling Christ helps the church resonate with the Spirit. After all, the Galatians and we are adopted by God through the Spirit of Christ, and we live lives of holiness and abide by the command of God, addressed by the word. For this reason, our freedom given by God "becomes the concrete determination of [our] own existence and the dominating factor in [our] own life-history" within the elected community; it is rooted in Jesus Christ, who was "justified before God and sanctified for Him."[126] This freedom is therefore a freedom of fellowship; it is both personal and communal freedom, bestowed for the whole community while each member is taken in all seriousness, prophetically in and with the life of the church. When each by faith serves the community, Barth utters that "no matter what may be the state of [a member's] inner conflict, the unity of the Church and the Spirit will necessarily be reflected and evinced and expressed microcosmically as [a member's] own personal unity."[127] Also,

> true and radical division amongst [us] begins only as [we] oppose or accept the command of God which is the command of [God's] goodness. This division does not consist in God, or in what is required of us. For it is always required of us that we ourselves should become and be good in correspondence with the goodness of God.[128]

Under the overlap of the Spirit/flesh (and a third way), then, hearing the command of God with our freedom or unfreedom yields divergent outcomes—the fruit of the Spirit on the one hand and the works of the flesh on the other—so our freedom or unfreedom makes an impact on all components of life. The results of each way are clear and have consequences in the service of the church's life in Galatia (and the present). Our freedom led by the Spirit is directly connected with the eschatological blessings (5:22–23). In contrast, the flesh-led life renounces the

---

126. *CD* IV/3, 663.

127. *CD* II/2, 730. Barth notes that "this unremitting commitment is obviously of advantage not only to the fellowship of Christians and non-Christians with each other but also to the inner unity of each individual Christian life" (*CD* II/2, 730).

128. *CD* II/2, 717.

eschatological promise of baptism.[129] Just as Paul alerts the Galatians (and us today), we lose our freedom and fall back into the yoke of slavery. Indeed, Martyn interprets 5:16–18 in responding to the works of the opponents as Paul rhetorically compares his teaching against theirs. In verse 16, Paul emphasizes that he is the one speaking to the Galatians, not the opponents. Employing the verb *peripateo*, "to walk," Paul refers to daily conduct in the Galatian churches.[130] This "walk" should be done with the Spirit of Christ, whom God has sent into the hearts of the Galatians so that the Spirit opposes the work of the flesh. This walk by the guidance of the Spirit is the command of God for a continuity of existence between God and us. As Martyn highlights Paul's intention of using the verb in the command, the verb *peripateo*, "to walk," is equivalent to the Hebrew *halak*, which means both "walk" and "conduct one's life" in Ezek 36:26–27, in which God promised to put a new heart and the Spirit in God's people so that we can walk in righteousness under God's commandments and follow God's ways.[131]

As a result of our sinful nature, we are in unfreedom and attend the restless third way and warfare. Yet, this unfreedom is awakened by the divine command as the indwelling of the Holy Spirit empowers us in rightly using our freedom.[132] As God-perceptivity originates from the Word, we are to obey the concrete divine command "walk by the Spirit," which takes our freedom in God who alone is free, pulling ourselves into the Spirit-led life instead of remaining in the flesh-led life. In accordance with the Spirit of Christ, we—died and rose in Jesus Christ—might also live with him in union by the power of the Holy Spirit. It is indeed the gospel of "Christ in us" that urges us to live life in the Spirit,[133] and the

129. Betz, *Galatians*, 277–90.

130. Martyn, *Galatians*, 492.

131. See also Ezek 11:19–20.

132. Emphasizing our freedom bounded by divine freedom, Barth writes that "as very God and very [human] He is the concrete reality and actuality of the divine command and the divine promise, the content of the will of God which exists prior to its fulfilment, the basis of the whole project and actualisation of creation and the whole process of divine providence from which all created being and becoming derives. Certainly the sin of [humankind] contradicts this first and eternal Word of God. But in the first and eternal Word of God the sin of [humankind] is already met, refuted and removed from all eternity. And in delivering and fulfilling this first and eternal Word in spite of human sin and its consequences, as He would in fact have delivered and fulfilled it quite apart from human sin, sin is also met, refuted and removed in time" (*CD* IV/1, 48).

133. See Gal 5:5, 16, 18, 22–23, 25; 6:1, 8.

The Church as a Third Way of Her Existence

freedom revealed in Jesus Christ will essentially further us to grateful service of the Lord as well as to preserve fellowship with others. We are encouraged to "walk by the Spirit" so that we are freed from the "basic principles of the world," which conflict with the life of the Spirit, and live the life of the members as one body of Christ in the harmony and peace of the Spirit. In unfreedom, by contrast, our persistent disobedience of the command entails the judgment of God, to which we are subject. On account of this, we as justified sinners are to be diligent in sanctification through the right use of our freedom, bounded by the covenant of grace revealed in Jesus Christ, so that we are companionable with the work of the Spirit. As Barth asserts,

> the law under which I stand is the law of my freedom, and therefore the law according to which I have to posit myself as the being whom I shall be, choosing the only possibility prescribed and offered me in my knowledge of God.[134]

As the command of God goes forth in the church, "walk[ing] by the Spirit" preserves the divine seal for the church, passing the third way and asserting the certainty of the eternal life that we are prepared and adapted for. With the Spirit dwelling in us, the word of God makes us free and necessitates responsibility and obedience to God. Undeniably, "the saving warfare of the Spirit against the flesh [was] waged (Gal. 5:17)"[135] by the law of love in Jesus Christ, in whom the one word of God is both gospel and law. The content of the word of God is the gospel through which we receive the gift of our freedom in Jesus Christ. At the same time, the form of the word of God is the law that we are freely obedient to Jesus Christ, in whom we have died and risen. Only through him, we achieve expectations of eschatological promise, becoming sanctified, bearing the fruit of the Spirit, and rendering holiness in our lives.

SUMMARY

This chapter first explores the exegetical accounts of the battleground (Gal 5:17) and its doctrinal understanding within an immediate context of 5:16–24. Second, a third way of the church's existence is assessed by means of the doctrine of nothingness. As this discussion is expanded to the doctrine of the word of God, entailing the doctrines of creation,

---

134. *CD* III/2, 181.
135. *CD* II/2, 729.

election, and providence, the theological claims of freedom and unfreedom of both Karl Barth and Søren Kierkegaard are investigated. Third, their claims are appraised by looking into divine freedom and ours, corresponding to the word as God's command in the third way or the overlap of the Spirit/flesh. It is accordingly affirmed that hearing the command, the church walks in the Spirit as she aligns her freedom with the freedom of the Trinity.

Chapter 3

The Word of God in Its Threefold Form

HAVING COME TO KNOW God (Gal 4:9a), this chapter first begins with hermeneutical approaches to God sending the Son (4:4–6) and the declarations of the preexistent Christ, discussing with the traditions of Wisdom and the Torah. Second, the threefold form of the word is dealt with in the context of the biblical notion of time as well as the God of Israel and the Trinity. Third, the word in its threefold form is explicated with doctrines of the *concursus Dei* and the I–Thou encounter.

THE PREEXISTENCE OF CHRIST AND THE BIBLICAL NOTION OF TIME

In Gal 4:4–6, the two expressions "God sent the Son" and "to redeem" make up an early Christian "sending formula." As Jesus Christ, who preexisted and arbitrated the creation, was "born of a woman" and "born under the law," he not only fulfilled the necessities of the law in his life but also endured the curse of the law on a tree. He will be, moreover, fully revealed in the fullness of time, which was set in the purpose of God. "The pre-existent Christ is," writes Fred Craddock, "involved in existence by his act of creation and by his act of redemption."[1] Christ was both the agent of creation and redemption, as creation has its fulfillment

---

1. Craddock, *Pre-Existence of Christ*, 91.

in redemption while redemption provides the proper understanding of creation. For the realm of redemption is coextensive with the realm of creation—the continuity of past-present-future in the history of salvation—the preexistence of Christ reveals the relationship between essence (who we are) and existence (how our lives are to be lived), as Craddock clarifies:

> Paul [speaks] of Christ's pre-existence to join essence and existence, to explain to his converts the real meaning of life, its essence, discovered and expressed in the context of their day-by-day existence. He explains what it means to be in Christ here and now, in the business of being a Christian where [we] are under any and all circumstances. He does so by reminding his readers of the incarnation, the coming into existence of the pre-existent, in whom one discovers and is apprehended by the true nature, the essence, of the authentic life. In Christ there is manifest in history, in time, now, the nature of life eternal. This is what is meant by saying that the pre-existent and existent Christ expresses essence within existence.[2]

In this essence within existence, the pre-existent and existent Christ not only lives in and with us but also stands before and beyond all the contingencies. Jesus Christ, a mediator of creation, is existent for the creature, finding its unity in him. He thus serves to join creation and redemption and to unite past and present in the continuous history of both Israel and the church, for he is not bound to time or place. In light of this, Paul unites the two realms with the preexistence of Jesus Christ.

R. G. Hamerton-Kelly observes not only the preexistent Christ and apocalyptic theology of a Hellenistic Jewish-Christian tradition[3] but also the preexistent Wisdom before the creation in the Palestinian Wisdom

---

2. Craddock, *Pre-Existence of Christ*, 98–99. Craddock highlights that "'the Christ is Jesus.' In this order, the expectation (Christ) is expressed prior to the fulfillment (Jesus)" (118n62).

3. See Hamerton-Kelly, *Pre-Existence, Wisdom, and the Son*. Hamerton-Kelly argues that "in Job 28, Wisdom is an uncreated, independent entity, which God used as the regulative principle in creation. Wisdom is not a person; it is fully subordinated to God's will" (19). Verse 27 reads that God "saw," "declared," "established," and "searched out" Wisdom for God's purpose of creation. Also, Prov 8:22–30 describes the process of Wisdom's personification, showing how Wisdom takes part in creation and how the myth of the first human contributed to this portrayal. In addition, "the influence of a foreign goddess, rival to Yahweh, probably played the major part in shaping the figure of personified Wisdom" (19).

traditions.[4] As stated by the wisdom tradition, God's plan is considered mysterious, and knowledge is given to the seer, to whom mysteries are disclosed.[5] These mysteries were believed to be written on heavenly tablets, which first contributed to the tradition of the Torah as the pre-existent plan of creation and then became the main contributor to the Wisdom tradition.[6] As rabbis and Hellenistic Jews, respectively, further developed the tradition of Wisdom (in early Judaism), Wisdom became the Torah amongst the Tannaim and Logos, which is evident in the writings of Philo, amongst the Alexandrian Jews.[7]

In addition, the formula of God sending the Son as a mediator is shaped by traditional understandings of preexistent divine Wisdom.[8] This is also connected to Paul's own understanding of the common apocalyptic belief of the early church that Jesus Christ from heaven, who was resurrected from the dead, would fulfill the promise for those who serve the true and living God.[9] According to Seyoon Kim, the sending formula in Gal 4:4–6 is similar to the sending formula of the Wisdom-Logos, as seen in Wis 9:10–17. Both passages are composed of the double sending: Galatians discusses the sending of the Son (v. 4) and the Spirit (v. 6), and Wis 9 speaks of the sending of Wisdom (v. 10) and the Spirit (v. 17). The sending formula of Galatians entails that the Son sent preexists, such as Logos, identified with preexistent Wisdom—meaning that divine Wisdom (Logos or Son) signifies Christ's preexistence and mediator role in creation. Paralleling the formula, the same verb is used in Wisdom and Galatians, in which the sending of the Son and the Spirit in Galatians (4:4,

---

4. Hamerton-Kelly, *Pre-Existence, Wisdom, and the Son*, 20.

5. Cf. Dan 2:19, 28–29.

6. Hamerton-Kelly, *Pre-Existence, Wisdom, and the Son*, 18–19.

7. Hamerton-Kelly, *Pre-Existence, Wisdom, and the Son*, 19–20.

8. See Kim, *Origin of Paul's Gospel*. Kim utters that "the same thoughts of Wisdom's pre-existence and mediatory role appear in Sir. 24:3ff., in which Wisdom praises herself alluding to the creation account of Gen. 1" (115). See also Prov 3:19.

9. See Hamerton-Kelly, *Pre-Existence, Wisdom, and the Son*. According to Hamerton-Kelly, the idea of preexistence is not explicitly expressed in 1 Thess 1:9b–10. But this passage supports Paul's arguments on the preexistent Jesus and apocalyptic theology of a Hellenistic Jewish-Christian tradition. Paul shares this knowledge with the churches in Thessalonica, Galatia, Corinth, Rome, and Philippi. Hamerton-Kelly argues that "the one whom the Christians await from heaven has already appeared on earth in great humility. The central apocalyptic reality is therefore the resurrected Messiah. . . . The earliest Christian theology used the Jewish apocalyptic scheme of things existing in heaven before their eschatological manifestation, in order to express their belief that in the period between the resurrection and the parousia Christ exists in heaven" (104–5).

6) aligns with the double sending of Wisdom and Spirit in Wisdom (9:10, 17).[10] The preexistent Christ, in Paul's account, reflects mediatorship in creation as he perceives that "God's sending the Son into the world" is equated with "God's sending Wisdom into the world." Kim claims "once Jesus Christ, like Wisdom in Jewish speculation, is conceived of as having existed in heaven from the beginning, his appearance on earth—again like Wisdom—is naturally regarded as God's sending him."[11]

James Dunn argues that the Son identified with heavenly Wisdom lacks a firm theory of preexistence, supported by the connection between Wis 9:10 and Gal 4:4. Primarily, "Wisdom is always a female [figure] and is never called God's 'son' in pre-Pauline literature,"[12] and the first time Paul identifies Christ as the Wisdom of God in 1 Cor 1:24. For Dunn, it is reasonable to assume that the preexistent Christ is identified with the Logos (the Word of God) and yet a Wisdom (or Logos) alluded to Gal 4:4 is unconvincing. Instead of looking into Gal 4:4 in the broader Hellenistic-Jewish context, Dunn acknowledges Jesus who speaks of himself as sent by God[13] and as God's Son and the last Adam, with respect to the phrase "last of all" (Mark 12:6). For instance, the sending formula of the Galatians passage should be read with the parable of the wicked tenants of Mark 12:1–12. Both passages have the structure of God sending the Son in the fullness of time. In his earthly ministry, Jesus was God's Son not because of his preexistence but by virtue of his commissioning from God. Dunn thus views Gal 4:4–5 as Adam's Christology–soteriology, with Christ as "the archetype of the first Adam, 'born of woman' (Gal. 4.4), 'in the (precise) likeness of sinful flesh' (Rom. 8.3). [Only] with the resurrection did Christ become himself archetype of a new man, eschatological

---

10. Kim, *Origin of Paul's Gospel*, 118. There is a parallel of using the verb ἐξαποστέλλω in Wis 9:10 and Gal 4:4, for the verb expresses the sending of both Wisdom and the Son.

11. Kim, *Origin of Paul's Gospel*, 119. Kim also notes that, "however, these parallels are not close enough or substantial enough for us to suppose that Paul was consciously dependent upon Wis. 9.10–17. Nevertheless, since it is clear that Paul thought of Christ's pre-existence and mediatorship in creation in terms of Wisdom's, it is natural to think that he thought of God's sending his Son into the world also in terms of his sending Wisdom into the world" (118–19).

12. Dunn, *Christology in the Making*, 39. Reading Luke 11:49, Dunn interprets the gospel Q, arguing that "Jesus quotes a saying of Wisdom in which divine Wisdom promises to send prophets (and apostles) to Israel" (201). Also, "Jesus *distinguished* himself from Wisdom as one of those sent by Wisdom (the climax of the prophetic appeal to Jerusalem)" (203). Italics his.

13. Dunn, *Christology in the Making*, 39–40; see also Mark 9:37, Luke 10:16.

man, last Adam."[14] In this sense, Mark 12:6 closely links to the ideas of sonship and inheritance in Gal 4:4–7, as Dunn emphasizes.

Nevertheless, Kim recognizes that wisdom is found in Christ, and it is also in the Torah, which has been traditionally equated with wisdom. In Sir 24:1–34, Wisdom self-reveals, and God commands Wisdom to dwell with the people of Israel (v. 8). Wisdom is identified as the Torah (v. 23), the heavenly tablets that are thought to have preexisted Wisdom. This preexistence of the law dominates as the heavenly is antecedent to the earthly. The early Jewish wisdom tradition accordingly identifies the Torah and wisdom as God's gift to Israel. Both the Torah and wisdom reveal the will of God for humanity, and we are obligated to keep the law and practice wisdom. To ancient Israel, thus, the law is considered divine wisdom and heavenly power as it was not only given by God, functioning as a system of conduct, but gave guidance for living a life by the will of God. The Torah was, however, set aside to witness the fulfillment of Jesus Christ through the Spirit, as Paul clarifies.[15] Reminding us of God sending the Son and the *telos* of the Torah to the Galatians, for Paul, is essential as law-observance deviates from the will of God, and the Galatians consequently become enslaved to the law, which is utilized as a means of making them righteous. As discussed in chapter 1, Paul metaphorically describes the Galatians as enslaved under the law, associating with the basic principles of the world (Gal 4:3) and with a relationship of minors and servants.[16] The terms minor, servant, and the principles can therefore be interpreted as referring to the pre-Christian situation binding to the law, in contrast with life after God sending the Son (vv. 4–6) as the predicament was released in the arrival of Jesus Christ.

Kim further claims that Paul attributes divine wisdom to Christ, who is preexistent, mediated in creation, revealed, and redeemed. Paul, rooted in Jewish wisdom theology, develops his own formula for God sending the Son—God's eschatological redemptive act for the world—by seeing wisdom as divine revelation.[17] Indeed, Kim's claim is relevant when reading 1 Cor 2:6–8,[18] where Paul depicts Jesus Christ as the secret and

---

14. Dunn, *Christology in the Making*, 127.
15. See "The Prophecy of Habakkuk and the Covenant of Grace" in the appendix.
16. See chapter 1; Macaskill, "Paul and the Torah," 323–38.
17. See Kim, *Origin of Paul's Gospel*, 100–136.
18. Paul's own use of the preexistent Jesus is particularly significant when he speaks to the churches in Corinthians to defend the gospel against the doctrines of his opponents. Galatians was written before Corinthians.

hidden wisdom of God: "Fallen human capacities cannot penetrate God's truth without the event of the cross and the work of the Holy Spirit."[19] The wisdom of God has been hidden before creation and from eternity, for it is a mystery, "which God decreed before the ages of our glory."[20] This hidden wisdom was indeed revealed in Jesus Christ. He, the image of the invisible God, is the perfect manifestation of God's nature and characteristics as well as the revelation of God's plan of salvation through his death and resurrection. In particular, God willed the manifestation and crucifixion of divine wisdom from the beginning, although wisdom never orients itself to the cross. We perceive not only the eternity of God, who is everlastingly wise, but also God's whole activity, willed by Godself.[21] For this reason, the wisdom of God inexplicably and divinely preserves us as it creates, maintains, and governs the world. Thus, God's wisdom, for Barth, is defined as "the proper instrument of divine providence."[22] Wisdom is indeed revealed in the divine act of reconciliation, in which incarnation is shifted to providence as the divine wisdom moves towards the world: wisdom and its relationship to the divine revelation are propounded to the elect who are covenanted with God. In Barth's acknowledgment, accordingly, the divine wisdom unveiled in Jesus Christ is fully disclosed as expressed in 1 Cor 1 and 2.[23]

Moreover, Barth speaks of the preexistence of Jesus Christ, founded in the doctrine of election, which declares the eternal basis of all divine election. For the preexistence of Jesus Christ is both the eternal Son of God as the subject of the election and the man Jesus as its object. In divinity, Jesus Christ is elected and willed by God, and we are elected and willed with him. He preexists as a designator of the eternal foundation: i.e., the eternity of the Word or Son. Barth claims, at the same time, that Jesus Christ is not only the Elected but the Elector, in whom we all are elected,[24] for God willed the preexistence of the man Jesus "before all things, even before the dawn of his own time."[25] The man Jesus is the basic reality of all reality "in his own way just as really before and with

---

19. Thiselton, *First Epistle to the Corinthians*, 241.
20. See 1 Cor 2:7.
21. Nimmo, "Divine Wisdom and Divine Economy," 416.
22. Nimmo, "Divine Wisdom and Divine Economy," 413.
23. *CD* III/1, 52–56.
24. See *CD* II/2, 94–145.
25. *CD* IV/2, 33.

God as God is in His."²⁶ Jesus Christ, as the primary object and content of God's determination, was predestined as the eternal foundation of all divine election. The first divine act—i.e., God's decision of election in Jesus Christ—therefore took place prior to creation. The preexistence of the man Jesus thus aligns with his predestination from prior to creation, to the revelation, to consummation. Creation is thus to be grasped based on its origin and destiny in Jesus Christ, in which it was included in the history of the person of Jesus, in and through him, because the divine decree of predestination is the very person of Jesus, which ensues to the eternal. Creation also subsists in Jesus Christ and is ordained by him to accomplish God's purpose of covenant partnership with humanity. Jesus Christ is both the subject and the object of predestination, for God's will and determinations are to create, reconcile, and redeem the world in him. He is the eternal Son of God, the objectivity of his election lying in the man Jesus, while, as the subject of election, Jesus Christ—in whom all are chosen—is the elected God.

Put another way, God has eternal coexistence with us, and we have eternal coexistence with God: the covenant is then the internal basis of creation. Thus, both creation and covenant are distinct and yet mutually interrelated with each other on both external and internal bases. Jesus Christ preexisted as the fundamental reality of the whole creation, which was ordained by the purpose of God's pretemporal decision. As the object of election, on the one hand, Jesus Christ, according to his human nature, was elected as the Son. He is the object of divine election in his obedience to the Father, who determines and wills the Son as the object of an election. On the other hand, the eternal Son as subject participates in the election of the Father, in which God accords with Jesus Christ. Also, the preexistent Jesus Christ was designated as the one to be incarnated²⁷ as

---

26. *CD* IV/2, 33.

27. For Barth, John's Gospel recognizes Jesus as the divine Word who existed from eternity (John 1:1), while Paul speaks of Jesus as "the first born of all creation" (Col 1:15), i.e., the mediator of creation. Also, Barth writes, "Jesus Christ was elected from all eternity [as] *Verbum incarnandum*, in his concrete humanity and visibility as the man Jesus of Nazareth" (*CD* IV/3, 724). See Smith, *Theology of the Third Article*; according to Smith, "there is a genuine correspondence to the Incarnation in the an/enhypostasis of God's Inverberation. John really does testify about the light and not just his own sense of illumination; it is really God who is present in the church's witness. In the same way that the flesh of Jesus did not preexist but was brought into being by the Spirit at a particular point in history as the medium of God's revelation, so, too, do the church's thoughts and words, as the collective vessel of God's presence, derive moment by moment from the Spirit's creative power" (121).

the work of God "precedes creation both eternally and in effect temporally, the incarnate Word of God, Christ."[28] The person of Jesus Christ is the Word, the decree of the beginning of all things, coinciding with eternal predestination; "[the] whole cosmos exists in no other way than by the Word of God, which is already the secret of [God's] creation, existence and nature. [We] may deny this Word, but by no denial can [we] remove or abrogate it,"[29] according to Barth.

This preexisting Jesus Christ knowingly involves infinity, for he not only includes "the election of Israel, of the Church, and of every individual member of [Christ's] body"[30] but also will be fully revealed in the fullness of time, which was set in the purpose of God. God sending the Son fulfilled the law and the curse, and Barth defines this time of revelation as the new time for us, which remains new. This time of fulfillment is distinct from God's created time and our time. Our time is in fact given by God and identified with respect to God's revelation, particularly the way in which God is knowable to us. It is constructed in God's existence, for God establishes the time for us.[31] The biblical notion of time is, for Barth, given by God in God's decisive act as God divides the concept of time into three domains—created time, fallen time, and revelation time. The fall lies between God-created time and our time, while God-created time remains a time hidden and withdrawn from us. Our existence in fallen time does not exclude the time of revelation because it is by God's revelation that God has time for us. In the theological sense, our time must be a different time, dissimilar from both the time originally created by God and the time conceptualized by us as fallen humans. Our time

---

28. *CD* II/2, 80.

29. *CD* III/1, 111. On account of this, the history of the covenant incorporates creation, necessitating the influence of divine providence.

30. *CD* III/2, 485.

31. As Barth notes, for Augustine, "[time] would be an intolerable anthropomorphism for God Himself to have to possess time and have time for us, by time becoming a determination of Himself in His revelation" (*CD* I/2, 46). So, revelation time, for Barth, includes a proper reality of our existence understood as accessible to God as is our (human) existence. According to Smith, "for Augustine, 'time' is simply the given distention of a human soul; the room of a soul's movement in the external world. It is composed of expectation and recollection, but one's own. It is not expectation and recollection of the incarnate Word, not a movement determined primarily by God and only secondarily by the human in relation to God, but of one's distinct past and future. Time is made by humanity in the acts of anticipation and memory" (Smith, *Theology of the Third Article*, 181). Cassidy, *God's Time for Us*; and Deng, "Eternity in Christian Thought."

The Word of God in Its Threefold Form

is described in that we live in the fallen time, in which the created and fallen times are superseded by the time of revelation, by God who reveals Godself in the event of Jesus Christ.[32]

We thus exist in fallen time and, simultaneously, a new time corresponding with the word—i.e., God who is present. The time of God—in the word by the Holy Spirit—recollects the time of Jesus Christ and anticipates his coming again, creating and sustaining the partnership. God creates a new time in each revelation where God encounters us in fallen time, in which we encounter Jesus Christ in faith and obedience. Put differently, we are in a new time in the word, in which *concursus* "is an operation in the Word and therefore by the Spirit, in the Spirit and therefore by the Word."[33] We confess the *concursus Dei* within the testimony of the prophets and apostles as we anticipate Jesus Christ by recollecting his life, death, and resurrection, which embraces the time of anticipation and fulfillment. With respect to the word in our time and space, accordingly, God (who accompanies us) has time for us and reveals Godself in hiddenness, in which our time triumphed by God's own time (the new time for us), existing as a transit "from the Old Testament to the New Testament, from the old aeon that ends with the cross of Christ to the new one that begins with His resurrection."[34] This transition is revelation (i.e., the light of fulfilled time), taking place of "our non-genuine and improper time as genuine, proper time."[35] In other words, the fulfillment of time by revelation does not signify completion but the announcement—the immediate imminence of the taking away of our time. The fulfillment of time by revelation is therefore to be completed.

With the grasp of the preexistent Christ and the biblical notion of time, we now turn to the doctrine of the word of God in its threefold form.

---

32. God has time for us, a fact that was revealed when Jesus Christ was present; God's revelation is seen in the presence of Jesus Christ, demonstrating that God has time for us. See *CD* I/2, 45–121.

33. *CD* III/3, 144.

34. *CD* I/2, 56.

35. *CD* I/2, 66.

THE THREEFOLD FORM OF THE WORD

The Time of Revelation

Barth ensures that God reveals Godself in a particular way. God promises to speak to us anew in the person of Jesus Christ when the church reads and preaches from Scripture. God is thus present for us in the threefold form of the word: proclamation, Scripture, and revelation. That is, the word of God entails the proclamation of the church, the reading of Scripture, the witness of prophets and apostles, and the events and acts of God in which God makes Godself known. The revelation in the definite sense is the Word made flesh in Jesus Christ. The Word was revealed in the life, death, and resurrection of the historical person Jesus, who established the reading of Scripture. This formation of Scripture and God's revelation in turn guides the church in preaching. The three forms of the word are thus interrelated and constitute the life and foundation of the church. Each of the forms has both fully human and wholly divine features. Proclamation, Scripture, and revelation are unified, much as the three forms of being of the Trinity are unified. As such, the word is one and threefold: the church's preaching, Scripture, and the revelation of Jesus Christ are one and the same word of God.[36]

It is inexplicable that each of the forms becomes the word of God just as the nature of this word is "the mystery of the Spirit who is the Lord."[37] In proclamation, a natural coherence not only arises between the space–time of the Testaments and the present context, but also formulates teleological arrays of meaningfulness—i.e., a meaningful agreement between proclamation and revelation attested in Scripture. In the context of space–time, coherence first takes place with respect to the time of revelation and God's eternity. On the one hand, the time God has for us is regarded as eternal time, different from our time, which comes into being and passes away. An ordinary notion of time is unable to use or discuss created time, fallen time, the time of revelation, and redeemed (fulfilled) time. Rather, we have the time God has for us. This means that, for Barth, we have no other time than the time of God's self-revelation, which is the event of Jesus Christ as fulfilled time—we only have the time of revelation. In light of this, God's time is not the same as our time. Our time is identified as allotted time, which is driven from the life of

---

36. See *CD* I/1, 88–124.
37. *CD* I/1, 186.

Jesus Christ—"the centre and the beginning and end of all the times of [all people's] lifetimes."[38] The allotted time is what God designated to establish the covenant: time implanted in God's eternity, in which we are elected in Jesus Christ by divine grace.[39]

On the other hand, God's time is eternity, including temporality. God's time can also denote "fulfilled time," which expected and recollected the event of Jesus Christ—not only the revelation time of the Old and New Testaments, but also the present with the past and the future. Fulfilled time thus incorporates pre-time, expectance-time, and revelation-time. In particular, pre-time is the time before Christ was born and also the time of the Old Testament, witnessing the expectation of revelation, which is neither merely future nor merely past—as both future and past, it is present. God's self-revelation in the Old Testament is a concrete act of God, establishing the covenant. In this revelation, though, God remains hidden and is simultaneously present to the human as the coming God, who is both the object and subject of Old Testament prophecy and eschatology. Like the Old Testament, the New Testament witnesses God's self-revelation as the hidden God. For the revealed time of the man Jesus is the time of the appearance and presence of God, while the time of revelation is not only the event of Jesus Christ but also the time of witness of this event. The New Testament indeed witnesses the incarnation as the fulfillment of this covenant—i.e., as the reception of God's grace and the fulfillment of God's law, while it is prevenient for the time of the revelation, conforming to the eternal God.

Eternity is accordingly the fulfillment of all time, embodying the secret and hidden wisdom of God in Jesus Christ. The fulfillment of all time by revelation denotes the proclamation, the immediate imminence when our time is occupied, although it does not signify completion because we are yet to understand our time in the flow of past, present, and future. The present of our time is actually in the past, for we never have the present. A norm of our time is, so to speak, the Word (Jesus Christ) speaking into our time, transforming it, redeeming it, and taking it up into the time of God's eternity. Barth articulates that the Word of God is never "not yet"

---

38. *CD* III/2, 440.

39. Additionally, Barth emphasizes that "the time we think we know and possess, 'our' time, is by no means the time God created" (*CD* I/2, 47). Also, "the grace and mercy of God, which become effective in that [God] has time for us, i.e., [God's] own time for us, answer to the long-suffering of God whereby [God] leaves us time, and our time at that, to adopt an attitude to this condescension, time, that is, to believe and repent" (*CD* I/2, 68).

or "no longer" as it is exposed to no becoming, no passing away, and therefore no change. The Word of God became flesh and therefore time.[40] The Word spoken from eternity thus raises time into God's own eternity as God's own time is the word in the very being of God. In the time of revelation (i.e., the word), we therefore grasp the meanings of our time, signifying created and eschatological, and yet fallen. We are in a fallen time (which God negates), but concurrently, our time is what God willed to restore the divine *telos* in us. Indeed, for Barth, "we are only in time as we are with God: God is the guarantee of the reality of our being in the past, the present and the future."[41]

Encountering God's time, our time (which is defined as a form of God's creation) is what God gave us, and a duration of our time posits the form of our existence. In other words, on the basis of God's gracious election, God has time in and of Godself. God has time for us, the time of revelation, and the time of Jesus Christ—God sending the Son who preexisted. Our existence is thus temporal in God's created time, and, in our temporal existence, God who is eternal knows and wills coexistence with us. This can happen only on the basis of time that is really God's time, in which God's being is both temporal and eternal. Indeed, Barth emphasizes that, in the Incarnation, God became temporal, became time, and took time unto Godself (i.e., the eternity of God), which makes coexistence possible for us by divine grace. Put differently, the Word became flesh (Incarnation God)—in Jesus Christ, "God takes time to Himself, that He Himself, the eternal One, becomes temporal."[42] This incarnation represents fulfillment in Jesus, in which God gives our time as the form of our existence and world. The divine presence of the incarnation is both eternal and temporal: "[God] was not only able to have and give time as the Creator, but in Jesus Christ He was able Himself to be temporal."[43] In the event of the Word (i.e., begotten Son), then, God's eternity consists of beginning, continuation, and a coming of an eschatological time. As the word of God constitutes the historicity of the being of God, God is present for all time and history in God's eternity. Jesus Christ, with his own time of life, death, and resurrection, lives beyond this time; the life of the man Jesus has a beginning, and his time was once past, once contemporary,

---

40. *CD* I/2, 52.
41. Nimmo, *Barth*, 93.
42. *CD* II/1, 616.
43. *CD* II/1, 617.

The Word of God in Its Threefold Form 95

and once future.[44] He lives in God's time of eternity, in which present, past, and future are simultaneous: eternity not only became time but also is timelessness, time without end. He is without ceasing, the eternal God, taking time and making it his own. Only in his own time, i.e., in the temporality of God's own eternity, does God choose to create time to *be*—yet he is before time, above time, and after time. Jesus's time is thus defined as both the time of a man and that of God who has eternal time.

For this reason, the notion of our time does not apply to the time of the human Jesus. Jesus is, for Barth, in time and has time like other men. At the same time, he is "the Lord of all time,"[45] with himself who became temporal and had time. Jesus's time is at the heart of all times created by him, even when his preexistence had time in himself before creation. His time in relation to our times acquires the character of God's eternity for Jesus lives in his time, which does not cease to be his time, and our times in him do not cease to be our times. His time is not only the time that he took to himself, granting it as a gift to all people of all time, but also the time he willed to have for us in order to inaugurate and establish the covenant with us. As Barth underlines, put differently, Jesus's time is therefore the time of all times because what God does in it is the goal of all creation and of all created time. For Jesus holds all time as he preexisted creation, existing in the present and beyond the end of time—the time of Jesus is equated with the time of God (i.e., eternity[46]), with the time of the covenant, and with fulfilled time for all other times for living creatures. Jesus Christ thus preexists as the eternal God of all time. His preexistence coincides with his eternal predestination and election, which comprises the preexistence of Israel, of the church, and of all members of his body. In him, the covenant is accomplished in time by his determination for reconciliation. Jesus Christ and his time are simultaneously eternal; he is always living, already living as the first, still living as the last, living in all real and conceivable times.

This grasp of the Lord—the Word as it is revealed—prepares us for the following discussion on the word as written, with a specific emphasis on how Scripture is perceived within the space–time[47] of the Old and

44. Life inevitably nears its end, even as time flows from yesterday, through today, and into tomorrow. See *CD* III/2, 437–640.

45. *CD* III/2, 441. Even as a man in his time, Jesus is the Lord of all time.

46. Eternity is equated with God's pretemporality, supra-temporality, and post-temporality, and therefore, the living God Himself (*CD* II/1, 638). See also *CD* II/1, 608–77.

47. In an alternative approach, Smith examines Thomas Torrance's discussion of

New Testaments, appraised through the compound portrayals of God—i.e., the God of Israel and the Trinity.

The God of Israel and the Trinity

We identify God as "the God of Israel" and "the Father, the Son, and the Holy Spirit." These two identifications are incompatible with each other.[48] In the Old Testament, the God of Israel is the One who elected Abraham, Isaac, Jacob, and their descendants to be God's people. This God gave the elect the law through Moses, anointed David king over Israel, and was involved with the redemptive history of the Israelites and their descendants. Since the coming of Jesus Christ—the promised Savior bearing the cross and resurrected by the Father in the Spirit—membership of God's people no longer mandates circumcision but depends upon faith in Jesus Christ. Consequently, the elect include all, beyond merely the fleshy descent. This God of Abraham, Isaac, and Jacob is the same God whom the church identifies as the Father, the Son, and the Holy Spirit. The Father in the Old Testament, though, does not appear in the way the New Testament sets out but appears as the One who sends the Son by the Spirit—i.e., the Father (as self-manifestation) is revealed in the incarnation of the Word via the Spirit.

---

how God's presence in space-time is constructed in relation to the incarnation. Smith disagrees with the "container" concept, arguing that the space for receiving and containing creates a disjunction between the finite and the infinite. Also, Smith adds, "Torrance contrasts the concept of space inherent in the Nicene affirmations of God's transcendence, on the one hand, and incarnational presence, on the other, with what he terms a 'receptacle' or 'container' notion of space and presence deriving from Hellenistic philosophy (pp. 1–22). In the former, God stands relative to space as its Creator and in the Incarnation engages it as the place of meeting and interface with the creature. Space does not exist except as the junction of being, the realm in and through which being stands relative to being; it is implicated by that relationship as its occasion. According to the latter, by contrast, particularly at the hands of Aristotle (in which space is the quantitative containment of substance), space is simply 'that which receives and contains material bodies.' In this concept, the Incarnation could only 'be thought of as an intrusion into the creation' (p. 24) as God merely enters a preexisting container for a period but has no real relation to it or its contents" (Smith, *Theology of the Third Article*, 129n37, referencing Torrance, *Space, Time and Incarnation*, 1–22, 24).

48. There are numerous terms for the God of Israel in the Old Testament and distinct terms for the Father, Son, and Holy Spirit in the New. When viewed from an Old Testament perspective, the terms for the God of Israel may refer to one, all, or none of the three persons of the Trinity.

The two distinctive descriptions—"the God of Israel" and "the Father, the Son, and the Holy Spirit"—are not identifiable so that the God of Israel is equated with the three persons in the Trinity. Rather, Bruce Marshall argues that Father, Son, and Spirit are the God of Israel, uttering that "the Father is the God of Israel, the Son is the God of Israel, and the Holy Spirit is the God of Israel, yet they are not three gods of Israel, but one God of Israel."[49] Put differently, the God of the church will be the same as YHWH, the God of Israel, as Johann Gerhard writes, "The Father is YHWH (*Jehovah*), the Son is YHWH, the Holy Spirit is YHWH, nevertheless they are not several YHWHs (*Jehovae*), but YHWH is one."[50] Namely, "one true YHWH is the Father, the Son, and the Holy Spirit, and these three persons are one true God."[51] In this light, some scholars support the claim that the Old and New Testaments have to attest the Trinity: As Augustine articulates,

> If the mystery of the Trinity [and not just of the Father] were entirely unknown in the Old Testament, then a new God would be introduced in the New Testament by the worship of the Son and the Holy Spirit. If the Son begins to be touched by divine worship only in the New Testament, then another God has been formed besides God the Father.[52]

For him, then, the Trinity (namely, the persons of the Son, the Holy Spirit, and the Father) is the one God who is equated with the God of Abraham, of Isaac, and of Jacob. He also notes that "we cannot possibly say that the God of Abraham and the God of Isaac and the God of Jacob is the Son of God but is not the Father. Nor will anyone dare to deny that the God of Abraham and the God of Isaac and the God of Jacob is the Holy Spirit, or the very trinity which we believe and recognize to be the one God."[53]

According to Irenaeus, Christ himself was with the Father, the God of the living, who spoke to Moses and Abraham. Christ was indeed known to Abraham (a prophet) who not only "saw in the Spirit the day of the Lord's advent" but also "learned about God from the Word and believed him."[54] Irenaeus here identifies the God of Israel as the second person

---

49. Marshall, "Israel," 258.
50. Marshall, "Israel," 259.
51. Marshall, "Israel," 259.
52. Marshall, "Israel," 251.
53. Rotelle, *Trinity*, 142.
54. Marshall, "Israel," 252. For Irenaeus and Luther, the God of Israel is primarily Christ or, at times, the Father.

of the Trinity, the Logos; namely, the God of Abraham is therefore Jesus Christ, the Father's Son (i.e., the Word). Augustine supports this perspective that "one and the same householder produced both covenants, the Word of God, our Lord Jesus Christ, who spake with both Abraham and Moses, and who has restored us anew to liberty, and has multiplied that grace which is from Himself."[55] In his sermon on the Beatitudes, Leo the Great illustrates that our Lord Jesus Christ honored Moses and spoke to him on that mountain. What Jesus Christ said to Moses was also spoken to the apostles inasmuch as "the swift hand of the Word, writing in the hearts of the disciples, established the precepts of the New Testament."[56] In the same vein, Luther agrees that our Lord Jesus of Nazareth, the Son of the Virgin Mary, is precisely "the God who led the children of Israel from Egypt and through the Red Sea [and] guided them in the wilderness by means of the pillar of cloud and the pillar of fire."[57] For Luther, this God of Israel, declaring, "I am the Lord, your God," is Jesus Christ, who died on the cross for us. Calvin explicitly takes this view, illustrating it with "the angel of the Lord" in Judg 6:11–12, 20–22: "[the] chief angel to be God's Word, who already at that time, as a sort of foretaste, began to fulfill the office of Mediator. For even though he was not yet clothed with flesh, he came down, so to speak, as an intermediary, in order to approach believers more intimately."[58] Thus, Calvin asserts that the God of Israel refers to the person of the word, clarifying that this word is not yet incarnate. Marshall argues that these interpretations are inconsistent with respect to the doctrine of the Trinity, however. In Mark 15:34, for instance, Jesus becomes one acting subject, a wholly divine person of the Word carrying the divine action in a fully human way. Jesus addresses the God of Israel, though. He does not talk to himself but cries out to the God of Israel on the cross: "My God, my God, why have you forsaken me?" On account of this, some of the interpretations "generate a more or less systematic incoherence in the basic New Testament narrative,"[59] as Marshall emphasizes.

---

55. Schaff, *Apostolic Fathers*, 787; according to Justin Martyr, there are hidden symbols of Jesus in the Old Testament. There are pieces of wood denoting the cross: e.g., the tree of life in Genesis, Moses's staff, the stick that Moses threw into the bitter waters (Exod 15:25), Jacob's walking stick, and the ladder Jacob saw in his dream, and more. See Graves, *Inspiration and Interpretation of Scripture*, 78.

56. Leo the Great, *Sermons*, 395.

57. Luther, *Notes on Ecclesiastes*, 313.

58. Calvin, *Institutes*, 133.

59. Marshall, "Israel," 248. Marshall raises a concern about this view when there

The Word of God in Its Threefold Form

Moreover, some make reference to Jesus Christ, which is sufficient and necessary to identify all three persons of the Trinity. Of these, Aquinas holds that the persons of the Trinity are expressed in many ways in the Old Testament. For him, Israel knew the Trinity at the very beginning of Genesis and even showed her faith to the incarnate and suffering Christ in the ceremonies of the law. For example, one's offering and sacrifice "for sin" signify forgiveness through Christ (Lev 4:25). One's peace offering of the sweetest odor to the Lord signifies the fragrance of the sacrifice of Christ's body (Lev 3:9). According to Jean-Pierre Torrell,

> this death [Christ's] was useful and necessary for us, and therefore the Apostle adds, "an offering and a sacrifice (*oblationem et hostiam*)." Here he uses an expression from the Old Law—Leviticus 4:25 ff.—according to which, when a person had sinned, an offering and sacrifice "for sin" was offered for him. Likewise, when someone wanted to give thanks to God or wished to obtain something, a peace offering had to be made—Leviticus 3:9—which oblation was the sweetest odor to the Lord. This was accomplished through Christ: so that we might be cleansed from sin and obtain glory, he "delivered himself up for us in sacrifice." . . . Clearly this odor was fragrant to God not in itself but rather by its signification, inasmuch as it signified the fragrance of the sacrifice of Christ's body, the Son of God. [Thus spoke Isaac of his son Esau]—Genesis 27:27—"The fragrance of my son is like the fragrance of a field which the Lord has blessed"; [and the spouse of the Canticle]—Canticle of Canticles 1:3—"Draw me!—We will run in the fragrance of your perfumes." This is the way in which we must offer God a spiritual sacrifice—Psalm 50:19—"My sacrifice to God is a contrite spirit."[60]

This recognition of Jesus during ceremonies advocates Aquinas's argument that "if one of the persons [of the Trinity] is taken away, the others are taken away because they are distinguished only by relations, which

---

is narrative incoherence. For instance, according to Isa 42:8, the God of Israel "claims exclusive rights to human worship." "If this God is simply identical with the Father, then the Son and the Spirit are not the God of Israel." This argument, for Marshall, means that "Christians would worship that which is not the God of Israel, and thus give their hearts to false gods" (Marshall, "Israel," 250). In doing so, it misconstrues the economic and the immanent Trinity.

60. Torrell, *Christ and Spirituality*, 140; Marshall posits, for Aquinas, that the mysteries of Jesus Christ were, on the one hand, revealed to the prophets and patriarchs in a certain generality. To the apostles, on the other, the mysteries were manifested with respect to specific circumstances (Marshall, "Israel," 253).

have to go together."⁶¹ This also implies that we are unable to discern any one of the persons in the Trinity without recognizing all three.

Other scholars observe that the Old Testament by itself is sufficient to show that God is triune. Israel knew the Trinity without any reference to Jesus Christ as there are many traces of the Trinity found in the Old Testament. Acknowledging that the definite revelation took place in the New Testament, for Gerhard, the revelation of the Trinity is established by both the New and the Old Testaments. Without any references in the New Testament, some texts speak that the Israelites acknowledged the Father, the Son, and the Holy Spirit as the texts often identify the Trinity with recognition of the second person. For instance, Gerhard designates "the sun of righteousness" (Mal 4:2) as Jesus Christ, who is the true God and Lord of Israel.⁶² Reading Exod 40:34–35, "The cloud covered the tabernacle, and Moses was unable to enter the tabernacle, because the cloud was overshadowing it."⁶³ For Gerhard, the Son of God (i.e., the Word) indwells God's special presence in the tabernacle of the covenant, which is compared to how the appearance in a cloud signifies "the incarnation of the Word that would follow in the fullness of time."⁶⁴ Considering the divine appearance and glory of Jesus Christ, Gerhard articulates that "in the Old Testament, when God wanted to reveal His majesty in a special manner so that mortals could endure it, [God] overshadowed it with the shadow of a cloud. So also in this supreme and singular manner of the presence and indwelling of the Word in the assumed flesh."⁶⁵ This overshadowing occurred in an explicable way in which the union of the divine majesty and human nature took place. In addition, Gerhard posits that it is the prefigured incarnation of the Son when the Son of God furnished the Israelites with a pillar of cloud and fire (Exod 13:21). This suggests that Moses witnessed the Son of God, which does not mean that he saw Jesus. Rather, Moses "beheld a temporary and prefigurative theophany of the incarnation to come."⁶⁶ Similarly, Augustine argues that the God of Israel must be the Trinity—who are inseparable and speak through created realities—although it is enigmatic to explain how the church identifies the three divine persons with the God of Israel. Augustine claims that

61. Marshall, "Israel," 243n17.
62. Gerhard, *Theological Commonplaces*, 48.
63. Gerhard, *Theological Commonplaces*, 100.
64. Gerhard, *Theological Commonplaces*, 100.
65. Gerhard, *Theological Commonplaces*, 100.
66. Marshall, "Israel," 253n45; see Gerhard, *Theological Commonplaces*, 101.

Christ is understood by the name "I am who I am" (Exod 3:14); "'God' refers to the Father who speaks through his Word. And yet because the Word or Son is equal to God he also has the name *idipsum*."[67] According to Lewis Ayres, Augustine understood this name as belonging to the entire Trinity, including Christ, rather than exclusively to the Father. Augustine also describes Moses speaking to the Lord "face to face" (Exod 33:11) as some form of physical manifestation and his anticipated vision from the Lord (33:13) as a true spiritual vision. What is significant about Augustine's interpretation is that "Moses knows that the purer the soul, the more the vision is desired. And yet even those whose vision rises towards the spiritual have only the sight of the 'back' of Christ, the flesh,"[68] as Ayres emphasizes.

Nevertheless, these claims are not sufficient to recognize the three persons of the Trinity, who are inseparably united. For instance, when we identify the God of Israel with the Son of the Trinity, the other persons—the Father and the Spirit—have to be identifiable in the same texts that the scholars claimed. The Son and the Spirit are not, though, referred to in the same way as the Father. Many are also of the view that offering christological interpretation of texts in the Old Testament is superfluous, as Jesus Christ is not the only subject matter of the Old Testament and some texts do not present the life, death, and resurrection of Jesus Christ and his teachings. It is therefore important to acknowledge that the Old Testament witnesses the triune God, instead of focusing on any particular member of the Trinity. Significantly, the Old Testament does not supersede the New Testament, nor does the New Testament supersede the Old. With this understanding, our primary aim lies in recognition of the God of Israel and the Trinity and their involvement with the word in its threefold form. The secondary aim presented here is to outline that we Christians worship the God of Israel and the Trinity, with each identifiable in its own depictions. We know the God of Israel, covenanting with the elect, who is indispensable to the church's identification of the God we worship. This covenantal history between YHWH and the elect is available to us only through the Old Testament, which gives a necessary condition for the church's individuation of the Trinity. A clear distinction thus exists between the Old and New Testaments, between the witness of expectation and that of recollection, and between the preparation

---

67. Ayres, *Augustine and the Trinity*, 205.
68. Ayres, *Augustine and the Trinity*, 161.

of witness and the accomplishment of the revelation achieved in Jesus Christ. The two Testaments are inseparable and must be acknowledged as the canonical unity of Scripture. As such, YHWH's engagement with Abraham and his children is indispensable to the Galatians and us because the God of Israel is to be identified for the church's continuation. In addition, YHWH's interaction with the elect is narrated in the historical covenant with them, which is a necessary condition for the church's individuation of the Trinity.

Furthermore, we can identify the whole Trinity without identifying all three or without making a reference to Jesus Christ. In other words, we can only refer to any one person of the Trinity if we know how to refer to the other two—that is, identifying any one person of the Trinity refers to the other two. The Nicene Creed unambiguously features the three persons. The Lord Jesus Christ was the only begotten Son of God, "begotten of the Father before all time [or before all worlds]"[69] and sent to become incarnate in time, while the Holy Spirit proceeds from the Father and the Son. The Father can send the Son, but not Himself, and the Father is never sent. Completing the redemptive mission, the Father sends the Spirit, presupposing the mission of the Son, which is sufficient to distinguish the persons of the Trinity from one another. We can accordingly identify the three via the missions. As Marshall indicates, "the relations to one another that their missions exhibit give us features not only unique to each, but which each has in all possible circumstances—regardless, in particular, of whether they decide to create a world and whether any of them are sent into that world."[70] According to George Lindbeck, the Nicene Creed is essential to mainstream Christian identity as the church recites the creed as a persistent symbol of unity in space and time. Lindbeck therefore highlights that "there may [be] complete faithfulness to the classical Trinitarianism and Christology even when the imagery and language of Nicaea and Chalcedon have disappeared

---

69. See the Nicene Creed of 381.

70. Marshall, "Israel," 238. The church "gratefully remembers that the incarnate Son completed his mission by his promise in the upper room and his free acceptance of death on Golgotha. In this way, the community joyfully recalls, the Son Jesus made his body and blood available for all time to his gathered people as the food and drink of their shared meal. [The church] calls upon the Father to send the Holy Spirit, whose work it is to join this people to the crucified and risen Jesus, who gives his very self in the elements they eat and drink" (238).

from the theology and ordinary worship, preaching, and devotion."[71] The Nicene Creed is remarkably distinguishable from the concepts in which it is formulated, for it can be described and redescribed in different ways without altering the fundamental principles.[72] Philosophical understandings and cultures have differently formulated and interpreted the crucial concepts of "one substance and three persons" or "two natures" of the ancient Trinitarian and christological creeds.[73] Nevertheless, the Nicene Creed demonstrates that the same content can be expressed in various formulations, and the expression has equivalent consequences, although each content is unidentifiable in the formulations. It is because the meaning of consubstantiality was expressed "in terms of the rule that whatever is said of the Father is said of the Son, except that the Son is not the Father."[74] Regardless of the fact that one substance and three persons or two natures are therefore no longer present, one and the same doctrine is effective in this new formulation, in which the same rules guided the making of the original doctrines. The Nicene Creed remains historically conditioned and formulated but unconditionally and permanently necessary for Christian identity.

We began this chapter with the preexistence of Jesus Christ and the biblical concept of time before entering into discussion about the doctrine of the word as proclamation, as Scripture, and as revelation—which is in its threefold form but one and the same word of God. Revealing the doctrine of the word, we first assessed a natural coherence between the space–time of the Testaments, examined through the biblical notion of revelatory time as well as the God of Israel and the Trinity. This assessment sets up the next discussion on the doctrine of the word by virtue of the *concursus Dei* and the I–Thou encounter.

The *Concursus Dei* and the I–Thou Encounter

Avowing *concursus* as an operation in the word and by the Spirit, we confess the *concursus Dei* within the testimony of the prophets and apostles as we anticipate the time of fulfillment in Jesus Christ by reminiscing

---

71. Lindbeck, *Nature of Doctrine*, 81.
72. Lindbeck, *Nature of Doctrine*, 78–82.
73. See comparison between the creed of 325 and the creed of 381 from Wikipedia, "Nicene Creed."
74. Lindbeck, *Nature of Doctrine*, 80.

about his life, death, and resurrection. In the *concursus Dei*, the word is to be witnessed via a natural coherence between the space-time of the Testaments and that of the present context, formulating teleological arrays of meaningfulness—i.e., a meaningful agreement between proclamation and revelation attested in Scripture. Meaningfulness is highlighted by the internal testimony of the Spirit, so the church may discern the written biblical word to be God's own word.[75] The Spirit's internal testimony enlightens the heart and mind to see insights into biblical words without adding new dimensions to the words themselves. These words are an indirect form of humans speaking about God's direct speaking, delivered by human mediators, whereas the words of the prophets and apostles speak of witnessing revelation.[76] Bruce McCormack asserts that "what God has said through the prophets and apostles to the Church in the past may give hints of what he will say through the same to the Church in our own day, but he is not bound to repeat himself."[77] God, who is free, addresses the church through the witness of Scripture in divine ways so that she hears God and discloses hidden layered meanings of biblical texts. Without doubt, there is a significant difference between the words of the prophets and apostles and those of human mediators; "the prophetic and apostolic word as the necessary rule of every word [is] valid in the Church."[78] This signifies that the mediators strive to achieve pure

---

75. See Smith, *Theology of the Third Article*. Smith observes a unity of Proclaimer and proclaimed between the witness to the word and the word, for God's divine action extends through Jesus Christ into testimony about Jesus Christ. "[When] we proclaim the Word of God, Jesus Christ, we are only acting in accordance with the verberate quality of the Word. Indeed, apart from that experience we cannot proclaim the Word. We can only think and speak as ones drawn into God's movement, as participants in his light. In this respect, we do not at one point hear and another believe. No, to hear just is to believe; one cannot hear except as a child of the Word. The witness to the Word lives and moves and has being in the Word [one]self. [One] becomes a child of God, reborn of the Son's obedience to the Father" (118).

76. See Warfield, *Inspiration and Authority of the Bible*. As Warfield asserts, "the apostles solemnly justified the Gospel which they preached, detail after detail, by appeal to the Scriptures. . . . Wherever they carried the gospel it was as a gospel resting on Scripture that they proclaimed it (Acts xvii. 2; xviii. 24.28); and they encouraged themselves to test its truth by the Scriptures (Acts xvii. 11). Every detail of duty was supported by them by an appeal to Scripture (Acts xxiii. 5; Rom. xii. 19). The circumstances of their lives and the events occasionally occurring about them are referred to Scripture for their significance" (80).

77. McCormack, "Historical Criticism and Dogmatic Interest," 333.

78. *CD* I/1, 104. "A real witness is not identical with that to which it witnesses, but it sets it before us" (*CD* I/2, 463), according to Barth. It is impossible that "there should be a direct identity between the human word of Holy Scripture and the Word of God, and

doctrines and dogmatics, focused on the centrality of Scripture. As Barth asserts, first, absolute doctrine removes false human reasoning: it must be free from added matter so that the present, living word of God can meet us through the preachers' words. This pure doctrine is possible insofar as preaching is purified by the measure of Scripture and revelation, and the measure is the work of dogmatics. Second, dogmatics set foundations for preachers and function to formulate statements for proclamation, moving beyond mere exposition to clarify and correct proclamation in light of church history and the present context. It is important to focus on the meaningful agreement between proclamation and revelation attested in Scripture because the interrelatedness of the doctrine, Scripture, and biblical interpretation can be naturally woven into preaching, in which "God speaks" is testified.

This denotes that the church's preaching, guided by the power of God, can become a living succession of the prophets and apostles as the task of human mediators articulates the divine ∞ as *the finitude*.[79] God's eternity is unlimited to both the infinite and the finite in relation to the attribution of God. Barth posits that God is infinite in God's own divine ways, as God is not bound to the limits of space and time or to the forms of space and time. At the same time, God is "infinite in a manner in which the antithesis and mutual exclusiveness of the infinite and the finite of non-spatiality and timelessness on the one hand and spatiality and temporality on the other."[80] God is certainly infinite as God is unbounded by basis, goal, standard, or law that is not Godself, while God is bounded in love that is unbounded. In this light, the church's preaching through the power of the Spirit testifies the living word as we, the hearers of the church, "believe in [Jesus' first witness] to the promise, and so to be witnesses of their witness, ministers of the *Scripture*."[81] This Scripture is

---

therefore between the creaturely reality in itself and as such and the reality of God the Creator" (*CD* I/2, 499). He also points out the truth of a miracle that "fallible [humans] speak the Word of God in fallible human words" (*CD* I/2, 529). Nimmo, *Being in Action*; Nimmo emphasizes that, "for Barth, then, there can no more be a divinization of the human word of the Bible than of the human nature of Jesus Christ Himself" (26).

79. Barth, *Word of God*, 190–91.

80. *CD* II/1, 467.

81. Barth, *Word of God*, 216. Italics his. See Smith, *Theology of the Third Article*. Smith indicates that "the Spirit brought the thought and speech of the prophets and apostles, after which our own thought and speech take shape, into conformity with the Word of God. In fact, it is in the ongoing act of making the prophetic and apostolic testimony true, one with the Word, that our thinking and speaking are grasped, taken up, and set into cadence after-Word" (190).

indeed sacred and canonical because it was written by the divine inspiration of the Holy Spirit. It is the divine communication indicating that God spoke, for God can be known only by God. By means of proclamation, Scripture attests past revelation, functions to govern the life of the church, and recounts promises of future revelation. Scripture becomes the word of God and, thereby, the church hears Scripture as the *viva vox Dei*[82] through the indwelling Spirit. Above all, God lives the fulfillment of the past in the present and the present in the future so as not to collapse into time but rather continue to the consummation.

Furthermore, Scripture and proclamation (which become the word) are distinguished from the absolute divine event of the Word in the person of Jesus Christ. The revelation of Jesus Christ is "God's own Word spoken by God Himself,"[83] giving rise to Scripture and calling forth proclamation. This word as revelation, taking place through Scripture and proclamation, is both unveiled and veiled, just as God gives Godself to be understood in a present but concealed way. This self-revealing God is not fully knowable to us and remains mysterious even though the word was revealed in the humanity of Jesus. God can therefore be both known and unknown. Accordingly, although it is revealed word, the word is veiled and unveiled, and hidden meanings of Scripture are both revealed and concealed. While veiling remains in revelation, unveiling may thus take place when our soul encounters the word[84]—what I call "the experience of coupling." Died and risen in Christ, we become "bearer[s] of the content of divine Spirit [in which we receive] the reality of experience of the Word of God."[85] Through this coupling, the possibility of knowing the Word emerges, and we are to be coupled with the Word, receiving God's revelation through the Spirit of God, who is also the Spirit of the word. We are not only brought to hear the word of God but also to become perceptually aware of the revealed word via the indwelling of the Spirit as a mode of divine action operating in us. Significantly, it is useful to note that coupling is *giving* via divine possibility, just as the word is *giving* to the hearing church: the revelation is not received by human possibility.

---

82. See Webster, *Holy Scripture*, 107–37.

83. *CD* I/1, 113.

84. It is indeed in the form of quite particular individual experiences, rooted in the concrete particularity of Jesus Christ. This mutual indwelling, the union of the divine and human logos in faith via the Spirit, for Barth, cannot be ignored or denied.

85. *CD* I/1, 212.

In particular, coupling occurs on the basis of the covenantal relationship. As the divine possibility actualizes the event of the word, the experience of the word of God, for Barth, takes place in an act of human self-determination: it is God who wills preceding our self-determination, which is subject to God's determination to experience the word. This experience is then the cooperation between God and us, which indicates that we freely partake in the event. The cooperation is thus described as "a simultaneity, interrelation and unity in tension between the divine and human determining: What is seen from one side as grace is freedom when seen from the other side and *vice versa*."[86] There is a clear distinction between divine determination and ours, as cooperation does not imply that we are competent to accomplish this experience. Nor is it within our capacities to experience the word. Rather, divine agency is absolutely sovereign for the event of the word, and we might fully engage in the covenant of grace. In the coupling, we may correspond to the word via cooperation—we stand in the event of the word of God, which is presented to us by Holy Scripture. We wholly engage with the word with our "own heart and soul and strength, as an independent subject who encounters and replies to God and is responsible to Him as His partner."[87] Barth explicitly advocates that the engagement of divine and human agencies is essentially enigmatic in nature, as well as facilitated by divine agency, which initiates and accords with human agency receiving God's initiation. This entails "a complementary human decision"[88] in our freedom conditioned by divine freedom, for, as Barth emphasizes, God permits cooperation between divine freedom and ours, which also includes the freedom for the fellowship. This harmony of double agency, according to George Hunsinger, is the "secretly identical" essence, bringing together the divine and human capacities—the divine capacity is "dialectically equated" with a capability inherent in us.[89] Hunsinger utters,

> God would be conditioned by a capacity in the partner, and the partner would condition God by this capacity. If divine precedence and human subsequence are complete, however, then the human partner receives a capacity that it did not bring to the event. It receives a capacity that is not given except in the event

---

86. *CD* I/1, 199. Italics his.
87. *CD* IV/2, 786.
88. *CD* II/2, 193.
89. Hunsinger, *How to Read Karl Barth*, 217.

by which it is actualized. The capacity is therefore entirely a consequence of, and in no sense a condition on, grace.[90]

This capacity does not lie in human nature but is granted in the event of the coupling that takes place by God (initiator) and the church (receiver of the initiation). Thus, our capability for this participation in union comes only by God's grace, which makes it possible for us to receive the word. Namely, grace is the only basis of capacity as, in the coupling, both the divine and human subjects are fully and spontaneously engaged.

In this relationship between God and partner, specifically, the experience of coupling, for Barth, is deliberated as "the encounter between nature and grace, or concretely, with the encounter between [human] and the Word of God."[91] The relationship is furthered by Hunsinger, who elucidates double agency, instituted by the Chalcedonian pattern[92]—asymmetry, intimacy, and integrity. First, it is the asymmetrical relationship of double agency. By God's grace, coupling "takes place in such a way that divine omnipotence and human freedom coexist in mutual love and freedom as the mystery of God with humanity and of humanity with God (particularism)."[93] Second, the intimate "living divine–human unity"[94] signifies that we are essentially dependent on God and, at the same time, hear the word via divine actions coinciding with human actions (and vice versa). Divine and human actions are discrete but coexist and coinhere within their historical interconnection, creating a unity rather than a separation. They are "necessarily two-sided, and its mystery must be thought of as the mystery of the human decision as well as the divine."[95] As the possibility of the encounter lies entirely in divine grace, actualizing human freedom is dependent on and mediated through Jesus Christ. We are contingent on the covenant of grace as our freedom is "real in the way in which [we] generally can only be in [our] relationship to the Creator."[96]

90. Hunsinger, *How to Read Karl Barth*, 216.
91. *CD* I/2, 791.
92. Hunsinger, *How to Read Karl Barth*. According to Hunsinger, "indeterminism violates the Chalcedonian stipulation of intimacy ('without separation or division'), and determinism violates that of integrity ('without confusion or change'), the dialectical option can be interpreted as violating the stipulation of asymmetry as Barth understood it ('complete in deity and complete in humanity'). (The relationship posited by the 'and' in the latter formula is to be interpreted asymmetrically)" (216).
93. Hunsinger, *How to Read Karl Barth*, 207.
94. Hunsinger, *How to Read Karl Barth*, 209.
95. *CD* II/2, 193.
96. *CD* II/1, 128.

The Word of God in Its Threefold Form

Third, double agency coexists without any confusion and with the integrity of divine–human unity, as Barth indicates that "what is theologically impossible is a study of these two realities as though they are on the same plane, as though there can be between them co-ordination, continuity or interchange, or as though in the last resort they are somehow identical."[97]

Hunsinger decisively renounces divine determinism in relation to humanity, particularly the way in which "metaphysical dogmas"[98] systematize how divine and human actions are interrelated. The dogmas assume that God is accessible to ordinary schemes of explanation, which are applied to divine actions and those of humans. For instance, we reduce God to a supreme subject—"a product of our own thinking, a concept and principle and therefore an instrument with the help of which we can master and solve any problem."[99] The sovereignty of God can not only be inaccurately portrayed as preceding and ruling us but also conceived as an impersonal, anonymous force. That is, divine authority is misrecognized as a tyrannical determination, rather than creating mutual, free response to the word. As Barth clarifies,

> in [God's] action He declares Himself and the purpose of what He does. His action is not, therefore, a mechanical operation in which the creature is simply the material used and has no understanding of what is done. He uses the creature as He speaks with it. The omnipotence of His action is the omnipotence of truth, which refuses to dominate by external means, but is ready to speak for itself, to teach, to convince, to seek and win recognition, and to conquer in this highly individual manner. What we have said about God's sovereign presence in the creaturely world is to be understood in this concrete way. It is not the presence of compelling fate, nor that of a higher power of nature. Nor is it the presence of a dictator and tyrant brutalising the world he controls.[100]

For Barth, God's sovereignty is thus the presence of the almighty word of God, speaking to us and heard by us. In this, there is our freedom: we hear it in a genuine freedom as we are consulted, permitted, and commanded in the church.[101] Double agency conjoins on the basis of divine

---

97. *CD* I/2, 790–91.
98. Hunsinger, *How to Read Karl Barth*, 207.
99. *CD* IV/3, 707.
100. *CD* III/2, 147–48.
101. *CD* I/2, 669. Barth does not speak of freedom as a choice of the Kantian term.

grace and freedom of unconditional sovereignty, which transcends all human dimensions and results in our freedom corresponding to what God wills for us. Aligning ourselves with the *concursus Dei*, put differently, we make use of the freedom that God presents, and this freedom does not suggest that we choose in our terms simply because we are conditioned by sovereign freedom. We are also responsible for this freedom as we freely correspond to the *concursus Dei* and, therefore, to the word by the power of the Spirit. We receive the word as active hearers, making our own responsible decisions, and our freedom concurs entirely within the covenant of grace—it is not compelled or ordered but joins in mutual correspondence with the word. In the covenant of grace, therefore, the receiving of the word of God

> does not take place in any mechanical way but in a spiritual communion corresponding to the individuality of the man Jesus and of all His witnesses, i.e., in the oneness of the many who as individuals are awakened to believe and testify, through the all-embracing oneness of Jesus Christ and the Holy Ghost.[102]

As divine freedom is independent of our freedom, subsequent to and dependent on grace, while influential on our freedom, the supremacy of the word and the Spirit confirms and establishes the autonomy, freedom, and responsibility of our own activity rather than prejudicing these.[103] Our freedom (necessitating autonomy and responsibility) thus naturally connects with obedience because "freedom is the logical precondition of obedience, even as obedience is the spontaneous expression of freedom."[104] With freedom and obedience, we correspond to what God wills in us: we are quickened by the Holy Spirit and move ourselves in obedience, "listening to the order and command of God."[105] Barth therefore asserts that there is no contradiction between divine sovereignty and our freedom, for

---

See Rauscher, "Kant's Social and Political Philosophy."

102. *CD* I/2, 703. It is to witness that "Christ in us and we in him" is renewed and refreshed.

103. *CD* III/3, 144–45.

104. Hunsinger, *How to Read Karl Barth*, 213.

105. *CD* IV/2, 800. According to Barth, we are obligated, in obedience, to use our freedom to love God and our neighbor and, in so doing, keep the two great commandments. For, he argues, our freedom is contingent upon divine freedom; without the latter, we are unfree.

The Word of God in Its Threefold Form

divine freedom cannot destroy and suspend human freedom. Always and in every respect the former draws the latter to and after itself. We ourselves are rooted in this genuine human freedom under the Word, prayerfully and thankfully, recognizing this reality as it wills to be recognized.[106]

Alongside this freedom, we indeed experience the word at the revelatory time, whereby the operation of *concursus* in the Spirit by the word takes precedence over our time. In other words, the word of God has spoken to us, and in our declaration, we freely receive the reality of the experience of the word. Barth declares that "the possibility of human experience of the Word of God [is] understood as the possibility of this Word itself [is] one that we can and must affirm with certainty, with final human seriousness."[107] This experience of the word (at the very revelatory time), with the help of the Spirit, engages in the three dynamic relationships between the word and the preacher, between the word and the church, and between the preacher and the church. In this experience, which is grounded in a mutual respect for each relationship and then unifying these relationships, God allows cooperation between divine freedom and a true communion, taking place in the freedom of the Spirit as we are in fellowship with one another when the word is heard.[108] God, indeed, meets us through the gospel of reconciliation in the divine work of self-manifestation, signifying the faithfulness of Jesus Christ. It is remarkable that there is a vital connection between the reality of experiencing the word and the unique Christian identity, formed to actualize the gospel of "Christ in us and we in Christ," in which the Spirit unites us with Christ. This connection is apparent when the church witnesses the word as preached, written, and revealed—hearing the announcement, the immediate imminence of the captivating time. Put another way, the church—a collective group of unique individuals—not only breathes in the word to live but also breathes it out to bear witness. Luke T. Johnson describes this as "the *texts of human lives* in a continuing process of self-revelation by the Living God."[109] Individuals (who have died and risen in Christ) breathe the word in and out, and the church (the body

---

106. *CD* I/2, 710.

107. *CD* I/1, 223–24.

108. As discussed in chapter 2, Barth indicates that the word, in its commands, grants us a freedom in fellowship but restricts all other freedoms. This liberty never permits us to destroy unity.

109. Johnson, *Scripture and Discernment*, 52. Italics his.

of Christ) witnesses communal experiencing of the reality of the word in light of individual experiences. The church's hearing of the revelation attested in Scripture demonstrates "an articulation of the church's faith in the Living God."[110] George Lindbeck also advocates that "when the text thus controls communal reading, Scripture can speak for itself and become the self-interpreting guide for believing communities amid the ever-changing vicissitudes of history."[111]

The experience of the word is, accordingly, a glimpse of the togetherness of God and the church, for the power of the Spirit is

> necessarily and irresistibly disruptive in the relationship of Jesus Christ to His community, namely, the divine working, being and action on the one side and the human on the other, the creative freedom and act on the one side and creaturely on the other, the eternal reality and possibility on the one side and the temporal on the other.[112]

That is, coupling (i.e., encountering revelation) entails reconciliation, which is the saving work of the Holy Spirit to bring God and believers together. This togetherness was once demonstrated in God's divine action of reconciliation through the power of the Holy Spirit, while sustaining the union between the begotten Son of God and his Father in heaven. Indeed, this salvific plan of reconciliation is persistently revealed in moments in the church's life, for God desires reconciliation and thus is present in moments of revelatory address. This makes revelation not a one-time event, but an ongoing one, and togetherness (i.e., union) continues to take place in the church by the Spirit through proclamation. In this way, the Spirit (of the subjective possibility) creates continuing possibilities of togetherness.[113] Hunsinger therefore underlines that, for Barth, "even human nature as created did not in itself possess a capacity of this kind for fellowship with God but could only receive it again and again *de novo* as an absolute gift."[114] Although we are flawed and sinful, we may therefore experience coupling with the word by God's grace in Jesus Christ through the Spirit. This also affirms that the church is the specific place where God makes Godself known and the Spirit unites

---

110. Johnson, *Scripture and Discernment*, 109.
111. Lindbeck, "Barth and Textuality," 362.
112. *CD* IV/3, 761.
113. See also *CD* I/2, 203–79.
114. Hunsinger, *How to Read Karl Barth*, 217.

The Word of God in Its Threefold Form

Christ with those who hear. Revelation is thus in giving even while we lack the capacity for God: God self-reveals to us in divine graceful action and is indeed "God for us, sinners." In revelation, therefore, the church hears the word through the activity of the Holy Spirit, and Barth asserts that "the constitution and preservation of the Church rests in [that we] hear God."[115] God truly speaks in Jesus Christ, in whom the revelation of reconciliation evinces via the church's proclamation as the Spirit unites Christ with the hearing church. By virtue of this, the church has come to know God and parallels God's will and purpose for her. That is, in faith and obedience, the church corresponds to what we hear in God's revelation, what we perceive in Scripture, and what we resonate in proclamation as one speech of the Father, the Son, and the Spirit.

As revelation surely meets us in its power and authority,[116] this disclosure, taking place as the revelation of reconciliation, entails knowledge of Christ and the confession of the church. We receive and acknowledge revelation by testimony, which has created the church and still preserves it; the church has sustained the testimony of those who have heard and seen it. In faith, we share and speak of the testimony. In return, confession awaits. When we come humbly in repentance and humility, reconciliation in revelation actualizes Christian life together as we witness the mystery of retrospective, imminent light. In other words, reconciliation in revelation witnesses not only the mystery concealed in the history of Jesus Christ but also the retrospective, imminent light that Christ discloses from the past, through the present, and toward the future. This admission embodies the meaning of knowledge in Scripture and Jesus Christ and the insight of the covenantal relationship between God and the church. This also includes relations with our neighbors.

On this basis, reconciliation establishes "Christian knowledge"[117] of Scripture and Jesus Christ in those who are brought to hear: the knowledge

---

115. Barth, *God in Action*, 22.

116. See Barth, *God in Action*, 3–19.

117. See McCormack, *Orthodox and Modern*, 21–39. McCormack identifies this, for Barth, as a special kind of knowledge with its source in an act of God, which is influenced by Kant. The unintuitive God is truly known in such a way that God makes Godself intuitable. The incomprehensible divine power was at work in raising Jesus from the dead: namely, the event of the cross is comprehensible. Revelation reaches its goal in the human recipient, and knowledge of God is realized. The significance of the event lies in the fact that God has entered the realm of historical intuitability. Put differently, God determines God's own being, and this determination is to be for us in Jesus Christ, who is the Self-revelation of God in the incarnation, life, death, resurrection, and ascension of the God-man. This divine act of God's Self-revelation means that the

arrives to us not only in terms of history and the present but also in terms of the future. Reconciliation signifies knowledge as its consequence; the church, by speaking and hearing God, engenders a reconciliation that deepens Christian knowledge. We therefore attain knowledge through self-revealing God: i.e., the word in the Spirit. Without this divine presence, there can be no knowledge of God. Only through this revelation is God knowable. This knowledge gained in revelation is thus true knowledge of God because we genuinely receive a share in divine knowledge,[118] in which God is an object of knowledge and we are its subject. In this simple subject–object relationship, we come to share the understanding through a transparent medium, which not only communicates knowledge of God to the church but also guides her to the deeper truth of enlightening the revelation, even though the medium does not fully disclose divine knowledge. Put another way, Jesus Christ is God's unveiling. In him, God reveals Godself, receivable to those in faith and obedience. At the same time, God takes on hiddenness in divine self-revelation and unveiling takes place with the concealment of Godself. This means that the knowledge we gain is indirect understanding of God while God's own direct knowledge is unveiled. God gives Godself to be known, and shared knowledge is gained by the work of the Spirit. We therefore come to apprehend the knowable God without ever comprehending God, who

---

unknowable God becomes knowable without setting aside God's incomprehensibility. God determines Godself for this gracious relationship to humankind and thus elects Godself for us in Jesus Christ. To speak of this Christology, the unity of divine and human nature in Christ is a unity of Subject, which is not the indwelling of a human subject by a divine Subject but the union of two natures in a single divine Subject (the Person of the Logos). The unfathomable God fully entered the realm of intuitability and yet God remains inexplicable even as God enters fully into knowability. Moreover, God is to be recognized not only as the Subject of this life but also as the medium of human flesh in which the veiled God becomes transparent. This recognition and transparency is achieved through the Holy Spirit, who draws believers into God's own Self-knowledge. This means that, on one hand, God makes Godself identifiable, for the unfathomable God is truly to be known, but in such a way that God does not yield Godself to believers. On the other hand, God remains inexplicable even as God enters fully into fathomability: the incomprehensible God fully entered the realm of intuitability. To substantiate this claim, Barth moves from a pneumatocentric to a Christocentric theology of revelation, specifically through a particular construal of the enhypostatic-anhypostatic Christology; see also *CD* IV/3, 38–367.

118. Barth asserts that we can recognize the reality of the word "as the present end and goal of the process whereby God's Word comes to [us] as a human word; not as ignorant but as sharing in the divine knowledge, as *conscientes*" (*CD* I/2, 710).

The Word of God in Its Threefold Form

remains veiled, because God is concealed in unveiling.[119] Without a veil, simultaneously, God is not knowable.

In the event of unveiling, put differently, God removes the incomprehensibility of the knowability of the word. This self-revealing God in hiddenness meets us in Jesus Christ, and the Spirit discloses the hiddenness in the veil by virtue of God's *telos*. Standing in revelation, the true knowledge we obtain is imparted to us by the power of the Spirit, and we can relate to the revelation of the living God, who remains concealed in this hidden subjectivity. The knowledge of God we gain is therefore indirect, and our knowing God is indirect. This knowing, nevertheless, entails a confession of faith based on the witness of Scripture as divine knowledge is unveiled. God's way of revealing Godself, momentously, is through the concealment of the subject–object relationship, and it is in Jesus Christ that we receive a share in divine knowledge. This shared insight is not knowledge that we can attain from our efforts. Only in revelation by the Spirit is this knowledge given to us, and this indirect, objective, shared knowledge of God is ours.

With this learning, the church participates in the revelation of Christ, as well as salvation. Our participation in reconciliation (through which only we can receive knowledge) bears witness and recognizes God-in-salvific-action for the church and in the world. Our participation forms the biblical construal that enables us to describe our lives within biblical narratives. This formation is acquired from understanding the covenantal relationship that we know to be immersed in knowledge of Scripture. This insight is received in revelation of reconciliation and therefore unveiled in coupling rather than in estrangement and a third way. The unveiling that comes from hearing the word is understood as our knowledge of Christ gradually deepens. From this knowability, we hear the word of God preached, written, and revealed. Indeed, hearing

---

119. According to Nimmo, "our capacity to know God by faith is one that we can only receive from God, for God cannot be apprehended by our own powers of cognition and would thus remain hidden if God did not intervene. This is not a reason for despair, however, but for gratitude and worship, because recognition of this hiddenness of God is actually the starting point for Barth's affirmation that true knowledge of God can and does exist" (Nimmo, *Barth*, 55); Barth, *Göttingen Dogmatics*, 325–50. For Barth, God, whose presence is hidden, finally and most completely meets us in the crucified Jesus Christ, a revelation that constitutes a different kind of hiddenness than his general presence in the world (335).

the word is a possibility for us as "we ourselves are [the Word's] actualisation in our entire existence."[120] Barth affirms,

> As the possibility which comes to us in the Word's reality it is our possibility, just as faith is our possibility as that which comes to us. It is really ours, the possibility of the entire creaturely and sinful [human]; yet not in such a way that contemplating [us we] can discover it or read it off somewhere in [us] or on [us]; only in such a way that this creaturely, sinful [human] waits for the Word that comes to [us] and therewith for [our] faith.[121]

On account of this possibility, the divine word revealed by the Spirit cultivates our knowledge of Jesus Christ. For we are bearers of the Spirit and thus experience the word of God, we can actually know God through the word, which also means that we know God because God reveals Godself to us. Indeed, God comes to us in the word and presents Godself to us in the word: "Hence the assurance of [our] affirmation of this possibility can only be that of the Word of God itself."[122] In faith and obedience, we affirm that objective knowledge of God comes to us and is achieved by the Holy Spirit.

What is crucial to grasp about this maneuver of the light in the revelation of the word springs from the essence of the covenantal relationship. It is rooted in the I–Thou encounter, belonging with the doctrine of the *concursus Dei*.[123] In the *concursus Dei*, as noted earlier, our free and self-governing activity by the covenant of grace is to parallel godly activity, regardless of the asymmetrical nature of divine and human. Established in the life and resurrection of Jesus Christ, God reveals Godself, "in willing and recognising the distinct reality of [the covenant partner], granting and conceding to it an individual and autonomous place side by side with [Godself]."[124] This God—who loves and redeems us—thus precedes our action as God undertakes to glorify it and follows it to conserve us in divine grace. God cooperates with us, preceding, accompanying, and

---

120. *CD* I/1, 224.

121. *CD* I/1, 237.

122. *CD* I/1, 224.

123. Nimmo, *Being in Action*. Nimmo indicates that the *concursus Dei* is, for Barth, a spiritual matter of faith. As Barth deems, "the concern of the *concursus Dei* is 'to find the description which can do justice in our thought and utterance to what we see and hear of the divine operation . . . it 'can never be perceived within the framework of a general philosophy'. Rather it must be revealed as 'the secret of grace,' and is thus 'not an assertion but a confession of the divine operation'" (124).

124. *CD* II/2, 178.

following all our activity to be primarily, simultaneously, and subsequently God's own activity, which reveals God's will in Jesus Christ.[125] In this, our hearing is accompanied by divine speech as we are dependent on God, and our freedom is guaranteed by God, who surrounds our activity. God, essentially, wills to preserve us in our time and space.

Within the very I–Thou relationship, then, we correspond to God's command, e.g., "walk by the Spirit." This does not mean that we are marionettes who move only at God's will.[126] Rather, we are able and willing to do what is appropriate, grounded in an ordered relationship—"God and divine freedom and action on the one hand, and [we and our] freedom and action on the other hand."[127] On this basis, the supremacy of the word and the Spirit establishes cooperation between double actions (the lordship of God and our participation) in Jesus Christ. This cooperation is, as previously stated, considered "a single action"[128] of the agencies of God and the covenant partner. Importantly, God concurs with us, but we do not give rise to the *concursus Dei*. The absoluteness of God carries human action in such a way that the word is revealed as irresistible to us. As Barth underlines, "we have to think of the majesty and absoluteness and irresistibility of the divine activity as the confirmation and continually renewed basis of the singularity of the creature to whom God is gracious, and of its worth, and independent activity."[129] Truly, divine freedom and ours can be paralleled.[130] God avows and respects autonomy, freedom, responsibility, and the life of the covenant partner, so we are not suppressed

---

125. See *CD* III/3, 90–154.

126. Barth, *Christian Life*, 153. McDowell, *Hope in Barth's Eschatology*, 137–40; McDowell agrees not only with Barth's rejection of "suspicions of divine coercion" but also with his emphasis of God's respect on human integrity and individuality, suggesting that "human and divine freedoms are a *co-operative*, rather than *competitive*, manner" (138); Italics his. McKenny, "Heterogeneity and Ethical Deliberation," 205–24; regarding the commandments and the word of God, McKenny holds the view that "one may derive substantive knowledge of the character and standards that the command of God will never violate" (217).

127. Nimmo, *Being in Action*, 135.

128. *CD* III/3, 132.

129. *CD* III/3, 118.

130. Nimmo, *Being in Action*. As Nimmo clarifies that "the operation of God is therefore 'absolutely above the power of the creature', being 'not merely done after a higher and superior fashion, but within a completely different order.' For Barth, then, 'An awareness of the supremacy of God over all the power of the creature, of the qualitative distinction between divine and creaturely potency, of the irreversibility of the order of precedence in divine and creaturely activity, must be brought into play and relentlessly kept in play at this juncture'" (123).

and extinguished but vindicated and valued. Since the authenticity of our freedom, absorbed into the covenant of grace, rests upon divine freedom in Jesus Christ, it can, indeed, concur with the divine. According to Barth,

> God controls the activity in its freedom no less than its necessity. The control of God is transcendent. Between the sovereignty of God and the freedom of the creature there is no contradiction. The freedom of its activity does not exclude but includes the fact that it is controlled by God. It is God who limited [the freedom of our activity] by [the command] and it is God who created it free.[131]

Therefore, we—in our freedom and responsibility—correspond to God who walks with us. With this *concursus Dei*, our freedom, attended by divine freedom, takes place by means of a "disciplined description of Christian discourse, normatively found in Holy Scripture,"[132] in which the true character of Christian thought and speech is analogous within the covenant of grace, unfolding "the history, encounter and decision between [God] and [humanity]."[133] The word comes to us in the power of the Spirit in such a way that we cannot determinedly resist it but are caused and freely moved to hear it. As the word is in the eternal election of Jesus Christ, in whom our freedom is revealed and constituted, we—freely and gratefully—align ourselves with the *concursus Dei* and confess that "we have listened to the Word of grace in which God has Himself revealed Himself in Jesus Christ."[134] We therefore stand in the relationship of revelation, in which the word spoken to us is received by us through the work of the Spirit.

Accordingly, only within this I–Thou relationship, *Deus dixit*—the Word, the Logos, and the inflexibility of God's revelation and infallibility—comes to us as a reality through Scripture. The I–Thou relationship explicitly articulates that God reveals Godself as subject. At the same time, God meets us objectively. God is subject and we are object. God speaks, and we are spoken to. We can know God who communicates with us, and Jesus Christ—the definite revelation of God—as a connection between subject and object. As indicated before, we relate to the actuality of the revelation of the living God, who remains hidden in unveiling. Put

---

131. CD III/3, 165–66.
132. Webster, *Barth's Moral Theology*, 102.
133. CD II/2, 177.
134. CD III/3, 109.

The Word of God in Its Threefold Form

differently, because of God's inexplicable nature, there are hidden subjectivities of God, which conceal the subject-object relationship in the act of unveiling. Yet, self-revealing God is knowable by us, for real knowledge of God is revealed even though God remains simultaneously veiled. This means that, on the one hand, *Deus dixit* is evident to the hearing church—that is, God actively relates to individuals in the church by revealing the word. In this way, God deliberately intervenes in the hearing church while remaining hidden. On the other hand, "God is completely inconceivable, concealed, and absent for those whom he does not address and who are not addressed by him."[135] Such an intervention has a certain pattern of the Spirit drawing us to God in the present. This pattern, according to David Kelsey, connects with an enigmatic "unsystematizable richness of what and who [we] are and how [we] are to be by virtue of God's ways of relating to [us]."[136] The pattern is visualized by means of "the language of popular piety [and] formal language of liturgy,"[137] in which the Spirit (who is within us) not only empowers the proclaiming and hearing of the gospel but also works in and through the faithful communal life of the church. Through these acts, the Spirit (with the Son sent by the Father) draws the church to live in God's self-involving covenant relationship, not only from a historical and current perspective but also with faith into eschatological time and space.[138] In the event of *Deus dixit*, the hearing church, therefore, witnesses the continuance of revelation, which she finds via the witness in Scripture. In that witness, she finds revelation, and a choice in our freedom lies in whether or not we respond to *Deus dixit* in faith and obedience.

Significantly, a pattern of *Deus dixit* includes a concrete and particular command of God, expressing permission and prohibition in Scripture, which communicates the specific meaning and purpose of God's

---

135. Barth, *Göttingen Dogmatics*, 58.

136. Kelsey, *Eccentric Existence*, 481. Kelsey also argues that God's intervention is a living contradiction, making us mysteries. For him, its inexplicable nature is opaque to human inquiry and ultimately defies logic.

137. Kelsey, *Eccentric Existence*, 444. Smith, *Theology of the Third Article*; for Smith, "the revelation of God is the event in which God causes himself to stand before us and causes us to stand before him. God has his existence in this event; his God-ness is just his freedom to move himself toward us and to turn us to him. He is Lord in this coordinated action, neither unable to move toward us because of his eternity nor unable to turn us to him because of our temporality. He reigns over eternity and time by being unconstrained by either in the event of revelation. He lives and reigns this way in the life and work of Christ and the Spirit" (173).

138. See Kelsey, *Eccentric Existence*, 441–542.

will and acts for the church in Jesus Christ, in whom "the right action of [humans] has already been performed and therefore waits only to be confirmed by our action."[139] Barth highlights that "in the one image of Jesus Christ we have both the Gospel which reconciles us with God and illumines us and consoles us, and the Law which in contradistinction to all the laws which we ourselves find or fabricate really binds and obligates us."[140] Once more, it is in Jesus Christ that the harmony of the word as both gospel and law is fulfilled. This harmonization depends on the whole relationship of God with us in the course of the covenant of grace, which not only "forms the true content and object of the biblical witness [but also] is continuously realised in the shape of the divine commanding and prohibiting, the divine ordering and directing."[141] God is the Subject of the command, and we are claimed for the cause of God,[142] who loves us and wills to make a covenant with us all through Jesus Christ—the Son of the everlasting Father, the very God and very man, the timeless Logos from all eternity, and "the eternal *testamentum*, the eternal *sponsio*, the eternal *pactum*, between God and [human]."[143] The covenant established through him between God and us all is "done in acts of grace and mercy, of judgment and punishment, and in [God's] Word as Gospel and Law, as comfort, admonishment and counsel."[144]

In light of this, the hearing church connects to the heart of the command as the living Lord Jesus Christ forms a covenantal relationship with her: God—the salvation and righteous judgment for us—makes Godself known to those who can hear the word. Within the I–Thou encounter, accordingly, the church as hearers experiences *Deus dixit*—God's spiritual reality is made known to us by the Holy Spirit, who works through the inspired words of Scripture. Indeed, the word does not fail us in our quest to know God, for it is presented to us as a promise and therefore

139. *CD* II/2, 543.
140. *CD* II/2, 539.
141. *CD* II/2, 672.
142. *CD* II/2, 682.

143. *CD* IV/1, 66. Barth reinforces our covenant with the Trinity, claiming that "to unite God in His attitude to [humans]—whether in respect of His properties, or as Father, Son and Holy Spirit—there is no need of any particular decree. God would not be God if He were not God in this unity. And a covenant with [humans] is not grounded merely in this unity of God in and with Himself. It is not self-evident but a new thing that in His unity with Himself from all eternity God wills to be the God of [humans] and to make and have [humans] as His [covenant partners]" (66).

144. *CD* IV/1, 35.

can only be received through faith.[145] This hearing excavates knowledge of Scripture and Jesus Christ, which signifies that true knowledge of God exists, and we gain that knowledge, although this comprehension of God is always indirect knowledge. As earlier mentioned, this indirect, objective knowledge of God arises from God in reconciling acts, meaning that, without the divine presence of the *concursus Dei*, there can be no knowledge of God. In the event of address, knowledge is shared by the church's participation in the covenantal relationship as the hearing church correlates the disclosure of self-revealing God and thus gains such indirect knowledge via the Spirit. This knowledge can appropriately become our knowability through *Deus dixit*, the revelation of the Father by the Son and of the Son by the Father, which takes place in the power of the Spirit. Knowledge of God in this relationship is the knowledge of Jesus Christ, which is not information that we can attain for ourselves. We can only receive this shared insight from God because the comprehension directly originates in God, who creates obedience of faith and causes the church to unveil the hiddenness of self-revealing God. Barth claims that

> [the] knowability of God's Word is really an inalienable affirmation of faith. [But] precisely as such it denotes the miracle of faith, the miracle that we can only recollect and hope for. [As] a final necessity we must also understand that [human] must be set side and God Himself presented as the original subject, as the primary power, as the creator of the possibility of knowledge of God's Word. Christ does not remain outside.[146]

In virtue of this miracle, the knowability of God's word thus not only takes place but also represents the possibility via church proclamation.[147] Namely, God can be known only by the Holy Spirit in Jesus Christ, in whom we join in divine knowledge, and the hearing church exists on the basis of knowledge of Jesus Christ, whereby we advance through the word of God. In revelation, then, and only in revelation, we grasp partial knowledge of God, without ever fully understanding God.

In the event of the word of God, therefore, we are summoned to the word and correspond to it. The *concursus Dei* is on one side and the childlike obedience of the covenant partner—i.e., the Galatians and all—on the other. There is also the Spirit, walking with the church while God

---

145. *CD* II/2, 603.
146. *CD* I/1, 247.
147. See *CD* I/1, 248–92.

accompanies our free, contingent, and autonomous activity, simply confirming the divine activity.[148] This "secretly identical" nature in distinctive but united double agency, without the event of the word, would have made it impenetrable for the Galatians (and all) to meet Jesus Christ, God sending the Son. In fact, the Galatians were more familiar with recognizing the God of Israel than Jesus Christ. Nevertheless, for God who reveals Godself to the Galatians, they have come to know God and share partial knowledge of the divine. As seen in chapter 1, we acknowledge God who first revealed Godself to us and call God "Abba Father" in our worship. This recognition is unreachable through the basic principles, the works of the law, or any mystic pursuit. Having died and risen in Christ, the Galatians (and all) are bearers of the Spirit of Christ, not only experiencing the reality of *Deus dixit* but also participating in shared knowledge of God; for the human possibility of knowing the word is only possible in light of the revelation of the word.

Moments of the communal life of the church, though, involve straying from the gospel and being led by the flesh. For this reason, as Paul urges, the church is to evoke the event of the word, encountering the living Lord Jesus Christ. After all, it is in the covenant of grace that the church hears the word and witnesses the *concursus Dei*. The sovereignty of God coexists and coinheres in the Galatians' and our lives, for the relationship that God establishes with us continues "a history of love and freedom."[149] It is truly the word of God that, in Jesus Christ, the Galatians and we hear and recognize. God, who speaks to us in the person of Jesus Christ, walks with us as God is present for us in the word as proclamation, as Scripture, and as revelation. In light of this, the church as hearers is historically interconnected with Jesus Christ and, without pausing, remains preserved in the covenantal relationship with God.

SUMMARY

In this chapter, we first explore God sending the Son, the preexistent Jesus Christ, by means of hermeneutics and its interconnected doctrinal engagement. On the basis of God being our God and us representing

---

148. See *CD* III/3, 90–154.

149. Hunsinger, *How to Read Karl Barth*, 31; besides, Barth notes that "the [human] mastered and compelled is precisely the [human] whom God loves, who is therefore set upon [our] own feet and made truly responsible" (*CD* I/2, 662).

God's Israel and God's church,[150] the theological concepts of time and the God of Israel and the Trinity are appraised. Second, the doctrine of the word in its threefold form is considered as we assess the God who accompanies us and meets us in the covenant of grace. The word of God comes to us as not only both the God of Israel and the Trinity but also the eternity of the compound of past–present–anticipated eschatological promises. In God's free election of grace, God, making us the covenant partners, is witnessed by us via the word of God as preached, written, and revealed. This discussion is advanced into the doctrines of the *concursus Dei* and the I–Thou relationship, for the word of God spoken from eternity not only addresses us all but also communicates with us about the inflexibility of God's revelation and infallibility, embodying the covenant of grace historically, currently, and for the future.

---

150. *CD* III/1, 26.

Conclusion

ON THE BASIS OF the relationship between the word of God and "Christ lives in us and we in him," we explore three characteristics of the church's existence—encountering, estrangement, and a third way, revealing each character by virtue of biblical exegesis and their doctrinal engagements. In encountering, on the one hand, we experience the word by the Spirit, which encourages us to live a communal life of the church bearing the fruit of the Spirit—i.e., one of the conditions for entering into the kingdom of God. In estrangement, on the other hand, Scripture is unheard, meanings veiled, and revelation disengaged. This estrangement is directly connected with the flesh-led life that would renounce the promise of baptism. Church life, therefore, does not include speaking fluent Christian narratives or persistently living our lives in ways that Scripture teaches. It is thus significant that the church needs to see her members under two opposing forces by repelling the powers of the flesh and aligning with the Spirit dwelling in us, for the decision to live by the flesh or live in the Spirit has an impact on all components of her existence. Paralleling these characteristics of the church, we also explicate the elected community of God as a twofold typology of Israel and the church, designated together in unity. The first typology portrays the disobedient church turning away from God, followed by its corresponding divine judgment. The second depicts that God's determination toward the church entails the mercy of God. The typology serves the eschatological *telos* of God through Jesus Christ and thus is one church in its distinctive features.

In addition to the polarity of the church, there is a third way of the church's existence, viewed neither as a community of sin nor a community of encountering revelation. We assess the third way through the doctrine

Conclusion

of nothingness and the biblical exegesis of Gal 5:17. The third way is furthered to discuss its nature with respect to the doctrine of election as well as that of justification, primarily avowed as *opus alienum Dei* attended by *opus proprium Dei*. We also acknowledge that the third way is perceived as the object ground of knowledge of sin and Jesus Christ. In light of this, the third way of the church's existence makes possible recognition of sin and the work of Jesus Christ, particularly the way in which the faith of the church—cultivated by Scripture—becomes an essential determinant to alter the church under both the overlap of the Spirit and the flesh and that of divine providence and nothingness. Accordingly, this third way is examined by the doctrine of the word as we emphasize the importance of the accord of the gospel (as content of the word) and law (as its form), so that the church remains the I-Thou relationship in the covenant of grace. Taking into account this harmony of the word, we appraise the third way and its relationship to freedom and unfreedom. Our freedom within divine freedom is revealed in Jesus Christ, and, for this reason, the determination of the church in her freedom or unfreedom takes her to diverse outcomes, either engaging an active dialogue with the word or leading to sin, the concrete form of nothingness. This determination of the church connects with the way she utilizes her freedom and unfreedom, in both 5:17 and a third way, resulting in the communal life of the church either led by the Spirit or the flesh. Moreover, in this treatment of freedom and unfreedom, we affirm that the church, corresponding to the word, is to grasp her freedom bound by divine freedom, signifying that we can know what freedom really is. In addition, unfreedom (i.e., the shadow side of freedom) negates the covenant partnership, which is only understood in light of impossible possibility, placing believers between possible obedience and impossible disobedience.

The church must therefore understand that her freedom and unfreedom lie in the knowledge of Christ and sin, in which our knowability of the word expands. That is, we recognize that we are grounded in the divine work of reconciliation through Jesus Christ, in whom resolution is achieved. This settlement was not only accomplished through Jesus Christ in the power of the Spirit but also continues—in the communal life of the church—to take place as a momentary union in which the Spirit brings together the presence of God and the church. It is in this revelation of reconciliation that we attain knowledge through self-revealing God. Put differently, by God's grace, the church as hearers grasps not only knowledge of both sin and Jesus Christ (in whom God reveals Godself in reconciling acts) but also her obligation to pursue God's will in faith and obedience. This understanding becomes more refined as our knowability increases, a process distinct from mere knowledge acquisition because it does not involve the human possibility of knowing the word but engages in discovering hidden meanings of the word. God creates the possibility of knowing God's word by the work of the Holy Spirit, so this awareness does not occur as a result of human effort. When we validate the experience of the word, knowability belongs to us as it becomes subjective even though it is objective. Subjective and yet objective knowability relates to receiving faith in God's grace, nurturing the church as she immerses herself in Scripture. Given our knowledge of Jesus Christ and the knowability of the word, we assert that the church can be reformed by the freedom Jesus Christ has granted it in our covenantal union: whether estranged or a third way, she can be brought to hear the word and exists as reconciled.

We also highlight that God's self-presence appears by the Holy Spirit, taking place through divine possibility. Corresponding to revelation, the hearing church thus demonstrates her comprehension of Scripture as a collection of revelatory occurrences. Indeed, Scripture speaks of God who not only intends to achieve God's salvific purposes for all but also gives the church an understanding of reality, willed and governed by God. As a result of this ideal, the hearing church is a competent participant engaging in revelatory saving events. Precisely at this point, we recognize that the "I" (died and risen in Christ) is not a condition to receive God who has revealed and reveals Godself in Jesus Christ. Baptized believers do not automatically encounter a self-revealing God: the baptized "I," receiving the Spirit in the faithfulness of Jesus Christ, does not become a channel to encounter God's revelation. Although eschatological promises are given to the "I," embodying the significance of baptism, the "I" is never a subject in relation to God's revelation but an object to be filled with content. God is the content and we are a vessel for the content. "There will then be revelation, that is, the establishment of fellowship between God and us by God's communication to us,"[1] as Barth affirms. We receive God, who reveals Godself in the Son and by the Spirit, and the church corresponds with faith and obedience to what we hear in God's revelation.

For the church as hearers, then, we hold the significance of the word of God in the unity of both gospel and law, as the discord of gospel and

---

1. Barth, *Göttingen Dogmatics*, 176.

law disintegrates the elected community of God rather than creating the communal life led by the Spirit. This discord, in our context of Galatians, ambiguously teaches the covenant of grace and interrupts the peace of the community. Entangled with false doctrines, moreover, the church not only fails to connect with the original meanings of Scripture but also distracts her from a truthful existence in Jesus Christ, and thus becomes estranged or a third way, contradicting God's self-manifestation in the incarnate Word. However, we deliberate that this negative side of the church's existence can be professed as the impossible possibility of aligning ourselves with the word. That is, the elected community necessitates her to profoundly engage with the word of God and participates in eternal election in Jesus Christ as she—under divine providence—sustains by faith within the history of one covenant.

Alongside these arguments, we are attentive in hearing the word commanding in the unity of gospel and law. This hearing connects to the sanctifying life of the church, especially when the command as God's judgment comes to us. We thus confirm that the command of God cannot be generalized and transformed into universal valid principles while it is "regarded as in some sense a legal text known to [us] and those whom [we have] to instruct."[2] The command of God "has eternal and valid content for us precisely in its temporary expression, and demands that we should hear and respect it in our very different time and situation."[3] This truth is the same for the Galatians and all of us. When the command of God confronts us as rules, principles, and general moral truths, we cannot merely perceive it as a prescribed text but are to understand it as "the ordering of [biblical characters] to conform in their actions at a definite time, in a definite place and in a definite way to the history of the covenant and salvation controlled by [God]."[4] In other words, we hear the command of God within the covenant of grace, for the function of Scripture "bears witness, not to an alien and dead, but to our own living Lord and

---

2. CD III/4, 6.

3. CD II/2, 707; Nimmo, *Being in Action*. The word of God lives, acts, and speaks in Scripture. So, too, the word of God commands. Accordingly, we would misunderstand the core relationship between God and us "as if the content of the command at a certain point in Scripture were in no way different from the command of God given today" (34). For this reason, Nimmo asserts that "Barth is determined to avoid: the Bible being conceived as a textbook of ethics in abstraction from the history of the covenant of grace" (34).

4. CD III/4, 12.

Commander and Judge."[5] This means that the command that was spoken to Abraham (and biblical characters) in Scripture is the command given to us even if we and the Galatians are in very different times, cultures, and situations. The word comes to us as "the real history which takes place between God and [human],"[6] and we hear the command of God in Scripture within the covenantal term in divine grace—that is, within the history of the Old and New Testaments. Indeed, the root of Paul's doctrine of justification lies in the essence of the covenant, in which the history of the one covenant and its divine *telos* are proclaimed. In this way, the church is preserved by the covenant of grace attested in Scripture. God as the Lord who rules over the church discloses the "divine existence in the act of His lordship and work, and His work as that of establishing, maintaining and confirming the covenant of grace."[7]

In covenanting with God, we therefore recognize that the God to whom Scripture bears witness gives the command. The command of God attested throughout Scripture determines our action freely as the hearing church obeys the word in the harmony of both gospel and law and thus keeps the commandments—i.e., love God and our neighbors. This recognition was significant to the Galatians, is true for us in the present, and will remain true for the future of the church as hearers. Indeed, "Scripture itself is a really truly living, acting and speaking subject"[8] in such a way that the word of God is addressed to us, and we hear it and seek the divine *telos* of the covenantal relationship. In the command of God, thus, "we are face to face with the person of God, with the action and revelation of this person, with God Himself"[9] whether the hearer of the command is Abraham, Moses, Jeremiah, Ezekiel, Paul, Israel, the church, or us today. Entrenched in the history and sequel of the covenant of grace, the command of God is heard in the Old Testament, continues into the New Testament and the letter to the Galatians, and is now at work in believers' lives, moving toward its final fulfillment. On this basis, we affirm that the conflicts of the Galatians are relevant to us, particularly the way in which the church necessitates gripping the divine *telos* of the covenant of grace.

5. *CD* II/2, 671.
6. *CD* II/2, 686.
7. *CD* II/2, 705.
8. *CD* I/2, 672.
9. *CD* II/2, 676.

Conclusion

The fundamental nature of the covenant is therefore unalterable by any forms of challenges that we have to deal with, such as commodities. In the life of commodities, a theological shift in the I–Thou relationship is noticeable. God becomes object as our belief promotes buying into faith and practices, and we "feel content and liberated" through consumption, while God is considered a material at our disposal. In this shift, the I–Thou relationship is fruitless. Deviated from the authenticity of the I–Thou encounter, an elusive covenantal relationship emerges. Put another way, the I–Thou relationship clearly articulates that self-revealing God is subject and content in light of the condition of the subjective-objective revelation. In revelation, God—who is knowable to us in hiddenness—meets us objectively. The vital theological existence of the church is that she is a vessel for revelation—i.e., God is subject and we are object; God speaks, and we are spoken to. We can know God who communicates with us, and Jesus Christ—the definite revelation of God—connects the subject and the object. When this fundamental shifts, however, there are consequences that affect the significance of hearing the word. The speech and life of the church drift from Scripture as the means through which we encounter the living God, nor are the messages rooted in the commodity relevant to the gospel of salvation. These kinds of missives do not properly reflect God meeting us through the life, death, and resurrection of Jesus Christ in the power of the Spirit. As a result, the particular characteristics of the church's existence—i.e., estrangement and a third way—are apparent, and the church circumscribes a graceful ambience in which "the Word proclaims and the church hears."

Countering this shift, restoring the I–Thou relationship in the life of commodities can be achieved by advancing ourselves in understanding Scripture in depth and nurturing with doctrines. Scripture and its doctrinal correlations contribute to expressing contextual reality through well-articulated human experiences within biblical narratives. As is apparent in the discussion presented throughout the book, doctrines and biblical interpretations are closely related to each other, correlating with both the individual and communal life of the church. The interrelatedness of the doctrine, Scripture, and the life of the elected community can be naturally woven into a proclamation where the church testifies that "God speaks." Enhancing the approach, first, pure doctrine should be attained. As shown in chapter 3, Barth accentuates absolute doctrine, removing false human reasonings. The doctrine must be free from added matter, not merely in exposition, but in clarification and correction of proclamation in the light of the church history and present contexts, while the meaningful agreement between proclamation and revelation attested in Scripture is emphasized. The present, living word of God can therefore meet us through the words of preachers, for truly absolute doctrine is possible insofar as proclamation is purified by the measure of Scripture and revelation. The measure is the work of dogmatics, as Barth highlights:

> Dogmatic work consists secondly of strictly and clearly relating the words of Christian preachers to the Word of God as it is spoken in revelation and as scripture bears witness to it. The autonomy of dogmatic thinking means that it is the thinking of faith and obedience, human thinking which at all costs has to orient itself to its theme, and finally the thinking of individuals who see themselves set before this theme. It does not mean that of ourselves we can or will think the truth of God. It means primarily the autonomy of the Holy Spirit.[10]

Another approach is David Kelsey's *discrimen*.[11] Kelsey suggests the *discrimen*, which is a freely given particular choice of arrangement, as reciprocal coefficients in order to counteract current forms of speech and life of the church. That is, the *discrimen* adopts a theological position of imaginative construal about God's presence as it determines a particular arrangement of justification, incarnation, atonement, and knowledge of God. In commodity life, for instance, the theological position can be formulated on the knowledge of God as a priority and then rearranged to teach justification, incarnation, and atonement. Regardless of the particular arrangement, the *discrimen* yields the same outcome—the authority and normativity of Scripture are understood as functions of Scripture in the common life of the church. In a similar fashion, John Webster proposes the centrality of Scripture, engaging in critical, theological biblical exegeses and doctrinal teachings. The proposal also improves the speech and life of the church, for the centrality of Scripture visualizes the divine work of self-manifestation through the gospel of reconciliation. By the work of the Spirit in God's grace, for Webster, the divine word evokes the individual's subjective act of faith within the church, and the church hears Scripture as the *viva vox Dei*.[12]

---

10. Barth, *Göttingen Dogmatics*, 298. Barth italicizes the passage.
11. See Kelsey, *Uses of Scripture*, 158–78.
12. See Webster, *Holy Scripture*, 107–35.

Conclusion

These approaches are effective in correcting the theological shift in the I–Thou relationship. After all, it is only within the I–Thou relationship that God has spoken. God reveals Godself to us and we to him: God as subject encounters us as object in the I–Thou relationship. On this basis, the church becomes not only a witness to *Deus dixit* but also experiences its reality through Scripture.[13] God promises to speak to us afresh in the person of Jesus Christ (who establishes our reading of Scripture) when the church reads and preaches from Scripture (which relates to the witness of God's revelation). Put differently, *Deus dixit*—the Word, the Logos, and the revelation—comes as a reality through Scripture. When *Deus dixit* interferes with us, a choice—freedom or unfreedom—lies in whether we respond to God's address. Corresponding in faith and obedience, the church unites with the *concursus Dei*: divine agency causes, and the church witnesses *Deus dixit* appearing as "the *particular* of God"[14] in specific moments of our life. That is, we witness the *telos* of God's command for Abraham in his particular background, which is relevant to the Galatians and even us today. Taking the word and resting upon God's promise, we hear the command of God in Jesus Christ, who accompanies us, continuing his presence into the future of the hearing church.

This elementary virtue of hearing *Deus dixit* notably attests a special way through the common life of the church whereby both individuals and the collective witness the living Christ by the Spirit. God actively relates to us by revealing narratives of what it means to exist in relation to God, and this God—the origin of the covenantal narratives—depicts how we (died and risen in Christ) live our lives in relation to the Son sent by God and contextual reality. Put another way, "we live by faith of Jesus Christ," and encountering *Deus dixit* engages us in the theological anthropology of David Kelsey, particularly the way in which he views "eschatological consummation."[15] This consummation speaks of the second aspect of the three distinct but interrelated ways of God relating to us: creating us, drawing us to eschatological consummation, and reconciling us. We are eschatologically consummated in God's self-involving covenantal relationship while living on borrowed time. God gives us time and space (that is our own) to live wisely for God's *telos*, accompanying the now-actual and not-yet-fully actualized eschatological blessing, which is freely given by God in the risen Jesus Christ. This blessing is therefore distinct from

---

13. See Barth, *Göttingen Dogmatics*, 45–68.
14. Barth, *Göttingen Dogmatics*, 60. Italics his.
15. See Kelsey, *Eccentric Existence*, 478–542.

both the primal blessing of creation and the blessing of reconciliation, for it is refined through sanctification by means of divine judgment. For this eschatological consummation, Kelsey places emphasis on the Spirit, who not only works in and through the faithful communal life of the church but also empowers the proclaiming and hearing of the gospel. Through these acts, the Spirit with the Son draws us deeply into a new creation—i.e., conformity by virtue of justification and sanctification. We are to live simultaneously according to the Spirit with the Son sent by the Father.

Finally, "God's own speech" invites us to reach for profound truth. We are faithful to God who speaks with authority and addresses us with captivating power, as Barth declares, "We need only dare to follow this [speech] to grow out beyond ourselves toward the highest [truth]. This daring is *faith*."[16] The risen Christ comes into the church through Scripture and proclamation, taken up by God through the Spirit, and the church reunites with Christ in the covenant of grace. Even if the church falls under the sway of a third way, of estrangement, or of the first typology, she can absorb the rays of Jesus Christ, which radiate not only the content for her but also the knowledge of the reconciling God, causing it to glitter. In this revelation of God, the church lives and continues to exist with the mighty act of the Holy Spirit. If we wish to merge with the absolute truth of holy revelation, then we must align ourselves with the I–Thou relationship, centering ourselves on Scripture and being attentive to pure doctrinal teachings. From incremental knowledge of Christ, we hear a momentary Scripture, participating in God who inexplicably makes Godself known in the divine way. As the gradation elevates through revelatory occurrences, by the power of the Holy Spirit, so does our knowing God, who self-reveals in reconciling acts through Jesus Christ. These acts demand gradual responses to the word as the hearing church in her freedom resonates with one speech of the Father, the Son, and the Spirit.

In this light, we may live because Christ lives in us. We live by faith of the Son of God who loved us and gave himself for us.

---

16. Barth, *Word of God*, 34. Italics his.

Appendix

The Prophecy of Habakkuk and the Covenant of Grace

THE FIRST CHAPTER FOCUSES discussions on Gal 2:15–21 and 3:10–14 in light of the antithesis of faith and law, particularly the way in which biblical interpretations and interconnected doctrinal understandings enable us to hear the word in both gospel and law within the covenant of grace. The passages underline Paul's theological claim that one is justified by faith through Jesus Christ in contrast to the false doctrine taught by the opponents, causing ambiguities in perceiving the history of the covenant of grace. Preserving the gospel, we argue that Paul speaks of the four scriptural texts in 3:10–13 to counter the opponents' claims.

Taking this into account, this chapter furthers Paul's declarations on Hab 2:4b, reading through the prophecy of Habakkuk, which delivers the oracle to the people of God. As the prophecy can speak of its broader historical context, we first examine both conventional interpretations and the commentary of Pesher Habakkuk (1QpHab).[1] We

1. The Habakkuk commentary was discovered in Qumran Cave 1 in 1947. The commentary is called the Pesher Habakkuk (1QpHab), dating to the first century. The pesher is a well-preserved scroll in the first two chapters of the prophecy of Habakkuk, which is made up of thirteen columns in total. Our discussion does not include chapter 3 of Habakkuk in the Bible. The prophecy closes with a psalm (chapter 3), constructed at the beginning and end in first-person speech as the prophet expresses his confidence in YHWH's restoration. Qumran commentators do not find the missing chapter strange as chapter 3 belongs to a completely different genre from the first two chapters.

then evaluate the function of Hab 2:4b within its wider context in the pesher and alongside Paul's specific intent for referencing the four texts in Gal 3:10–13. In detail, the prophecy of Hab 2:4b serves as a significant proof-text in the construction of the doctrine of justification. A literal interpretation of the law-gospel contrast, as some commentators contend, easily misses the prophetic intention behind Paul's words. This section therefore explores the Habakkuk prophecy, its historical context, false teachings, and the doctrine of justification as outlined in 3:10–14. It also draws a parallel between the wicked priest and Paul's opponents, emphasizing their similar deeds. Furthermore, the two contrasting doctrines of Paul and his opponents are shown to be mirrored by the different uses of Scripture taught by the teacher of righteousness and the wicked priest. As established in chapter 1, Paul teaches the covenant of grace in opposition to his opponents, who advocate for a works-based covenant and assert that adherence to the law's ordinances is necessary to become—and remain—descendants of Abraham. This chapter, in turn, examines how the authentic knowledge of the covenant fundamentally differentiates the priest from the teacher. Our discussion then advances to acknowledge two points: first, the *telos* of the covenant; and second, the overarching unity and continuity of God's covenant across the Old and New Testaments. These two aspects inform how hearing the word in the harmony of gospel and law leads to an understanding of justification in the covenant of grace.

TRADITIONAL VIEWS

The prophecy involves a complaint from Habakkuk, as it appears Jehoahaz was dethroned and replaced by Jehoiakim. Habakkuk is distressed because the nation faces the breakdown of law and order and the prophecy that he received earlier is unfulfilled. Faced with the destruction of Judah, Habakkuk hears YHWH and the oracle, in response, affirms YHWH established that the power of Chaldeans (1:6) will be raised to restore the righteous and overthrow the wicked. This anticipated downfall of the wicked and rise of the righteous was slowed. At the end of the complaint, though, the attitude of the prophet changes with his trust in YHWH, and he waits for another oracle. Standing on his watchtower, the prophet waits for the second oracle, expressing his trust in YHWH (2:1). The divine response comes back and affirms that the delay is over and the original prophecy will be forthcoming, as the prophet writes down the oracles, the salvation of the righteous, and the judgment on the wicked. YHWH brings life to the righteous—those who are faithful. The prophet and his readers are to wait for fulfillment at the appointed time. A series of woes follows. The grievances of Habakkuk are written in both singular and plural form, expressing complaints that are communal in nature, for the prophet speaks as an individual on behalf of the community. In view of this prophecy, Hab 2:4b is particularly important to Jewish apocalyptic understandings—the prophet declares the salvation of the righteous from God's judgment to those who keep the divine commandments. The prophet emphasizes that righteousness comes only through faith, and proclaims the holy almighty Lord, who engages in salvation for the righteous as well as judgment for the wicked. Alternatively, God will chastise the Chaldeans for their iniquity. In the meantime, as some scholars argue, "the righteous will live by their faithfulness," meaning that they will survive the invasion and return to their own land (e.g., the exile is over). That is, the righteous will "live"[2] and there will be life after the Chaldean invasion. In this sense, the prophecy not only speaks of how one becomes righteous but also declares the assurance of YWHW that the righteous of Judah will live through judgment and ultimately be vindicated. Those who continue to trust in God, on account of their faithfulness, will therefore survive the hardship. Thus, they (i.e., the remnant) will return to their homes, which is their justification as the righteous people of God.

THE PESHER HABAKKUK

According to the pesherist, Hab 1:6 speaks of the foreign invaders, the Chaldeans—i.e., the Babylonians that YHWH chose to apply justice to the elect. However, the pesherist implies the Kittim (i.e., the Romans), who intervened in the affairs of Judea in 63 BCE.[3] Under the dominion of the Kittim, some did not remain faithful to covenantal law. The pesherist interpreted them as "the wicked ones." When Hab 2:3 states that a

2. Hunn, "Habakkuk 2.4b in Its Context," 228–32. Nebuchadnezzar conquered Judah in 586 BCE. The Medo-Persians entered Babylon and killed Belshazzar in 539 BCE. Then, Habakkuk and the righteous waited at least forty-seven years to see the fulfillment of the vision. This implies that some of the righteous were young when the oracle (Hab 2:3) was spoken, and others died before 539 BCE. The remnant, therefore, saw the fulfillment of the vision, and the life they lived must be resurrection life: "The text thus speaks of the eschaton" (231).

3. Lim, *Earliest Commentary*, 7–10, 21–24, 55–56.

previous vision was unfulfilled, the pesherist asserts that God's revelation is yet to come. For the pesherist, the sectarians viewed revelation as not ceased but continuous, as in Habakkuk's own day.

In column 4:16—5:8,[4] interpreting Hab 1:12b–13, God gives judgment to all the nations, all the wicked who rebuke, and all the righteous who keep God's commandments in their distress. God will not destroy "His people by the hand of the nations" (5:3), meaning that the Kittim were not raised to annihilate the chosen ones. The pesherist therefore addresses a concern about the rise of the Kittim army and the commanders leading them. As he assures his readers, God will not destroy the elect through the nation (the Kittim), which serves to reprove and correct the wicked ones among the elect—namely, those who did not keep the divine commandments. Divine judgment falls upon both the Kittim and God's people, as God judges the wicked nations and all the wicked of God's people. God's people (who are chosen) are then divided between those who keep God's commandments and those who turn to the wicked ones. Accordingly, God's people are reidentified as those who observe the law and remain faithful to the commandments during their suffering: their spirits are thus upright with YHWH. Regarding the fall of the Kittim and the deliverance of God's people, the sectarians understood that YHWH has placed God's people for judgment and correction, but not for destruction. The Kittim (like the Chaldeans) serve the divine purpose of correcting the people, some of whom are wicked, and others who keep the commandments.[5] When the pesherist reflects the sectarian view of the end-time in column 12:10—13:4,[6] citing Hab 2:18–20, he accentuates that, on the Day of Judgment, God will destroy all nations who worship idols because these nations are wicked and will be demolished from the land.

The pesherist also notably interprets the prophecy of Habakkuk in the two eras of the prophet's own time and his own time, as well as in a future beyond his time—an eschatological understanding. In this light, the pesherist is of the view that Scripture embodies layered significance for different times with respect to all those who did and did not remain faithful to the covenant of God.

---

4. Lim, *Earliest Commentary*, 76.
5. Lim, *Earliest Commentary*, 77.
6. Lim, *Earliest Commentary*, 160.

MEANING OF THE LAW AND FOUR FIGURES

Hab 2:4b
וצדיק באמונתו יחיה
ὁ δὲ δίκαιος ἐκ πίστεως ζήσεται
but the righteous live by their faithfulness.

According to Hab 2:4b in Greek (ὁ δίκαιος ἐκ πίστεως ζήσεται), Paul's citation of Hab 2:4b in Gal 3:11 does not follow the Hebrew textual form. Paul adds the conjunction (δέ) but does not use the possessive pronoun "your" (σου), while the LXX keeps the Hebrew pronoun suffix but changes it from a *vav* (ו: "his/its"), or "your" (σου) to a *yod* (י), which is "my" (i.e., μου).[7] The LXX thus means "my faithfulness" in the text, and the NRSV uses the third person plural "their." Both the MT and LXX of Hab 2:1–4 translate that the end-time takes longer and the righteous will wait for it on account of their faithfulness. The MT understands באמונתו as the faithfulness or loyalty of the righteous, while the LXX interprets it as πίστεώς μου—the trust of the righteous in the divine.[8] With this, reading the Pesher Habakkuk, the text of 1 QpHab 7:17—8:3 is presented and its interpretation of Hab 2:3–4 is as follows:

Column 7:17—8:3
Column 7   [וצדיק באמונתו יחיה   ] 17
Column 8   x   פשרו על כול עושי התורה בבית יהודה אשר 1
            יצילם אל מבית המשפט בעבור עמלם ואמנתם 2
            במורה הצדק 3

Col. 7 [¹⁷ **But the righteous will live by his faithfulness**] (Hab 2:4b) Col. 8¹ Its interpretation concerns all doers of the law in the house of Judah whom ² God will deliver from the house of judgment on account of their suffering and their faithfulness ³ in the Teacher of Righteousness.[9]

The pesherist connects the verb "will live" (יחיה) with divine deliverance from the house of judgment (מבית המשפט). Those who keep the law

---

7. Lim, "Why Did Paul Cite Habakkuk?," 227–29; see Hunn, "Habakkuk 2.4b in Its Context," 220–24.

8. Lim, "Why Did Paul Cite Habakkuk?," 229.

9. Lim, *Earliest Commentary*, 107; bolds his. Fitzmyer interprets the same of column 7:17—8:2: "[¹⁷ ; *but (the) righteous one because of his fidelity shall find life*]. ⁸:¹ The interpretation of it concerns the observers of the Law in the house of Judah, whom ² God shall deliver from the house of judgment because of their struggle and their fidelity to the Teacher of Righteousness" (Fitzmyer, *To Advance the Gospel*, 239).

make them righteous and are called "the doers of the law." The righteous are justified by both their suffering (עמלם) and their faithfulness (אמנתם) to the Teacher of Righteousness (במורה הצדק) and thus will surely be saved from the house of judgment. Notably, the pesherist describes "the doers of the law" (עושי התורה) as men of truth (אנשי האמת), referring to the men of YHWH because they observe the law and remain faithful to the covenant of God even in the midst of their hardship.[10] They can be identified as men of the law, or as Essenes, which has its etymological meaning of "doer."[11] Significantly, Timothy Lim argues that "the *torah* or *nomos*, however, is not about the Jewish law or its observance. The term is more akin to the rule of law that becomes slack in the midst of destruction and violence perpetrated by the wicked."[12] The content of the law in Habakkuk is therefore aligned with Lev 18:5 and Deut 27:26. The three passages convey the same message that those who keep the law are identified as the righteous, who will accordingly be justified by their faith. This interpretation thus contradicts the literal approach of viewing the relationship between the law and faith in the Galatians passage. Moreover, Lim argues that Hab 2:4b is less interested in salvation or law-observance as the intention of the prophet is to contrast the righteous with the proud (2:4a).[13] The righteous would indeed live but the proud are defeated.

The prophecy of Habakkuk, furthermore, speaks of four primary figures—the wicked, the righteous, the wicked priest, and the Teacher of Righteousness. The doers of the law (עושי התורה) keep the divine commandments (Hab 2:12–13) and are called the righteous. The righteous are identified as covenant keepers in a wider sense and can also be recognized as royal figures. The prophecy underlines that the righteous not only believe in the education of the Teacher of Righteousness but will also be justified through their faithfulness and suffering. God will deliver the righteous from the house of judgment (column 2:1–10).[14] In addition to what it says about the righteous, the prophecy articulates very little about the Teacher of Righteousness. It is, though, worthwhile to note that the authority of the Teacher comes from God, as the pesherist emphasizes the authenticity of the Teacher's education and the Teacher speaking "from

10. See Lim, *Earliest Commentary*, 104–10; Hunn interprets the verb as "to live" (חיה). See Hunn, "Habakkuk 2.4b in Its Context," 228–32.
11. Brownlee, *Midrash Pesher of Habakkuk*, 119.
12. Lim, "Why Did Paul Cite Habakkuk?," 229.
13. Lim, "Why Did Paul Cite Habakkuk?," 229.
14. Lim, *Earliest Commentary*, 42.

the mouth of God." This phrase aligns with "from the mouth of YHWH" (מפי יהוה) in Jer 23:16, signifying that true prophets speak from the mouth of YHWH.[15] God gave understanding of the word to the Teacher, who pays close enough attention to the biblical text and receives the word as revelation. The Teacher not only interprets the oracles of the prophets but also perseveres against evil deeds and blesses those who are faithful in the covenant of God (column 2:8–9). Lim accentuates that

> in 1QpHab 7 the prophetic words of Habakkuk are characterized as "mysteries" which the Teacher of Righteousness has interpreted in association with the fulfillment of eschatological events that will affect the sectarian community. Accordingly, the prophet Habakkuk knew only in part what his own words prophesied, whereas the Teacher of Righteousness knew more completely how they would be fulfilled. The pesherist followed this method of the Teacher and wrote what can be described as an ancient commentary of the prophecy of Habakkuk.[16]

The next figure is the "wicked," referring to several different figures throughout the prophecy, including a royal figure. The Kittim are used to serve the divine purpose to reprove the wicked, which does not make the Kittim righteous. Also, the prophet speaks of "the righteous" ruler having been replaced by "the wicked ruler."[17] Some royal figures are thus described as both "the wicked one" and "the righteous one." In addition, the pesherist identifies "the wicked" with "the Man of the Lie" (column 1:13, 2:1–2)[18] and with nations who worship idols.

Finally, "the wicked priest" is a critical figure for the pesherist. The priest occupies a high role (i.e., reigning high priest) and can be referred to as a single person or a group. The priest is portrayed as greedy and arrogant and called by the name of truth (column 8:9),[19] which can be mistakenly taken as meaning righteous. The priest was disobediently rebellious against God as he not only deceitfully robbed and amassed the wealth of the people but also exalted himself when he ruled Israel (during the Hasmonean period).[20] He was unfaithful to the covenantal relation-

15. Lim, *Earliest Commentary*, 45.
16. Lim, "Habakkuk (Book and Person)," 1044.
17. See Haak, *Habakkuk*, 107–30.
18. Lim, *Earliest Commentary*, 36, 42.
19. Lim, *Earliest Commentary*, 110.
20. "The office of the priest-king reflected in the pesher," writes Lim, "is consistent with the role of the Hasmonean high priests who also ruled the kingdom" (Lim, *Earliest Commentary*, 125).

ship with both YHWH and God's elect and consequently broke the divine commandments. In the third woe oracle (column 10:5—11:2),[21] the pesherist notably depicts the Preacher of the Lie building a city, inferring that the preacher's teaching and deception misled the elect. According to Lim, "the Man of the Lie or the Preacher of the Lie has associates, followers or a congregation, and the opposition to the Teacher of Righteousness and God's elect takes the form of teachings that are considered lies."[22] The Man and the Preacher—as a rival pedagogue rather than a ruling high priest—is therefore distinguished from the wicked priest although they have many deeds in common. Nevertheless, the Man, Preacher, and priest are involved in building projects and come to fiery judgments. In column 11:17—12:10,[23] the wicked priest defiles the temple of Jerusalem and destroys the poor, and Lim clarifies the meaning of the "poor" that refers to a figurative community:

> The term "poor" need not be understood literally. It occurs only three times in Pesher Habakkuk, all in column 12 (lines 3, 6, and 10), and self-designates the community. In the War Scroll, the term אביונים denotes the oppressed community that will be delivered by the mighty hand of God (1QM 13:13–14). Written anarthrously all three times in column 12 of Pesher Habakkuk the term reflects the sectarians' perception of themselves as a community that has experienced duress and hardship. They are not necessarily poor materially.[24]

God judges the priest because he not only oppressed the poor but also destroyed the community. For this reason, God's judgment upon the wicked priest is therefore announced because they are defiant against God, they deceive the elect, they disbelieve the words of the Teacher of Righteousness, and they even persecute the Teacher. The deeds of the priest result in their being sent to the house of Judah—they are condemned in the house of judgment and led to the judgment of fire. Yet, Lim indicates that "the expression 'the house of judgment' (בית המשפט) is not found

---

21. Lim, *Earliest Commentary*, 136–37.

22. Lim, *Earliest Commentary*, 145. Regarding "The Disbelief of the Traitors" (1:16—2:10) and "The House of Absalom and the Men of their Council" (5:8–12), traitors and men are referred to one and the same individual who is not the wicked priest (as a ruling high priest) but a rival pedagogue (144–45). Also "the identification of the wicked priest and Liar as one or more of the Hasmonean high priests and kings, known for their building activity in Jerusalem" (141).

23. Lim, *Earliest Commentary*, 152.

24. Lim, *Earliest Commentary*, 158.

in the biblical texts. In Second Temple Jewish literature various sources refer to the temporary holding-place of the wicked or locate the place of condemnation in Sheol and Hades."[25] The pesherist uses the expression to construct a punishment at the end-time despite the fact that it is not explicitly drawn from the texts. Lim therefore clarifies that "the comment is extraneous to Hab 2:10b, but little historical information can be extracted, apart from the general hope that the wicked priest will be punished for his oppression and robbery in the afterlife."[26]

On this basis, we appraise that the wicked priest and Paul's opponents in the Galatian community have deeds in common. Just as the prophet concerns himself with the priest, Paul concerns himself with his opponents, who falsely teach the Galatian Christians. First, the prophecy indicates an incident that took place on Yom Ha-Kippurim (the Day of Atonement), when the wicked priest chased after the Teacher of Righteousness to his house of exile. The wicked priest is also accused of observing a different calendar or defiling the day of rest.[27] Concerning calendrical customs, the opponents persuade that the Galatians should observe certain calendrical occasions to show their full participation as God's people. Indeed, observing the proper calendar is significant because it was believed that God preserves remnants among Israelites: "God established his covenant with those who remained faithful and revealed to them 'secret things' (III, 14), which are related to the observance of

---

25. Lim, *Earliest Commentary*, 135.

26. Lim, *Earliest Commentary*, 136.

27. According to Lim, Shemaryahu Talmon indicates that the sectarian community followed one ephemeris and the wicked priest another. The wicked priest (the high priest of the Jerusalem temple) did not travel to Qumran on Yom Kippur because "he would have been needed for the ritual of atonement" (Lim, *Earliest Commentary*, 148). Indeed, the sons of Zadok followed a different calendar from the "wicked priest" and his followers, meaning that this difference of calendrical observance was "not a polemical issue among sectarian writings" (149). The sectarian did not therefore consider the priest as wicked "because [the priest] travelled on the most solemn day of the religious year. Rather, he travelled to Qumran because it was not his Yom Kippur" (148). On the other hand, Sacha Stern argues that the wicked priest is not accused of observing a different calendar but of troubling the Teacher and his followers. It is possible that "the wicked priest might have been accused of 'desecrating the day of rest' if he had travelled from Jerusalem to Qumran" (149). Stern claims, however, that there is no evidence that the wicked priest traveled from Jerusalem to Qumran. Lim thus posits that the interpretations of Talmon and Stern "remain possible since the pesherist comments allusively about the event, using biblical language that is likewise vague and ambiguous. Talmon, but not Stern, has to assume that the place of exile is Qumran" (149).

the proper calendar."[28] F. F. Bruce argues that the Galatians were taught that these ritual requirements and observances would bring them closer to perfection in their Christian lives, while they still pursued pagan ways of life.[29] So, the Galatians followed mixed religious requirements of both Jews and pagans, which caused their observance to deviate from what was originally intended, as Bruce points out. Tying the principles to the four terms (Gal 4:10), Paul's vague references to Jewish religious celebrations contrasted with the insistence of his opponents, who upheld them as terms stipulated by the law. Martinus de Boer advocates that Paul "intentionally uses terms that cover both Jewish and pagan calendrical observances, for he wants the Galatians to realize that, by turning to the law, they are going back to where they came from."[30] In the same view, Calvin notes that

> the false apostles not only attempted to lay the yoke of Jewish bondage on the neck of the church, but filled their minds with wicked superstitions. To bring back Christianity to Judaism, was in itself no light evil; but far more serious mischief was done, when, in opposition to the grace of Christ, they set up holidays as meritorious performances, and pretended that this mode of worship would propitiate the divine favor. When such doctrines were received, the worship of God was corrupted, the grace of Christ made void, and the freedom of conscience oppressed.[31]

Second, just as the wicked priest troubles the Teacher and accuses the Teacher of preaching lies, the opponents accused Paul of preaching "a false gospel"[32] (Gal 1:10). The opponents not only challenged the authenticity of Paul's ministry but also argued that he had merely human authority from Jerusalem, and he was subject to it, regardless of the divine origin of Paul's apostolic ministry, not "from a human being" but "through a revelation of Jesus Christ" (1:12). The gospel Paul preached came to him by revelation, in the same way as the prophets in the Old Testament are attributed to have received the oracle.[33] That is, unlike false prophets "speak[ing] visions of their own minds (חזון לבם ידברו)," Paul, as a teacher of righteousness, speaks the words "from the mouth of YHWH" (מפי יהוה)—just as

28. Wold, "Revelation's Plague Septets," 283–84.
29. See Bruce, *Galatians*, 315–19.
30. de Boer, *Galatians*, 276.
31. Calvin, *Galatians and Ephesians*, 100.
32. See Sandnes, *Paul—One of the Prophets?*, 57.
33. See 1 Cor 2:6–16 where Paul speaks of revealed wisdom in hiddenness.

The Prophecy of Habakkuk and the Covenant of Grace 143

the Teacher of Righteousness, who rightly guides the elect, is attributed with speaking these messages.[34] Moreover, the opponents accused Paul of modifying the message in order to attract the Galatians by omitting circumcision, thus failing to keep the law and the covenant. In Paul's defense, ironically, the prophecy predicts that the heart of the wicked priest is necessary to receive the divine circumcision, which his opponents need to hear the judgment of God. In column 11:8–17,[35] citing Hab 2:16, the pesherist mentions the "drink and wobble" (column 11:9) of the wicked whose hearts are not right with God. The pesherist thus figuratively calls to have the priest's heart circumcised, removing the foreskin of stubbornness (column 11:13). Otherwise, the cupful of God's wrath will swallow him up.[36]

Third, the prophecy has foreseen and is primarily distressed about the deeds of the wicked, especially the wicked priest who opposes the Teacher, defiles the temple, and deceptively teaches the community. Similarly, the teaching of the opponents influences the Galatians not only to turn back on serving the basic principles of the world (Gal 4:3) but also to turn away from obeying the truth (5:7). Thus, their teaching contaminates the whole community (5:9).[37] The opponents consequently bear the appropriate penalty (5:10). With respect to "the poor" in the prophecy, Paul recounts that the Jerusalem apostles asked him and Barnabas not to forget the poor as they preached the gospel to the gentiles, a duty Paul was already eager to fulfill (2:6–10). Fred Craddock suggests that the rich–poor contrast in the biblical narrative conveys a spatial picture of heaven–earth, so the "poor" (2:10) do not solely experience material poverty but also spiritual poverty, which lacks the nature of the church, her unity, her fellowship, and her authenticity in Jesus Christ.[38]

---

34. Lim, *Earliest Commentary*, 32–33, 42–53.
35. Lim, *Earliest Commentary*, 149.
36. See Lim, *Earliest Commentary*, 149–51.
37. "A little yeast works through the whole batch of dough" (5:9): Paul addresses the Corinthians with the same proverb in 1 Cor 5:6 as he repudiates a false theology held by his opponents, which is corrupting the entire Corinthian church. Betz also elucidates that "the negative symbolism of leaven is well documented in Philo and Plutarch, who also interprets it as 'spoiling the dough'" (Betz, *Galatians*, 266). In the words of Plutarch, "Yeast is itself also the product of corruption, and produces corruption in the dough with which it is mixed; for the dough becomes flabby and inert, and altogether the process of leavening seems to be one of putrefaction; at any rate, if it goes too far, it completely sours and spoils the flour" (266n128).
38. Craddock, *Pre-Existence of Christ*, 101–4.

This leads us to our next point, which we will explore the overarching unity and continuity of God's covenant across the Old and New Testaments; a key component of this exploration is a recap of the history of the covenant, with a particular focus on the word in unifying the gospel and the law within the covenant of grace.

THE COVENANT OF GRACE

Paul declares that the Galatians entered the eschaton as having died and risen in Christ. They were obedient to the truth and heard the good news as they knew God. They were to walk by the Spirit and enjoy freedom achieved in the death and resurrection of Jesus Christ, in whom both the form and content of the word of God is harmonized—i.e., the gospel is actualized in Jesus Christ, in whom the law is not only established but also fulfilled. Distinguished from the way Paul uses Scripture, his opponents misconstrue the word as God's command in Scripture, resulting in fluctuating the *telos* of the covenant between God and the elect. In light of this, it is significant that the one word of God in both gospel and law embodies the covenant of grace, where our attention now turns to tracing the history of a single covenant and its divine *telos* for the Galatians and us.

In the beginning, YHWH initiated the covenant without needing to make a pledge with Israel. In the fullness of his sovereignty, God chose to be with her and accept the obligation of that covenantal relationship. Israel, exercising her freedom of choice, could then accept or reject YHWH's overture. In committing to a pledge with YWHW, Israel declared that she would be God's people and thus keep God's commandments. God's law, rooted in divine grace, was perceived as a special revelation—an expression of YHWH's will. It was YHWH, the source of justice and security, binding community and individual alike. As evident in the Sinai commitment, the fundamental principles for human life are stated: the first four commandments clarify specific obligations of the covenant partners toward YWHW, while the last six deal with responsibilities toward other persons. YHWH initiated the formation of a covenant community, which became the norm as Israel moved toward the theocratic nation that YWHW intended. The commitment concerns Israel's earliest ethical formulations and is typical of biblical religion throughout as it focuses on the responsibilities of human beings to a deity believed to be both Creator and Redeemer. In addition to the Sinai covenant, the

The Prophecy of Habakkuk and the Covenant of Grace

covenantal codes represent an accumulation of laws from various periods in Israel's history. In fact, Deuteronomy sets a high moral standard, describing harsh treatment for the disobedient and their enemies while encouraging the faithful elect to a solemn relationship of obligation and obedience with YHWH. Features within the covenant code, such as legislation on altars, sacrifices, slavery, strangers, and capital crimes, suggest it was formulated for a later, more settled society rather than for a nomadic one. Thus, the obligations of the elect were codified within the body of Israelite law and its forms of worship. This framework, particularly the Deuteronomic code, later proved critical in Israelite history during periods that called for a renewed proclamation of the law. In a covenantal relationship, YHWH exhorted Israel to remain obedient and faithful to the divine commitments, and Israel's destiny was thus secured through her faithfulness to YHWH. Through the history of Israel, the elect constantly failed to keep the covenant. Nevertheless, YHWH waited for the elect and reaffirmed his claim on their loyalty when they turned from evil, renewed their vows, and again became YHWH's people. The story of Israel was increasingly one of judgment and salvation. In the midst of recurring disobedience, however, YWHW sent prophets with an oracle of the everlasting covenant.

Jeremiah 31:31–34 prophesies a new covenant in which YHWH would write the law on the hearts of his people, thereby superseding the Sinai covenant. This internalization of the law is central to establishing the eternal covenant. As declared, the divine prophecy was fulfilled in Jesus Christ; he not only forgave our sins but redeemed us through his faithful obedience. Also, the prophecy of Ezek 36:26–27 professes a similar renewal of the covenant, announcing the promise of a new heart and spirit for the elect. Because of the rebellious, stubborn, and disobedient nature of the elect, and their inability to keep God's decrees and laws,[39] this renewal of heart and spirit is necessary. Through the promised Spirit of God, a new heart and spirit are created, which reestablishes an everlasting covenant between YHWH and the people; the Spirit bestows a new, circumcised heart, empowering the elect to keep God's commandments.

The two prophecies therefore express the covenant differently but inaugurate the same promise of YHWH. Indeed, these allusions of Jer 31:31–34 and Ezek 36:26–27 are evident in Gal 3–5. The law (the

---

39. See Brueggemann, *Hopeful Imagination*. Brueggemann writes that "Israel never obeyed, according to Ezekiel, not even from the very beginning. Israel was always challenging, profaning, trivializing, mocking, exploiting" (77).

importance of the Mosaic covenant) and its significance for the new covenant are contented by the Spirit, which is the gift to every believer. Paul identifies the Galatian Christians as the heirs of Abraham (Gal 3:6–9 and 16–18), the people of the new covenant who belong to Christ (2:20, 4:6–7), and for whom the Spirit of Christ is present. Paul also contrasts the Mosaic Law with the new covenant in 4:21–31, referring to Abraham's two wives, Sarah and Hagar, as representatives of the two covenants. Hagar represents the Sinai covenant, associated with children under the law, while Sarah symbolizes the new covenant, ensuing the heir of God's promise through the Spirit.[40] The Galatians are like Isaac, born by the Spirit, for God sent the Spirit of the Son into their hearts. As a result, the Galatians are to walk with the Spirit, transforming them into a new creation, and bear the fruit of the Spirit rather than the unruly conduct of the flesh. As the Spirit assists in fulfilling the law of the new covenantal promises, it is not the law that conquers the battle of the flesh against the Spirit but Jesus Christ who accomplished the perfect covenant, embodying the law without losing the significance of the Mosaic covenant.

Indeed, Paul reveals the two covenants in depth when he illustrates the ministry of Moses in 2 Cor 3:7–18 and counters the ministry of his opponents, centered on the Torah. In the Corinthians passage, Paul draws our attention to the story of the new stone tablets (Exod 34:1–35)

---

40. Trible, *Hagar, Sarah, and Their Children*, 33–69. Trible reinterprets familiar texts and considers neglected ones to discover and recover traditions that challenge cultures. Looking into the conflict relationship between Hagar and Sarah and the story of Hagar, Sarah, and their children, Trible highlights that traditional interpretations, by ignoring or justifying the suffering of female characters, have often perpetuated the misogyny inherent in some of the texts. Countering patriarchal interpretations, Trible retells the story. First, Trible points out that Hagar is the only character about whom God does not use the word "bless," nor does God ensure Hagar's life continues until death. Though there is no blessed life and no resting place for Hagar, she is a figure of many firsts: the first person to flee oppression, the first runaway slave, the first person to be visited by a messenger of God, and the first woman to receive a divine promise of descendants. Second, Trible notes that while Abraham mistreats his wife, Sarah, he also obeys her. Conversely, Sarah, a patriarchal wife, orders her husband and mistreats Hagar. Third, Trible observes that both Isaac and Ishmael are blessed by God, but not to the same degree of blessing—the blessing of Isaac is greater than that of Ishmael. Trible thus argues that the text is biased, treating some people and women with inferiority and subordination. While acknowledging Trible's valuable insights into the text, this interpretation, in my view, affects the fundamental nature of the covenantal term less than Paul emphasizes. The covenant formula—"Obey my voice, and I will be your God, and you shall be my people. And walk only in the way that I command you, that it may be well with you" (Jer 7:23)—remains the same to all of us; for an alternative approach, see Greene-McCreight, "Figured In," 339–52.

where God renewed the covenant that the Israelites broke before it was even completed. Paul, in his insightful wisdom, reads the Exodus text to defend the authenticity of his ministry. First, Paul peculiarly calls the ministry of Moses the ministry of death and condemnation. However, he affirms that the old covenant was a covenant of the law given through Moses at Mount Sinai, and this law was pointing to the way of true salvation. Second, Moses took a veil off when speaking with God. After speaking with God, divine glory was made known through Moses, whose face radiated with this reflected divine glory—he had been filled with God's own glory. When Moses addressed the Israelites, he wore a veil, which raises the question of why he veiled the glory. According to Brevard S. Child, the biblical account is not concerned with whether the tradition resisted Moses speaking while he wore a veil because its emphasis is on unveiling God's glory.[41] Also, Paul argues that "their minds were hardened" (2 Cor 3:14), suggesting that, by reading Moses in a flawed way, the super-apostles obscured the set-aside glory of the Old Testament, foreshadowing the New Testament. Moses veiled his shining face, and so, the Israelites could not see the divine *telos* of the set-aside glory of the old covenant. Nevertheless, behind Moses's veil was dazzling glory even the Israelites could see, but their minds were hardened to perceive the *telos* of set-aside glory just as a veil rested on the hearts of the super-apostles when reading Scripture. This is also true for us in the present time when we do not see the divine *telos* in the old covenant.

Paul furthers the exegesis on the Exodus text. Moses turned to the Lord, and he alone was infused with God's set-aside glory and transfigured as a reflection of God's glory. Unlike the ministry of Moses, which has a temporary removal of the veil, the veil of "all of us" (2 Cor 3:18) who died and rose with Christ has been taken away. When we—unconditionally elected by God's grace—turn to God, all of us, with unveiled faces, gaze at "the light of the knowledge of the glory of God in the face of Christ" (2 Cor 4:6).[42] In this gaze, we grasp the *telos* of God's everlasting glory in Jesus Christ, for the new covenant Paul proclaims is the glory of God in the person of Jesus Christ, the source of divine glory. For Paul, accordingly, Exod 34 exposes hidden meanings in Scripture. Moses—an agent of both the old and the new covenants—was the minister obeying God's purpose in the set-aside glory until God revealed mysterious

---

41. Childs, *Exodus*, 619.

42. Through this gaze, we are transformed into God's image seen in Jesus Christ, in whom the eschatological community makes such transformation visible to others.

(secret and hidden) eschatological glory in Jesus Christ. The purpose of the law and the old covenant is Jesus Christ, and the old covenant is thus understood as witnesses to the gospel of Christ, manifested in the power of God, in which Paul proclaims the new covenant for an eschatological community. The new covenant cannot be broken because it was sealed by the blood and body of Christ, for it does not originate from the effort of flesh but is a gracious gift of God made possible through Jesus Christ. That is, Jesus Christ—in whom God has taken upon Godself, making the execution as God's own decision—is the revelation of the new covenant for all, whose heart is written by the divine law (Jer 31:33) and received the gift of God's Spirit (Ezek 36:26–27). Paul, therefore, knowingly calls the Corinthians "a letter of Christ" (2 Cor 3:3) inscribed by the Spirit of the living God. They (and all) are invited to participate in a new relationship with God, establishing "an eschatological community actually brought into being through the agency of Jesus Christ."[43] This community enables God's Good News "to be known and read by all" (2 Cor 3:2).[44]

Alternatively, the covenant in the Old Testament incorporates the historical events between the God of Israel and the people as it depicts the acts of God and their choices. In God's free grace, the very divinity of God speaks to the covenant partner, and Israel is actual in its history in their obedience and disobedience.[45] As Barth accentuates,

> the covenant relationship between *Yahweh* and Israel, which is the presupposition of everything that takes place in the relations between these two partners, and, without denying its exclusiveness, to understand it inclusively, as that which points to a covenant which was there at the beginning and which will be there at the end, the covenant of God with all [people].[46]

Jesus Christ discloses the particular covenant with Israel alongside the new covenant that wages the sin of disobedience and bears its corresponding judgment of God. The old covenant is therefore integrated into

---

43. Hays, *Letters of Paul*, 127.
44. See Hays, *Letters of Paul*, 122–53.
45. *CD* IV/4, 18.
46. *CD* IV/1, 31–32, Italics his. Marked by a sacred ritual, God's covenant with Abraham represented divine grace and the promise of salvation. Yet, this initial agreement proved insufficient to establish a lasting relationship for all people. Consequently, a new, definitive, and unshakable covenant became necessary. To accomplish this, God himself personally took part in the covenant-making rite, establishing a final, perpetual, and unbreakable agreement for all time.

The Prophecy of Habakkuk and the Covenant of Grace 149

this new covenant as the event of the cross completes the history in the old form of the covenant and the divine reaction against it, and thus the old covenant becomes the new, perfect covenant. As Barth affirms, "God [breaks] the opposition of His people, creating and giving a new heart to [all] of His people, putting His Spirit in [our] inward parts, making the observance of His commandments self-evident to [all of us]."[47] By virtue of the divine eschatological *telos*, therefore, Jesus Christ is called to be the mediator of the covenant, and, in this mediator's capacity, he reveals this covenant with Israel, which is made for the whole race. Jesus Christ thus stands amongst the nations Israel elected, and the covenant of grace is founded in him, representing the history of the one covenant attested by the knowledge of Scripture from both the Old and New Testaments.

Placing our justification in Jesus Christ (in whom we died and rose), we are in this covenantal relationship by the grace of God. The proposition of law in this covenant between God and all is not merely the law of God but primarily speaks of God's forgiveness of our sin and justification through the intervention of Jesus Christ. The gifted righteousness of law is Jesus Christ, God's promise to those who have faith in Christ, in whom judgment and sanctification are demonstrated. As seen in chapter 1, although Paul's opponents are in a sense of loyalty to the command of God in Scripture, their covenant is superimposed by the law and works of the law. The discord of gospel and law causes undesirable consequences because the history of Jesus Christ becomes a secondary, subsequent divine arrangement. The discord misdirects us as if righteousness is achieved by our works. The significance of sin is also reassessed; human sin is measured by law-keeping, and the grace of God becomes a subordinate significance within a covenantal relationship, resulting in negligence of the historical relationship between God and all.

For this reason, the word commanding necessitates that we are grounded in the history of the one covenant, regardless of inhabiting a different time and place. Whenever God commands according to the witness of Scripture, we listen to the meaningfulness of its concrete, historical reality and "learn by the direct instruction of God or His messengers and servants, of Jesus Himself or the Holy Spirit."[48] We hear the divine command from our individual moments in the history of God's own action, in which revelation continues to complete God's redemptive

---

47. *CD* IV/1, 33.
48. *CD* III/4, 12.

purpose, settling the authoritative ordinance on all accounts.[49] The hearing church—"an expression of the true Israel and the true Church"[50]—witnesses the history of God for certain people at particular times, rooted in the concrete particularity of Jesus Christ.[51] We thus hear God as the same and not the same in different times and circumstances, for the word, through the power of the Spirit, yields the equivalent influence on the communal life of the church. By virtue of this, the *telos* of the divine command for Abraham is thus the particular commands of God in Scripture, different and yet relevant to the Galatians and us today. We also hear the command "as a direction to make use of [the] freedom which is given us once and for all in Jesus Christ,"[52] and this hearing demands our responses to a covenantal relationship, to which we must advance ourselves in careful reading of Scripture and commit ourselves to thinking and acting in accordance with Scripture within the covenant of grace.

In this covenant, after all, the experience of the word is elevated, and so is our hearing of God, the Father with the Son by the Spirit, speaking to the church presently. Through the very divine speech, may the church witness: "Let the ancient law and custom to a newer rite now yield."[53] As well, may her walk be close with God, for the proclamation "walk by the Spirit" reaches us who died and rose in Christ—the unending, never wavering, forever love covenant written on our hearts. This covenant of free and perfect love has indeed continued to be part of the Galatians and all walking with Christ, who accompanies us as the reality encompassing the antecedent cause, the concurrent movement, and the immanent presence. Walk by the Spirit: the word commanding comes to us as both gospel and law, which is in principle inexplicable and yet heard by faith.

---

49. *CD* IV/1, 25.

50. *CD* II/2, 703.

51. Revelation, while universal in its divine origin, is not generalized; rather, it is actualized through specific individual experiences that particularize the universal truth of God.

52. *CD* IV/1, 102.

53. Aquinas, "Tantum Ergo," c. 1264.

Bibliography

Adams, Robert Merrihew. *Finite and Infinite Goods: A Framework for Ethics*. Oxford: Oxford University Press, 2002.
Anderson, Clifford B., and Bruce L. McCormack, eds. *Karl Barth and the Making of Evangelical Theology: A Fifty-Year Perspective*. Grand Rapids: Eerdmans, 2015.
Anderson, R. Dean. *Ancient Rhetorical Theory and Paul*. Revised ed. Leuven, BE: Peeters, 1999.
Arnold, Clinton E. "'I Am Astonished That You Are So Quickly Turning Away!' (Gal 1.6): Paul and Anatolian Folk Belief." *NTS* 51 (2005) 429–49.
———. "Returning to the Domain of the Powers: *Stoicheia* as Evil Spirits in Galatians 4:3, 9." *Novum Testamentum* 38 (1996) 55–76.
Asano, Atsuhiro. *Community-Identity Construction in Galatians Exegetical, Social-Anthropological, and Socio-Historical Studies*. London: T&T Clark, 2005.
Assel, Heinrich, and Bruce McCormack, eds. *Luther, Barth, and Movements of Theological Renewal (1918–1933)*. Berlin: DeGruyter, 2020.
Asselt, Willem J. van. *The Federal Theology of Johannes Cocceius: (1603–1669)*. Translated by Raymond A. Blacketer. Leiden: Brill, 2001.
Attridge, Harold W., et al., eds. *The HarperCollins Study Bible: NRSV*. Revised ed. San Francisco: HarperOne, 2006.
Augustine. *Augustine's Commentary on Galatians*. Translated by Eric Plumer. Oxford: Oxford University Press, 2003.
Aune, David E. *The Westminster Dictionary of New Testament and Early Christian Literature and Rhetoric*. Louisville: Westminster John Knox, 2003.
Avis, Paul, ed. *The Oxford Handbook of Ecclesiology*. Oxford: Oxford University Press, 2018.
Ayres, Lewis. *Augustine and the Trinity*. Cambridge: Cambridge University Press, 2010.
Bacote, Vincent E., et al. *Evangelicals and Scripture: Tradition, Authority and Hermeneutics*. Downers Grove: IVP, 2004.
Baggett, David, and Jerry L. Walls. *Good God: The Theistic Foundations of Morality*. Oxford: Oxford University Press, 2011.
Banks, Robert. *Paul's Idea of Community: The Early House Churches in Their Cultural Settings*. Ebook ed. Grand Rapids: Baker, 2012.
Barclay, John M. G. "Mirror-Reading a Polemical Letter: Galatians as a Test Case." *JSNT* 31 (1987) 73–93.

———. *Obeying the Truth: A Study of Paul's Ethics in Galatians*. Edited by John Riches. Edinburgh: T&T Clark, 1988.

———. *Paul and the Power of Grace*. Grand Rapids: Eerdmans, 2020.

Barnett, Paul. *The Second Epistle to the Corinthians*. New International Commentary on the New Testament. Grand Rapids: Eerdmans, 1997.

Barr, James. *The Semantics of Biblical Language*. Oxford: Oxford University Press, 1961.

Barrett, C. K. *Freedom and Obligation: A Study of the Epistle to the Galatians*. London: SPCK, 1985.

Barter, Jane A. "A Theology of Liberation in Barth's Church Dogmatics IV/3." *SJT* 53 (2000) 154–76.

Barth, Karl. *The Christian Life*. Translated by Geoffrey W. Bromiley. London: T&T Clark, 2017.

———. *The Church and the Churches*. Grand Rapids: Eerdmans, 2005.

———. *Church Dogmatics*. 4 vols. in 13 parts. Edited by G. W. Bromiley and T. F. Torrance. Translated by G. W. Bromiley et al. Edinburgh: T&T Clark, 1956–75.

———. *Community, State, and Church: Three Essays by Karl Barth with a New Introduction by David Haddorff*. Eugene, OR: Wipf & Stock, 2004.

———. *God Here and Now*. Translated by Paul M. van Buren. London: Routledge, 2003.

———. *God in Action*. Manhasset, NY: Round Table, 1963.

———. *The Epistle to the Romans*. Translated by Edwyn C. Hoskyns. Oxford: Oxford University Press, 1968.

———. *The Faith of the Church: A Commentary on the Apostles' Creed According to Calvin's Catechism*. Edited by Jean-Louis Leuba. Translated by Gabriel Vahanian. London: Collins, 1958.

———. *The Göttingen Dogmatics: Instruction in the Christian Religion*. Vol. 1. Edited by Hannelotte Reiffen. Translated by Geoffrey W. Bromiley. Grand Rapids: Eerdmans, 1991.

———. *The Holy Spirit and the Christian Life: The Theological Basis of Ethics*. Louisville: Westminster John Knox, 1993.

———. *The Word of God and the Word of Man*. Translated by Douglas Horton. New York: Harper & Brothers, 1957.

Bavinck, Herman. *Sin and Salvation in Christ*. Reformed Dogmatics 3. Edited by John Bolt. Translated by John Vriend. Grand Rapids: Baker, 2006.

Bayer, Oswald. *Living by Faith: Justification and Sanctification*. Minneapolis: Fortress, 2017.

Benckhuysen, Amanda W. "Reading Between the Lines: Josephine Butler's Socially Conscious Commentary on Hagar." In *Recovering Nineteenth-Century Women Interpreters of the Bible*, edited by Christiana De Groot and Marion Ann Taylor, 135–48. Atlanta: SBL, 2007.

Bender, Kimlyn J. *Karl Barth's Christological Ecclesiology*. Eugene, OR: Cascade, 2013.

———. *Reading Karl Barth for the Church: A Guide and Companion*. Grand Rapids: Baker, 2019.

Bender, Kimlyn J., and D. Stephen Long, eds. *T&T Clark Handbook of Ecclesiology*. London: T&T Clark, 2020.

Bergmann, Michael, and Patrick Kain, eds. *Challenges to Moral and Religious Belief: Disagreement and Evolution*. Oxford: Oxford University Press, 2014.

Berkouwer, G. C. *The Triumph of Grace in the Theology of Karl Barth*. Grand Rapids: Eerdmans, 1956.

Bibliography

Berzon, Todd S. "'O, Foolish Galatians': Imagining Pauline Community in Late Antiquity." *CH* 85 (2016) 435–67.
Best, Ernest. *One Body in Christ: A Study in the Relationship of the Church to Christ in the Epistles of the Apostle Paul*. London: SPCK, 1955.
Betz, Hans Dieter. *Galatians: A Commentary on Paul's Letter to the Churches in Galatia*. Philadelphia: Fortress, 1979.
Biggar, Nigel. "Barth's Trinitarian Ethic." In *The Cambridge Companion to Karl Barth*, edited by John Webster, 212–27. Cambridge: Cambridge University Press, 2000.
———. "A Case for Casuistry in the Church." *MT* 6 (1989) 29–51.
———. *The Hastening That Waits: Karl Barth's Ethics*. Oxford: Oxford University Press, 1993.
———, ed. *Reckoning with Barth: Essays in Commemoration of the Centenary of Karl Barth's Birth*. London: Mowbray, 1988.
Bindley, T. Herbert. *The Oecumenical Documents of the Faith: The Creed of Nicaea, the Epistles of Cyril, the Tome of Leo, the Chalcedomian Definition*. 4th ed. London: Methuen, 1950.
Bobrinskoy, Boris. "God in Trinity." In *The Cambridge Companion to Orthodox Christian Theology*, edited by Mary B. Cunningham and Elizabeth Theokritoff, 49–62. Cambridge: Cambridge University Press, 2008.
Boccaccini, Gabriele, et al. *Paul the Jew: Rereading the Apostle as a Figure of Second Temple Judaism*. Minneapolis: Fortress, 2016.
Boesel, Chris. *Reading Karl Barth: Theology That Cuts Both Ways*. Eugene, OR: Cascade, 2023.
———. *Risking Proclamation, Respecting Difference*. Cambridge, UK: James Clark, 2010.
Boulton, Matthew Myer. *Life in God: John Calvin, Practical Formation, and the Future of Protestant Theology*. Grand Rapids: Eerdmans, 2011.
Bouyer, Louis. *Eucharist: Theology and Spirituality of the Eucharistic Prayer*. Notre Dame: University of Notre Dame Press, 1989.
Bowden, Hugh. *Mystery Cults of the Ancient World*. London: Thames & Hudson, 2023.
Bowlin, John. "Barth and Aquinas on Election, Relationship, and Requirement." In *Thomas Aquinas and Karl Barth: An Unofficial Catholic-Protestant Dialogue*, edited by Bruce McCormack and Thomas Joseph White, 237–61. Grand Rapids: Eerdmans, 2013.
Brecht, Martin. *The Preservation of the Church, 1532–1546*. Martin Luther 3. Translated by James L. Schaaf. Minneapolis: Fortress, 1999.
Bretall, Robert. *A Kierkegaard Anthology*. Princeton: Princeton University Press, 1973.
Breukelman, Frans H. *The Structure of Sacred Doctrine in Calvin's Theology*. Edited by Rinse H. Reeling Brouwer. Grand Rapids: Eerdmans, 2010.
Brinsmead, Bernard Hungerford. *Galatians, Dialogical Response to Opponents*. Dissertation Series 65. Chico, CA: Scholars, 1982.
Bromiley, Geoffrey W. *Introduction to the Theology of Karl Barth*. Edinburgh: T&T Clark, 1979.
Brondos, David. "The Cross and the Curse: Galatians 3.13 and Paul's Doctrine of Redemption." *JSNT* 81 (2001) 3–32.
Brown, Raymond E. "The Pre-Christian Semitic Concept of 'Mystery.'" *CBQ* 20 (1958) 417–43.
Brownlee, William H. *The Midrash Pesher of Habakkuk*. Atlanta: SBL, 1979.
———. "The Placarded Revelation of Habakkuk." *JBL* 82 (1963) 319–25.

———. "The Wicked Priest, the Man of Lies, and the Righteous Teacher: The Problem of Identity." *JQR* 73 (1982) 1–37.
Bruce, F. F. *The Epistle to the Galatians: A Commentary on the Greek Text*. Milton Keynes, UK: Paternoster, 1982.
Brueggemann, Walter. *Hopeful Imagination: Prophetic Voices in Exile*. Philadelphia: Fortress, 1986.
———. *Returning from the Abyss: Pivotal Moments in the Book of Jeremiah*. Louisville: Westminster John Knox, 2022.
———. *The Theology of the Book of Jeremiah*. Cambridge: Cambridge University Press, 2007.
———. *To Pluck Up, to Tear Down: A Commentary on the Book of Jeremiah 1–25*. Grand Rapids: Eerdmans, 1988.
Brueggemann, Walter, et al. *Struggling with Scripture*. Louisville: Westminster John Knox, 2002.
Brunner, Emil. *The Divine Imperative*. Translated by Olive Wyon. Philadelphia: Westminster, 1947.
Brunner, Peter. *Worship in the Name of Jesus*. Translated by M. H. Bertram. St. Louis: Concordia, 1980.
Buber, Martin. *I and Thou*. Translated by Ronald Gregor Smith. Edinburgh: T&T Clark, 1923.
Buckley, James J. "Christian Community, Baptism, and Lord's Supper." In *The Cambridge Companion to Karl Barth*, edited by John Webster, 195–211. Cambridge: Cambridge University Press, 2000.
Buckley, James J., and David S. Yeago, eds. *Knowing the Triune God: The Work of the Spirit in the Practices of the Church*. Grand Rapids: Eerdmans, 2001.
Bultmann, Rudolf, et al. *Kerygma and Myth: A Theological Debate*. Edited by Hans Werner Bartsch. London: SPCK, 1962.
———. *Theology of the New Testament*. Vol. 1. Translated by Kendrick Grobel. New York: Charles Scribner's Sons, 1951.
Burrell, David B. "Freedom and Creation in the Abrahamic Traditions." In *Faith and Freedom: An Interfaith Perspective*, 143–55. Malden, MA: Wiley-Blackwell, 2004.
Burton, Ernest DeWitt. *A Critical and Exegetical Commentary on the Epistle to the Galatians*. New York: Charles Scribner's Sons, 1920.
———. *Spirit, Soul, and Flesh: The Usage of Pneuma, Psyche, and Sarx in Greek Writings and Translated Works from the Earliest Period to 225 A.D., and of Their Equivalents Ruah, Nefesh and Basar in the Hebrew Old Testament*. Chicago: University of Chicago Press, 1918.
———. *Syntax of the Moods and Tenses in New Testament Greek*. Edinburgh: T&T Clark, 1894.
Busch, Eberhard. "The Covenant of Grace Fulfilled in Christ as the Foundation of the Indissoluble Solidarity of the Church with Israel: Barth's Position on the Jews During the Hitler Era." *SJT* 52 (1999) 476–503.
———. *The Great Passion: An Introduction to Karl Barth's Theology*. Translated by Geoffrey W. Bromiley. Edited by Darrell L. Guder and Judith J. Guder. Grand Rapids: Eerdmans, 2010.
Calvin, John. *Commentary on Galatians and Ephesians*. Grand Rapids: Christian Classics Ethereal Library, 1999.
———. *Commentary on the Epistle to the Romans*. Grand Rapids: Christian Classics Ethereal Library, 1999.

Bibliography

———. *Concerning the Eternal Predestination of God*. Translated by J. K. S. Reid. London: James Clarke, 1961.

———. *Institutes of the Christian Religion*. Vol. 1. Edited by John T. McNeill. Translated by Ford Lewis Battles. Revised ed. Louisville: Westminster John Knox, 2006.

———. *Writings on Pastoral Piety*. Edited and translated by Elsie Anne McKee. Mahwah, NJ: Paulist, 2001.

Caneday, Ardel. "'Redeemed from the Curse of the Law': The Use of Deut 21:22–23 in Gal 3:13." *TrinJ* 10.2 (1989) 185–209.

Capes, David B. *Old Testament Yahweh Texts in Paul's Christology*. Tübingen: Mohr Siebeck, 1992.

Carmichael, Calum M. *Law, Legend, and Incest in the Bible: Leviticus 18–20*. Ithaca, NY: Cornell University Press, 1997.

Carr, Amy, and Christine Helmer. "Law-Gospel Theologies of a State of Exception." *Dialog: A Journal of Theology* 60 (2020) 54–64.

Carson, Donald A., and John D. Woodbridge, eds. *Hermeneutics, Authority, and Canon*. Eugene, OR: Wipf & Stock, 2005.

Cassidy, James J. *God's Time for Us: Barth's Reconciliation of Eternity and Time in Jesus Christ*. Bellingham, UK: Lexham, 2016.

Charlesworth, James H., ed. *The Old Testament Pseudepigrapha*. Peabody, PA: Hendrickson, 2013.

Chester, Stephen. "When the Old was New: Reformation Perspectives on Galatians 2:16." *ET* 119 (2008) 320–29.

Childs, Brevard S. *The Book of Exodus: A Critical, Theological Commentary*. Philadelphia: Westminster, 1974.

Ciampa, Roy E. "Deuteronomy in Galatians and Romans." In *Deuteronomy in the New Testament: The New Testament and the Scriptures of Israel*, edited by Steve Moyise and Maarten J. J. Menken. London: T&T Clark, 2007.

———. *The Presence and Function of Scripture in Galatians 1 and 2*. Tübingen: Mohr Siebeck, 1998.

Clough, David. *Ethics in Crisis: Interpreting Barth's Ethics*. London: Routledge, 2016.

Cocceius, Johannes. *The Doctrine of the Covenant and Testament of God*. Translated by Casey Carmichael. Grand Rapids: Reformation Heritage, 2016.

Cocksworth, Ashley. *Karl Barth on Prayer*. London: T&T Clark, 2015.

Coe, David Lawrence. "Law and Gospel, Distinction and Dialectic: C. F. W. Walther, Søren Kierkegaard, and the Rich Young Ruler." *Kierkegaard Studies Yearbook* 27 (2022) 403–18.

Coggins, Richard, and Jin H. Han. *Six Minor Prophets Through the Centuries—Nahum, Habakkuk, Zephaniah, Haggai, Zechariah and Malachi*. Malden, MA: Wiley-Blackwell, 2011.

Cole, R. Alan. *Galatians*. 2nd ed. Downers Grove, IL: IVP, 2015.

Colwell, John E. *Living the Christian Story: The Distinctiveness of Christian Ethics*. Edinburgh: T&T Clark, 2001.

Coogan, Michael, et al., eds. *The New Oxford Annotated Bible with the Apocrypha: NRSV*. 5th ed. Oxford: Oxford University Press, 2018.

Cook, Richard B. "Paul and the Victims of His Persecution: The Opponents in Galatia." *BTB* 32 (2002) 182–91.

Cosgrove, Charles H. *The Cross and the Spirit: A Study in the Argument and Theology of Galatians*. Macon, GA: Mercer University Press, 1988.

Couenhoven, Jesse. "Grace as Pardon and Power: Pictures of the Christian Life in Luther, Calvin, and Barth." *JRE* 28 (2000) 63–88.

———. *Stricken by Sin, Cured by Christ: Agency, Necessity, and Culpability in Augustinian Theology*. Oxford: Oxford University Press, 2013.

Cousar, Charles B. *Galatians: A Bible Commentary for Teaching and Preaching*. Louisville: Westminster John Knox, 1982.

Cowan, J. Andrew. "The Curse of the Law, the Covenant, and Anthropology in Galatians 3:10–14: An Examination of Paul's Use of Deuteronomy 27:26." *JBL* 139 (2020) 211–29.

Craddock, Fred B. *The Pre-Existence of Christ in the New Testament*. Nashville: Abingdon, 1968.

Crane, Ashley S. *Israel's Restoration: A Textual-Comparative Exploration of Ezekiel 36–39*. Leiden: Brill, 2008.

Cremer, Hermann. *The Christian Doctrine of the Divine Attributes*. Translated by Robert B. Price. Eugene, OR: Pickwick, 2016.

Cudworth, Ralph. *A Treatise Concerning Eternal and Immutable Morality: With A Treatise of Freewill*. Edited by Sarah Hutton. Cambridge: Cambridge University Press, 1996.

Cullmann, Oscar. "The Significance of the Qumran Texts for Research into the Beginnings of Christianity." *JBL* 74 (1955) 213–26.

Cummins, Stephen A. *Paul and the Crucified Christ in Antioch: Maccabean Martyrdom and Galatians 1 and 2*. Cambridge: Cambridge University Press, 2004.

Darwall, Stephen L. *The Second-Person Standpoint: Morality, Respect, and Accountability*. Cambridge: Harvard University Press, 2009.

Das, A. Andrew. *Galatians*. St. Louis: Concordia, 2014.

———. *Paul and the Stories of Israel: Grand Thematic Narratives in Galatians*. Minneapolis: Fortress, 2016.

Davies, Horton. *The Vigilant God: Providence in the Thought of Augustine, Aquinas, Calvin, and Barth*. 2nd ed. Compiled by Marie-Hélène Davies. New York: Peter Lang, 2018.

Davies, W. D. *Paul and Rabbinic Judaism: Some Rabbinic Elements in Pauline Theology*. 2nd ed. London: SPCK, 1962.

Dawkins, Richard. *The God Delusion*. London: Bantam, 2006.

de Boer, Martinus C. *Galatians: A Commentary*. Louisville: Westminster John Knox, 2011.

———. "The Meaning of the Phrase τά στοιχεῖα τοῦ κοσμοῦ in Galatians." *NTS* 53 (2007) 204–24.

Deddo, Gary. "The Grammar of Barth's Theology of Personal Relations." *SJT* 47 (1994) 183–222.

Deng, Natalja. "Eternity in Christian Thought." Stanford Encyclopedia of Philosophy, Aug. 24, 2023. https://plato.stanford.edu/entries/eternity/

deSilva, David A. *Global Readings: A Sri Lankan Commentary on Paul's Letter to the Galatians*. Eugene, OR: Cascade, 2011.

Dewhurst, Russell. "Ecclesiastical Law Society Day Conference: Gospel and Law in Theological Education." *ELJ* 20 (2018) 336–46.

Dolamo, Ramathate T. "The Continued Debate on Law and Gospel Among Selected Lutheran Scholars within the Change Agency Paradigm." *HTS Teologiese Studies* 74 (2018) 1–8.

Bibliography

Donaldson, James. *The Westminster Confession of Faith and the Thirty-Nine Articles of the Church of England: The Legal, Moral, and Religious Aspects of Subscription to Them.* London: Longmans, Green, 1905.

Donaldson, Terence L. *Paul and the Gentiles: Remapping the Apostle's Convictional World.* Minneapolis: Fortress, 1997.

Dunn, James D. G. *Baptism in the Holy Spirit.* London: SCM, 1970.

———. *Beginning from Jerusalem: Christianity in the Making.* Vol. 2. Grand Rapids: Eerdmans, 2009.

———, ed. *The Cambridge Companion to St. Paul.* Cambridge: Cambridge University Press, 2003.

———. *Christology in the Making: A New Testament Inquiry into the Origins of the Doctrine of the Incarnation.* 2nd ed. London: SCM, 1989.

———. *The Epistle to the Galatians.* London: A&C Black, 1993.

———. *Jesus, Paul, and the Gospels.* Grand Rapids: Eerdmans, 2011.

———. "The Justice of God: A Renewed Perspective on Justification by Faith." *JTS* 43 (1992) 1–22.

———. "'The Letter Kills, but the Spirit Gives Life' (2 Cor. 3:6)." *Pneuma* 35 (2013) 163–79.

———. *The New Perspective on Paul.* Revised ed. Grand Rapids: Eerdmans, 2008.

———. *The Theology of Paul's Letter to the Galatians.* Cambridge: Cambridge University Press, 1993.

———. *The Theology of Paul the Apostle.* Grand Rapids: Eerdmans, 1998.

Ebeling, Gerhard. *The Truth of the Gospel: An Exposition of Galatians.* Philadelphia: Fortress, 1985.

Eisenman, Robert H., and Michael Wise. *The Dead Sea Scrolls Uncovered.* New York: Penguin, 1992.

Elliott, Mark W. *The Heart of Biblical Theology: Providence Experienced.* London: Routledge, 2016.

———. *Providence Perceived: Divine Action from a Human Point of View.* Berlin: DeGruyter, 2015.

Elliott, Mark W., et al., eds. *Galatians and Christian Theology: Justification, the Gospel, and Ethics in Paul's Letter.* Grand Rapids: Baker, 2014.

Elliott, Susan M. "Choose Your Mother, Choose Your Master: Galatians 4:21—5:1 in the Shadow of the Anatolian Mother of the Gods." *JBL* 118 (1999) 661–83.

———. *Cutting Too Close for Comfort: Paul's Letter to the Galatians in Its Anatolian Cultic Context.* London: T&T Clark, 2008.

Ellis, Earle E. "Paul and His Opponents." In *Christianity, Judaism and Other Greco-Roman Cults, Part 2: Early Christianity*, edited by Jacob Neusner, 264–98. Studies in Judaism in Late Antiquity 12. Leiden: Brill, 1975.

———. *Paul's Use of the Old Testament.* Eugene, OR: Wipf & Stock, 2003.

Ellul, Jacques. *The Humiliation of the Word.* Grand Rapids: Eerdmans, 1985.

Elmer, Ian J. *Paul, Jerusalem and the Judaisers: The Galatian Crisis in Its Broadest Historical Context.* Tübingen: Mohr Siebeck, 2009.

Ensiminger, Sven. *Karl Barth's Theology as a Resource for a Christian Theology of Religions.* London: T&T Clark, 2016.

Erasmus, Desiderius. *Paraphrases on Romans and Galatians.* Edited by Robert D Sider. Translated by John B. Payne et al. Toronto: University of Toronto Press, 1984.

Esler, Philip F. *Galatians.* London: Routledge, 1998.

———. "Making and Breaking an Agreement Mediterranean Style: A New Reading of Galatians 2:1–14." *BI* 3 (1995) 285–314.
Evans, C. Stephen. *God and Moral Obligation*. Oxford: Oxford University Press, 2014.
Fee, Gordon D. *God's Empowering Presence: The Holy Spirit in the Letters of Paul*. Peabody, MA: Hendrickson, 1994.
———. *Paul, the Spirit, and the People of God*. Peabody: Hendrickson, 1996.
Fergusson, David A. *Creation*. Grand Rapids: Eerdmans, 2014.
———. "Divine Providence and Action." In *God's Life in Trinity*, edited by Miroslav Volf and Michael Welker, 153–65. Minneapolis: Fortress, 2006.
———. "The Doctrine of the Incarnation Today." *ET* 113 (2001) 75–79.
———. "Interpreting the Resurrection." *SJT* 38 (1985) 287–305.
———. "Providence." In *The Oxford Handbook of Karl Barth*, edited by Paul Dafydd Jones and Paul T. Nimmo, 373–88. Oxford: Oxford University Press, 2019.
———. *The Providence of God: A Polyphonic Approach*. Cambridge: Cambridge University Press, 2018.
———. "The Theology of Providence." *TT* 67 (2010) 261–78.
Fergusson, David, and Bruce McCormack, eds. *Schools of Faith: Essays on Theology, Ethics and Education in Honour of Iain R. Torrance*. London: T&T Clark, 2019.
Fitzmyer, Joseph A. *To Advance the Gospel: New Testament Studies*. 2nd ed. Grand Rapids: Eerdmans, 1998.
Flanders, Henry Jackson, et al. *People of the Covenant: An Introduction to the Hebrew Bible*. 4th ed. Oxford: Oxford University Press, 1996.
Flett, John G. *The Witness of God: The Trinity, Missio Dei, Karl Barth, and the Nature of Christian Community*. Grand Rapids: Eerdmans, 2010.
Fredriksen, Paula. *Paul: The Pagans' Apostle*. New Haven, CT: Yale University Press, 2017.
Frei, Hans W. *The Eclipse of Biblical Narrative: A Study in Eighteenth and Nineteenth Century Hermeneutics*. New Haven, CT: Yale University Press, 1974.
———. *The Identity of Jesus Christ: The Hermeneutical Bases of Dogmatic Theology*. Eugene, OR: Cascade, 2013.
Frymer-Kensky, Tikva, et al. *Christianity in Jewish Terms*. Boulder, CO: Westview, 2000.
Furnish, Victor Paul. *II Corinthians*. The Anchor Bible. New Haven, CT: Yale University Press, 2005.
Fung, Ronald Y. K. *The Epistle to the Galatians*. Grand Rapids: Eerdmans, 1988.
Gadamer, Hans-Georg. *Truth and Method*. Revised 2nd ed. Translation revised by Joel Weinsheimer and Donald G. Marshall. London: Bloomsbury, 2004.
Garlington, Don B. *The Obedience of Faith: A Pauline Phrase in Historical Context*. Tübingen: Mohr Siebeck, 1991.
———. "Role Reversal and Paul's Use of Scripture in Galatians 3.10–13." *JSNT* 65 (1997) 85–121.
Gathercole, Simon. "Pre-Existence and the Freedom of the Son in Creation and Redemption: An Exposition in Dialogue with Robert Jenson." *IJST* 7 (2005) 38–51.
Gaventa, Beverly Roberts. *Our Mother Saint Paul*. Louisville: Westminster John Knox, 2007.
———. *When in Romans: An Invitation to Linger with the Gospel According to Paul*. Grand Rapids: Baker, 2016.
Gerhard, Johann. *Theological Commonplaces: On the Person and Office of Christ*. Edited by Benjamin T. G. Mayes. Translated by Richard J. Dinda. St. Louis: Concordia, 2009.

Bibliography

Gibbs, J. G. "A Secondary Point of Reference in Barth's Anthropology." *SJT* 16 (1963) 132–35.
Gibson, David. *Reading the Decree: Exegesis, Election and Christology in Calvin and Barth.* London: T&T Clark, 2009.
Gockel, Matthias. *Barth and Schleiermacher on the Doctrine of Election: A Systematic-Theological Comparison.* Oxford: Oxford University Press, 2006.
Goodenough, Erwin R. *By Light, Light: The Mystic Gospel of Hellenistic Judaism.* Amsterdam: Philo, 1969.
Gorner, Paul. *Heidegger's Being and Time: An Introduction.* Cambridge: Cambridge University Press, 2007.
Gorringe, Timothy J. *Karl Barth: Against Hegemony.* Oxford: Oxford University Press, 1999.
Goshen-Gottstein, Alon. "The New Covenant—Jeremiah 31:30–33 (31:31–34) in Jewish Interpretation." *SCJR* 15 (2020) 1–31.
Gottwald, Norman K. *The Hebrew Bible: A Socio-Literary Introduction.* Philadelphia: Fortress, 1985.
Grant, Robert M. *A Historical Introduction to the New Testament.* New York: Harper & Row, 1963.
Graves, Michael. *The Inspiration and Interpretation of Scripture: What the Early Church Can Teach Us.* Grand Rapids: Eerdmans, 2014.
Grebe, Matthias. *Election, Atonement, and the Holy Spirit: Through and Beyond Barth's Theological Interpretation of Scripture.* Cambridge, UK: James Clarke, 2014.
Green, Christopher. *Doxological Theology: Karl Barth on Divine Providence, Evil, and the Angels.* London: T&T Clark, 2011.
Green, Joel B., et al., eds. *Dictionary of Jesus and the Gospels.* 2nd ed. Downers Grove, IL: InterVarsity, 2013.
Greene-McCreight, Kathryn. "Figured In: Nonliteral Reading, the Rule of Faith, and Galatians 4." In *The Identity of Israel's God in Christian Scripture*, edited by Don Collett, et al., 339–52. Atlanta: SBL, 2020.
Grice, Paul. *Studies in the Way of Words.* Cambridge: Harvard University Press, 1991.
Grillmeier, Aloys. *Christ in Christian Tradition: From the Apostolic Age to Chalcedon (451).* London: Sheed and Ward, 1965.
Gunther, John J. *St. Paul's Opponents and Their Background: A Study of Apocalyptic and Jewish Sectarian Teachings.* Leiden: Brill, 1973.
Gunton, Colin E., ed. *The Cambridge Companion to Christian Doctrine.* Cambridge: Cambridge University Press, 1997.
———. "The Triune God and the Freedom of the Creature." In *Karl Barth: Centenary Essays*, edited by S. W. Sykes, 46–68. Cambridge: Cambridge University Press, 1989.
Gunton, Colin E., and Daniel W. Hardy, eds. *On Being the Church: Essays on the Christian Community.* Edinburgh: T&T Clark, 1989.
Gustafson, James M. *Can Ethics Be Christian?* Chicago: University of Chicago Press, 1977.
———. *Christ and the Moral Life.* New York: Harper & Row, 1968.
———. *Ethics from a Theocentric Perspective.* Chicago: University of Chicago Press, 1983.
———. "Ways of Using Scripture." In *From Christ to the World: Introductory Readings in Christian Ethics*, edited by Wayne G. Boulton, et al., 21–26. Grand Rapids: Eerdmans, 1994.

Haak, Robert D. *Habakkuk*. Leiden: Brill, 1992.

Habermas, Jürgen. *Knowledge and Human Interests*. Translated by Jeremy J. Shapiro. Boston: Beacon, 1971.

Haddorff, David W. "The Postmodern Realism of Barth's Ethics." *SJT* 57 (2004) 269–86.

Hamerton-Kelly, R. G. *Pre-Existence, Wisdom, and the Son of Man: A Study of the Idea of Pre-Existence in the New Testament*. Cambridge: Cambridge University Press, 1973.

Hancock, Angela Dienhart. "Barth and Preaching." In *The Oxford Handbook of Karl Barth*, edited by Paul Dafydd Jones and Paul T. Nimmo, 580–93. Oxford: Oxford University Press, 2019.

Hansen, G. Walter. *Abraham in Galatians*. Sheffield, UK: Sheffield Academic, 1989.

Hanson, Anthony Tyrell. *Jesus Christ in the Old Testament*. London: SPCK, 1965.

———. *The New Testament Interpretation of Scripture*. London: SPCK, 1980.

Hardin, Justin K. *Galatians and the Imperial Cult: A Critical Analysis of the First-Century Social Context of Paul's Letter*. Tübingen: Mohr Siebeck, 2008.

Hare, John E. *God's Call: Moral Realism, God's Commands, and Human Autonomy*. Grand Rapids: Eerdmans, 2000.

———. *God's Command*. Oxford: Oxford University Press, 2015.

Hare, R. M. *Practical Inferences*. Berkeley: University of California Press, 1972.

Harmon, Matthew S. *She Must and Shall Go Free: Paul's Isaianic Gospel in Galatians*. Berlin: DeGruyter, 2010.

Harrison, Jim. *Paul's Language of Grace in Its Graeco-Roman Context*. Tübingen: Mohr Siebeck, 2019.

Hauerwas, Stanley. *Character and the Christian Life: A Study in Theological Ethics*. Notre Dame: University of Notre Dame Press, 1975.

———. *The State of the University: Academic Knowledges and the Knowledge of God*. Malden, MA: Blackwell, 2007.

Hays, Richard B. *Echoes of Scripture in the Gospels*. Waco, TX: Baylor University Press, 2016.

———. *Echoes of Scripture in the Letters of Paul*. New Haven, CT: Yale University Press, 1989.

———. *The Faith of Jesus Christ: The Narrative Substructure of Galatians 3:1—4:11*. 2nd ed. Grand Rapids: Eerdmans, 2002.

———. *Reading with the Grain of Scripture*. Grand Rapids: Eerdmans, 2020.

Healy, Nicholas M. "Karl Barth's Ecclesiology Reconsidered." *SJT* 57 (2004) 287–99.

———. "The Logic of Karl Barth's Ecclesiology: Analysis, Assessment and Proposed Modifications." *MT* 10 (1994) 253–70.

Hector, Kevin W. *Theology Without Metaphysics: God, Language, and the Spirit of Recognition*. Cambridge: Cambridge University Press, 2011.

Hegel, G. W. F. *Phenomenology of Spirit*. Translated by Peter Fuss and John Dobbins. Notre Dame: University of Notre Dame Press, 2019.

Helm, Paul. *Eternal God: A Study of God Without Time*. Oxford: Oxford University Press, 1997.

Hengel, Martin. *The Pre-Christian Paul*. In collaboration with Roland Deines. Philadelphia: Trinity Press International, 1991.

Hengel, Martin, and Anna M. Schwemer. *Paul Between Damascus and Antioch: The Unknown Years*. Louisville: Westminster John Knox, 1997.

Heppe, Heinrich. *Reformed Dogmatics*. Revised ed. Edited by Ernst Bizer. Translated by G. T. Thomson. Eugene, OR: Wipf & Stock, 2008.

Hesselink, John. "Law and Gospel or Gospel and Law? Karl Barth, Martin Luther and John Calvin." *Nederduitse Gereformeerde Teologiese Tydskrif* 53 (2012) 62–80.

Hick, John. *An Interpretation of Religion: Human Responses to the Transcendent*. 2nd ed. New Haven, CT: Yale University Press, 2004.

Hietanen, Mika. *Paul's Argumentation in Galatians: A Pragma-Dialectical Analysis*. London: T&T Clark, 2007.

Hogeterp, Albert L. A. "'Our Freedom in Christ': Revisiting Pauline Imagery of Freedom and Slavery in His Letter to the Galatians in Context." *Religions* 14 (2023) 672.

Holladay, William L. *Jeremiah 2: A Commentary on the Book of the Prophet Jeremiah, Chapters 26–52*. Edited by Paul D. Hanson. Minneapolis: Fortress, 2016.

Holmes, Christopher R. J. "The Shape of God's Providence: Some Reflections in Dialogue with Barth and Thomas." *Pro ecclesia* 31(2002) 196–207.

Honderich, Ted, ed. *Morality and Objectivity: A Tribute to J. L. Mackie*. Abingdon, UK: Routledge, 2011.

Horgan, Maurya P. *Pesharim: Qumran Interpretations of Biblical Books*. Eugene, OR: Pickwick, 2023.

Horton, Michael Scott. *Covenant and Eschatology: The Divine Drama*. Louisville: Westminster John Knox, 2002.

Howard, George. *Paul Crisis in Galatia*. 2nd ed. Cambridge: Cambridge University Press, 1990.

Hultgren, Stephen. *Habakkuk 2:4 in Early Judaism, in Hebrews, and in Paul*. Cahiers de la Revue Biblique 77. Pendé, FR: J. Gabalda & Cie, 2011.

Hunn, Debbie. "Habakkuk 2.4b in Its Context: How Far Off Was Paul?" *JSOT* 34 (2009) 219–39.

Hunsinger, George. *Disruptive Grace: Studies in the Theology of Karl Barth*. Grand Rapids: Eerdmans, 2000.

———. *Evangelical, Catholic, and Reformed*. Grand Rapids: Eerdmans, 2015.

———, ed. *For the Sake of the World: Karl Barth and the Future of Ecclesial Theology*. Grand Rapids: Eerdmans, 2004.

———. *How to Read Karl Barth: The Shape of His Theology*. Oxford: Oxford University Press, 1991.

———, ed. *Thy Word Is Truth: Barth on Scripture*. Grand Rapids: Eerdmans, 2012.

Hursthouse, Rosalind. *On Virtue Ethics*. Oxford: Oxford University Press, 2002.

Hutter, Reinhard. "Karl Barth's 'Dialectical Catholicity': Sic Et Non." *MT* 16 (2000) 137–57.

Janzen, J. Gerald. "Habakkuk 2:2–4 in the Light of Recent Philological Advances." *HTR* 73 (1980) 53–78.

Jehle, Frank. *Ever Against the Stream: The Politics of Karl Barth, 1906–1968*. Translated by Richard and Martha Burnett. Eugene, OR: Wipf & Stock, 2012.

Jenson, Matt. *Gravity of Sin: Augustine, Luther, and Barth on homo incurvatus in se*. London: T&T Clark, 2006.

Jenson, Robert W. *God After God: The God of the Past and the God of the Future, Seen in the Work of Karl Barth*. Indianapolis: Bobbs-Merrill, 1969.

Jerome, Saint. *St. Jerome's Commentaries on Galatians, Titus, and Philemon*. Translated by Thomas P. Scheck. Notre Dame: University of Notre Dame Press, 2010.

Jervis, L. Ann. *Galatians*. Grand Rapids: Baker, 1999.

Jewett, Robert. "The Agitators and the Galatian Congregation." *NTS* 17 (1971) 198–212.

———. *Paul's Anthropological Terms: A Study of Their Use in Conflict Settings*. Leiden: Brill, 1971.

Jones, Cheslyn, et al., eds. *The Study of Liturgy*. Revised ed. Oxford: Oxford University Press, 1992.
Jones, Gareth, ed. *The Blackwell Companion to Modern Theology*. Malden, MA: Blackwell, 2004.
Jones, Paul Dafydd. *The Humanity of Christ: Christology in Karl Barth's Church Dogmatics*. London: T&T Clark, 2008.
Jones, Serene. *Calvin and the Rhetoric of Piety*. Louisville: Westminster John Knox, 1995.
Johnson, Elizabeth A. *She Who Is: The Mystery of God in Feminist Theological Discourse*. 25th anniversary ed. New York: Crossroad, 2017.
Johnson, Keith L., and David Lauber, eds. *T&T Clark Companion to the Doctrine of Sin*. London: T&T Clark, 2016.
Johnson, Luke Timothy. *Scripture and Discernment: Decision Making in the Church*. Nashville: Abingdon, 1996.
Johnson, William Stacy. *The Mystery of God: Karl Barth and the Postmodern Foundations of Theology*. Louisville: Westminster John Knox, 1997.
Jüngel, Eberhard. *God's Being Is in Becoming: The Trinitarian Being of God in the Theology of Karl Barth—A Paraphrase*. Translated by John Webster. Edinburgh: T&T Clark, 2001.
———. *Justification: The Heart of the Christian Faith—A Theological Study with Ecumenical Purpose*. Translated by Jeffrey F. Cayzer. London: T&T Clark, 2001.
———. *Theological Essays II*. Translated by Arnold Neufeldt-Fast and J. B. Webster. London: T&T Clark, 2014.
Kahl, Brigitte. *Galatians Re-Imagined: Reading with the Eyes of the Vanquished*. Minneapolis: Fortress, 2010.
Kampen, John, and Moshe J. Bernstein, eds. *Reading 4QMMT: New Perspectives on Qumran Law and History*. Boston: Scholars, 1996.
Käsemann, Ernst. *New Testament Questions of Today*. London: SCM, 1969.
Keener, Craig S. "A Comparison of the Fruit of the Spirit in Galatians 5:22–23 with Ancient Thought on Ethics and Emotion." In *The Language and Literature of the New Testament*, edited by Lois Fuller Dow, et al., 574–98. Leiden: Brill, 2016.
———. *The Mind of the Spirit: Paul's Approach to Transformed Thinking*. Grand Rapids: Baker, 2016.
Keller, Catherine. *Face of the Deep: A Theology of Becoming*. London: Routledge, 2003.
Kelsey, David H. *Eccentric Existence: A Theological Anthropology*. Louisville: Westminster John Knox, 2009.
———. *The Uses of Scripture in Recent Theology*. Philadelphia: Fortress, 1975.
Kennedy, Darren. *Providence and Personalism: Karl Barth in Conversation with Austin Farrer, John Macmurray and Vincent Brümmer*. New York: Peter Lang, 2011.
Kennedy, George A. *New Testament Interpretation Through Rhetorical Criticism*. Chapel Hill: University of North Carolina Press, 1984.
Kern, Philip H. *Rhetoric and Galatians: Assessing an Approach to Paul's Epistle*. Cambridge: Cambridge University Press, 2004.
Kierkegaard, Søren. *The Concept of Dread*. Translated by Reider Thomte and Albert Anderson. Princeton: Princeton University Press, 1946.
———. *Philosophical Fragments: Or a Fragment of Philosophy*. 2nd ed. Translated by Howard V. Hong. Princeton: Princeton University Press, 1962.
———. *The Sickness Unto Death*. Translated by Walter Lowrie. Princeton: Princeton University Press, 1941.

———. *Works of Love*. Kierkegaard's Writings 16. Edited and translated by Howard V. Hong and Edna H. Hong. Princeton: Princeton University Press, 1995.

Kilcrease, Jack D. "The Challenge of Karl Barth's Doctrine of the Word of God." *CTQ* 84 (2020) 59–81.

Kim, Seyoon. "God Reconciled His Enemy to Himself: The Origin of Paul's Concept of Reconciliation." In *The Road from Damascus: The Impact of Paul's Conversion on His Life, Thought, and Ministry*, edited by Richard N. Longenecker, 102–24. Eugene, OR: Wipf & Stock, 2002.

———. *The Origin of Paul's Gospel*. 2nd ed. Tübingen: Mohr Siebeck, 2019.

———. *Paul and the New Perspective: Second Thoughts on the Origin of Paul's Gospel*. Grand Rapids: Eerdmans, 2002.

Kim, Sung-Sup. *Deus Providebit: Calvin, Schleiermacher, and Barth on the Providence of God*. Minneapolis: Fortress, 2014.

King, John B. "Toward Law–Gospel Harmony in Lutheran Theology and Ethics." *Dialog: A Journal of Theology* 59 (2020) 225–32.

Kittel, Gerhard, and Gerhard Friedrich, eds. *Theological Dictionary of the New Testament*. Translated by Geoffrey W. Bromiley. Grand Rapids: Eerdmans, 1985.

Klempa, William. "The Concept of the Covenant in Sixteenth- and Seventeenth-Century Continental and British Reformed Theology." In *Major Themes in the Reformed Tradition*, edited by Donald K. McKim, 94–107. Eugene, OR: Wipf & Stock, 1998.

Klooster, Fred H. *The Significance of Barth's Theology; An Appraisal: With Special Reference to Election and Reconciliation*. Grand Rapids: Baker, 1961.

Knight, Douglas A., and Gene M. Tucker, eds. *The Hebrew Bible and Its Modern Interpreters*. Philadelphia: Fortress, 1985.

Koch, John D. *The Distinction Between Law and Gospel as the Basis and Boundary of Theological Reflection*. Tübingen: Mohr Siebeck, 2016.

Kolb, Robert. *Martin Luther and the Enduring Word of God: The Wittenberg School and Its Scripture-Centered Proclamation*. Grand Rapids: Baker, 2016.

———. *Martin Luther as Prophet, Teacher, Hero: Image of the Reformer, 1520–1620*. Ebook ed. Grand Rapids: Baker, 2012.

Kooi, Cornelis van der. *As in a Mirror: John Calvin and Karl Barth on Knowing God—A Diptych*. Translated by Donald Mader. Leiden: Brill, 2005.

Kozman, Rony. "Ezekiel's Promised Spirit as *adam*'s Revelatory Spirit in the Hodayot." *Dead Sea Discoveries* 26 (2019) 30–60.

Krause, Joachim J. "'Writing on the Heart' in Jeremiah 31:31–34 in Light of Recent Insights into the Oral–Written Interface and Scribal Education in Ancient Israel." *ZAW* 132 (2020) 236–49.

Krötke, Wolf. "Barth and Evil on Nothingness." In *Barth and Dogmatics*, edited by George Hunsinger and Keith L. Johnson, 207–16. The Wiley Blackwell Companion to Karl Barth 1. Hoboken, NJ: Wiley-Blackwell, 2020.

———. "The Humanity of the Human Person in Karl Barth's Anthropology." In *The Cambridge Companion to Karl Barth*, edited by John Webster, 159–76. Cambridge: Cambridge University Press, 2000.

———. *Sin and Nothingness in the Theology of Karl Barth*. Translated and edited by Philip G. Ziegler and Christina-Maria Bammel. Princeton: Princeton Theological Seminary, 2005.

Lambrecht, Jan. "The Line of Thought in Gal. 2.14b–21." *NTS* 24 (1978) 484–95.

———. "Paul's Reasoning in Galatians 2:11–21." In *Paul and the Mosaic Law*, edited by James D. G. Dunn, 53–74. Tübingen: Mohr Siebeck, 1994.

———. "The Right Things You Want to Do: A Note on Galatians 5,17d." *Biblica* 79 (1998) 515–24.

———. "Transgressor by Nullifying God's Grace: A Study of Gal 2:18–21." *Biblica* 72 (1991) 217–36.

Lategan, Bernard. "Is Paul Defending His Apostleship in Galatians?" *NTS* 34 (1988) 411–30.

Lavender, Jordan. "*Nomos* and the Dispute in Galatians 2: A Case of Conflicting By-Laws." *Religions* 14.12 (2023) 1449.

Layton, Bentley, and David Brakke, eds. *The Gnostic Scriptures*. New Haven, CT: Yale University Press, 2021.

Lee, Boyung. "When the Text Is the Problem: A Postcolonial Approach to Biblical Pedagogy." *RE* 102 (2007) 44–61.

Lee, Jung Young. "Karl Barth's Use of Analogy in His Church Dogmatics." *SJT* 22 (1969) 129–51.

Leith, John. H. *John Calvin's Doctrine of the Christian Life*. Louisville: Westminster John Knox, 1989.

Leo the Great. *Sermons*. The Fathers of the Church 93. Translated by Jane Patricia Freeland and Agnes Josephine Conway. Washington, DC: Catholic University of America Press, 1996.

Levenson, Jon D. *Creation and the Persistence of Evil: The Jewish Drama of Divine Omnipotence*. Princeton: Princeton University Press, 1994.

Levy, Ian Christopher, ed. *The Letter to the Galatians*. Grand Rapids: Eerdmans, 2011.

Lim, Timothy H. *The Earliest Commentary on the Prophecy of Habakkuk*. Oxford: Oxford University Press, 2020.

———. "Habakkuk (Book and Person)." In *Encyclopedia of the Bible and Its Reception*, 10:1041–46. Berlin: DeGruyter, 2015.

———. "Qumran Scholarship and the Study of the Old Testament in the New Testament." *JSNT* 38 (2015) 68–80.

———. "Why Did Paul Cite Habakkuk 2:4b?" *ET* 133 (2022) 225–32.

Lincicum, David. *Paul and the Early Jewish Encounter with Deuteronomy*. Tübingen: Mohr Sieback, 2010.

Lindars, Barnabas. *New Testament Apologetic: The Doctrinal Significance of the Old Testament Quotations*. London: SCM, 1961.

Lindars, Barnabas, and Stephen S. Smalley, eds. *Christ and Spirit in the New Testament*. Cambridge: Cambridge University Press, 1973.

Lindbeck, George Arthur. "Barth and Textuality." *TT* 43 (1986) 361–76.

———. *The Nature of Doctrine: Religion and Theology in a Postliberal Age*. 25th anniversary ed. Louisville: Westminster John Knox, 2009.

Lindsay, Mark R. *Barth, Israel, and Jesus: Karl Barth's Theology of Israel*. Burlington, VT: Ashgate, 2007.

Lloyd, Genevieve. *Providence Lost*. Cambridge: Harvard University Press, 2008.

Locatell, Christian. "Jeremiah 31:34, New Covenant Membership, and Baptism." *Scriptura* 114 (2015) 1–14.

Lohse, Bernhard. *Martin Luther's Theology: Its Historical and Systematic Development*. Translated and edited by Roy A. Harrisville. Minneapolis: Fortress, 2011.

Longenecker, Bruce W. *Remember the Poor: Paul, Poverty, and the Greco-Roman World*. Grand Rapids: Eerdmans, 2010.

Longenecker, Richard N. *Galatians*. World Biblical Commentary 41. Grand Rapids: Zondervan, 1990.

Lovin, Robin W. *Christian Faith and Public Choices: The Social Ethics of Barth, Brunner, and Bonhoeffer*. Philadelphia: Fortress, 1984.

———. *Christian Realism and the New Realities*. Cambridge: Cambridge University Press, 2008.

Lull, David John. *The Spirit in Galatia: Paul's Interpretation of Pneuma as Divine Power*. Chico, CA: Scholars, 1980.

Luther, Martin. *Galatians*. Edited by Alistor McGrath and J. I. Packer. Wheaton, IL: Crossway, 1998.

———. *Lectures on Galatians 1535: Chapters 1–4*. Luther's Works 26. Edited by Jaroslav Pelikan. St. Louis: Concordia, 1963.

———. *Notes on Ecclesiastes, Lectures on the Song of Solomon, Treatise on the Last Words of David*. Luther's Works 15. Edited by Jaroslav Pelikan. St. Louis: Concordia, 1972.

Lyons, George. *Galatians*. Kansas City: Beacon Hill, 2012.

Macaskill, Grant. "History, Providence and the Apocalyptic Paul." *SJT* 70 (2017) 409–26.

———. "Paul and the Torah: Framing the Question Christianly." In *The Identity of Israel's God in Christian Scripture*, edited by Don Collett, et al., 323–38. Atlanta: SBL, 2020.

MacDonald, Neil B., and Carl Trueman, eds. *Calvin, Barth, and Reformed Theology*. Eugene, OR: Wipf & Stock, 2008.

Macken, John. *The Autonomy Theme in the Church Dogmatics: Karl Barth and His Critics*. Cambridge: Cambridge University Press, 1990.

Mangina, Joseph L. "Bearing the Marks of Jesus: The Church in the Economy of Salvation in Barth and Hauerwas." *SJT* 52 (1999) 269–305.

———. *Karl Barth on the Christian Life: The Practical Knowledge of God*. New York: Peter Lang, 2001.

———. *Karl Barth: Theologian of Christian Witness*. Louisville: Westminster John Knox, 2004.

———. "The Stranger as Sacrament: Karl Barth and the Ethics of Ecclesial Practice." *IJST* 1 (1999) 322–39.

Manson, T. W. "The Son of Man in Daniel, Enoch and the Gospels." In *The Son of Man Problem: Critical Readings*, edited by Benjamin Reynolds, 322–38. London: T&T Clark, 2018.

Massmann, Alexander. *Citizenship in Heaven and on Earth: Karl Barth's Ethics*. Minneapolis: Fortress, 2015.

Marius, Richard. *Martin Luther: The Christian Between God and Death*. Cambridge: Harvard University Press, 1999.

Marshall, Bruce D. "Israel." In *Knowing the Triune God: The Work of the Spirit in the Practices of the Church*, edited by James J. Buckley and David S. Yeago, 231–64. Grand Rapids: Eerdmans, 2001.

———. *Trinity and Truth*. Cambridge: Cambridge University Press, 2004.

Marshall, Peter. *Enmity in Corinth: Social Conventions in Paul's Relations with the Corinthians*. Tübingen: Mohr Siebeck, 1987.

Martínez, Florentino García, and Eibert J.C. Tigchelaar, eds. *The Dead Sea Scrolls*. Study ed. Leiden: Brill, 1999.

Martyn, J. Louis. *Galatians*. The Anchor Bible 33A. New York: Doubleday, 1997.

———. "A Law-Observant Mission to Gentiles: The Background of Galatians." *SJT* 38 (1985) 307–24.
Matera, Frank J. *Galatians*. Edited by Daniel J. Harrington, SJ. Collegeville, MN: Liturgical, 1992.
McCormack, Bruce L., ed. *Engaging the Doctrine of God: Contemporary Protestant Perspectives*. Grand Rapids: Baker, 2008.
———. "Historical Criticism and Dogmatic Interest in Karl Barth's Theological Exegesis of the New Testament." In *Biblical Hermeneutics in Historical Perspective*, edited by Mark S. Burrows and Paul Rorem, 322–38. Grand Rapids: Eerdmans, 1991.
———. *The Humility of the Eternal Son: Reformed Kenoticism and the Repair of Chalcedon*. Cambridge: Cambridge University Press, 2021.
———, ed. *Justification in Perspective: Historical Developments and Contemporary Challenges*. Grand Rapids: Baker, 2006.
———. *Karl Barth's Critically Realistic Dialectical Theology: Its Genesis and Development, 1909–1936*. Oxford: Oxford University Press, 1997.
———. *Orthodox and Modern: Studies in the Theology of Karl Barth*. Grand Rapids: Baker, 2008.
McCosker, Philip, and Denys Turner, eds. *The Cambridge Companion to the Summa Theologiae*. Cambridge: Cambridge University Press, 2016.
McDowell, John C. *Hope in Barth's Eschatology: Interrogations and Transformations Beyond Tragedy*. Burlington, VT: Ashgate, 2000.
———. "Much Ado About Nothing: Karl Barth's Being Unable to Do Nothing About Nothingness." *IJST* 4 (2002) 319–35.
McFarland, Ian A. "The Body of Christ: Rethinking a Classic Ecclesiological Model." *IJST* 7 (2005) 225–45.
———. *The Divine Image: Envisioning the Invisible God*. Minneapolis: Fortress, 2005.
———. *From Nothing: A Theology of Creation*. Louisville: Westminster John Knox, 2014.
———. *In Adam's Fall: A Meditation on the Christian Doctrine of Original Sin*. Malden, MA: Wiley-Blackwell, 2010.
———. *The Word Made Flesh: A Theology of the Incarnation*. Louisville: Westminster John Knox, 2019.
McFarland, Ian A., et al. *The Cambridge Dictionary of Christian Theology*. Cambridge: Cambridge University Press, 2011.
McGlasson, Paul. *Karl Barth and the Scriptures: A Study of the Biblical Exegesis in Church Dogmatics I and II*. Ann Arbor, MI: UMI, 1986.
McKenny, Gerald. *The Analogy of Grace: Karl Barth's Moral Theology*. Oxford: Oxford University Press, 2010.
———. "'Freed by God for God': Divine Action and Human Action in Karl Barth's Evangelical Theology and Other Late Works." In *Karl Barth and the Making of Evangelical Theology: The Fifty-Year Perspectives*, edited by Clifford B. Anderson and Bruce L. McCormack, 129–49. Grand Rapids: Eerdmans, 2015.
———. "Heterogeneity and Ethical Deliberation: Casuistry, Narrative, and Event in the Ethics of Karl Barth." *ASCE* 20 (2000) 205–24.
———. *Karl Barth's Moral Thought*. Oxford: Oxford University Press, 2021.
McKnight, Scot, et al., eds. *Dictionary of Paul and His Letters*. Revised, 2nd ed. Downers Grove, IL: IVP, 2023.

Bibliography

McLean, Stuart D. *Humanity in the Thought of Karl Barth*. Edinburgh: T&T Clark, 1981.
Mendenhall, George E. *Law and Covenant in Israel and the Ancient Near East*. Pittsburgh: Biblical Colloquium, 1955.
Mendenhall, George E., and Gary A. Herion. "Covenant." In *The Anchor Bible Dictionary 1: A–C*, edited by David Noel Freedman, et al., 1179–202. New York: Doubleday, 1992.
Mezei, Balázs M. *Radical Revelation: A Philosophical Approach*. London: T&T Clark, 2017.
Milbank, John. *Being Reconciled: Ontology and Pardon*. London: Routledge, 2003.
———. "Can a Gift Be Given? Prolegomena to a Future Trinitarian Metaphysic." *MT* 11 (1995) 119–61.
Miner, Robert. *Truth in the Making: Creative Knowledge in Theology and Philosophy*. London: Routledge, 2004.
Molnar, Paul D. *Divine Freedom and the Doctrine of the Immanent Trinity: In Dialogue with Karl Barth and Contemporary Theology*. 2nd ed. London: T&T Clark, 2017.
———. *Karl Barth and the Theology of the Lord's Supper: A Systematic Investigation*. New York: Peter Lang, 1996.
Moo, Douglas J. *Galatians*. Grand Rapids: Baker, 2013.
Mouw, Richard J. *The God Who Commands*. Notre Dame: University of Notre Dame Press, 2020.
Mozley, J. B. *A Treatise on the Augustinian Doctrine of Predestination*. Eugene, OR: Wipf & Stock, 2004.
Mtshiselwa, Ndikho. "Reading Jeremiah 31:31–34 in Light of Deuteronomy 29:21—30:10 and of *Inqolobane Yesizwe*: Some Remarks on Prophecy and the Torah." *OTE* 30 (2017) 403–20.
Murphy, Mark C. *An Essay on Divine Authority*. Ithaca, NY: Cornell University Press, 2002.
Myers, Jason A. "Law, Lies and Letter Writing: An Analysis of Jerome and Augustine on the Antioch Incident (Galatians 2:11–14)." *SJT* 66 (2013) 127–39.
Nanos, Mark D., ed. *The Galatians Debate: Contemporary Issues in Rhetorical and Historical Interpretation*. Peabody, MA: Hendrickson, 2002.
———. *The Irony of Galatians: Paul's Letter in First-Century Context*. Minneapolis: Fortress, 2002.
Neder, Adam. *Participation in Christ: An Entry into Karl Barth's Church Dogmatics*. Louisville: Westminster John Knox, 2009.
Neil, William. *The Letter of Paul to the Galatians*. Cambridge: Cambridge University Press, 1967.
Neusner, Jacob, ed. *Christianity, Judaism and Other Greco-Roman Cults, Part 2: Early Christianity*. Studies in Judaism in Late Antiquity 12. Leiden: Brill, 1975.
———. *Christianity, Judaism and Other Greco-Roman Cults, Part 4: Judaism After 70 Other Greco-Roman Cults Bibliography*. Studies in Judaism in Late Antiquity 12. Leiden: Brill, 1975.
Ngewa, Samuel. *Galatians*. Grand Rapids: Zondervan, 2010.
Niang, Aliou Cissé. *Faith and Freedom in Galatia and Senegal: The Apostle Paul, Colonists and Sending Gods*. Leiden: Brill, 2009.
Nimmo, Paul T. *Barth: A Guide for the Perplexed*. London: T&T Clark, 2017.
———. *Being in Action: The Theological Shape of Barth's Ethical Vision*. London: T&T Clark, 2007.
———. "The Divine Wisdom and the Divine Economy." *MT* 34 (2018) 403–18.

———. "Karl Barth." In *T&T Clark Companion to the Doctrine of Sin*, edited by Keith L. Johnson and David Lauber, 285–99. London: T&T Clark, 2016.

———. "Karl Barth and the *Concursus Dei*—A Chalcedonianism Too Far?" *IJST* 9 (2007) 58–72.

———. "The Orders of Creation in the Theological Ethics of Karl Barth." *SJT* 60 (2007) 24–35.

Nimmo, Paul T., and David A. S. Fergusson, eds. *The Cambridge Companion to Reformed Theology*. Cambridge: Cambridge University Press, 2016.

Novak, David. "Karl Barth on Divine Command: A Jewish Response." *SJT* 54 (2001) 463–83.

Oakes, Peter. *Galatians*. Grand Rapids: Baker, 2015.

Oaks, Linda Frances. *Karl Barth's Hermeneutic of Election: Romans 9–11 as a Theological Paradigm*. Ann Arbor, MI: UMI, 1993.

Oberman, Heiko A. *Luther: Man Between God and the Devil*. Translated by Eileen Walliser-Schwarzbart. New Haven, CT: Yale University Press, 1989.

O'Donovan, Oliver. "Flesh and Spirit." In *Galatians and Christian Theology: Justification, the Gospel, and Ethics in Paul's Letter*, edited by Mark W. Elliot, 271–84. Grand Rapids: Baker, 2014.

O'Neill, J. C. *The Recovery of Paul's Letter to the Galatians*. London: SPCK, 1972.

Owens, Mark D. *As It Was in the Beginning: An Intertextual Analysis of New Creation in Galatians, 2 Corinthians, and Ephesians*. Eugene, OR: Pickwick, 2016.

Paddison, Angus. "Karl Barth's Theological Exegesis of Romans 9–11 in the Light of Jewish-Christian Understanding." *JSNT* 28 (2006) 469–88.

Pannenberg, Wolfhart. *Anthropology in Theological Perspective*. Translated by Matthew J. O'Connell. Edinburgh: T&T Clark, 1985.

———. *Systematic Theology*. 3 vols. Translated by Geoffrey W. Bromiley. London: T&T Clark, 2004.

Perkins, Pheme. *Abraham's Divided Children: Galatians and the Politics of Faith*. Harrisburg, PA: Trinity Press International, 2001.

Perry, Edmund. "The Meaning of 'emuna in the Old Testament." *JBR* 21 (1953) 252–56.

Placher, William C. *The Domestication of Transcendence: How Modern Thinking About God Went Wrong*. Louisville: Westminster John Knox, 1996.

Polanyi, Michael. *Knowing and Being: Essays*. Edited by Marjorie Greene. Chicago: University of Chicago Press, 1969.

Popkes, Wiard. "Two Interpretations of 'Justification' in the New Testament Reflections on Galatians 2:15–21 and James 2:21–25." *Studia Theologica* 59 (2005) 129–46.

Porter, Stanley E., ed. *Handbook of Classical Rhetoric in the Hellenistic Period: 330 B.C.–A.D. 400*. Leiden: Brill, 2001.

Porter, Stanley E., and Matthew Brook O'Donnell, eds. *The Linguist as Pedagogue: Trends in the Teaching and Linguistic Analysis of the Greek New Testament*. Sheffield, UK: Sheffield Phoenix, 2009.

Preus, James S. *From Shadow to Promise: Old Testament Interpretation from Augustine to the Young Luther*. Cambridge: Harvard University Press, 1969.

Price, Daniel J. *Karl Barth's Anthropology in Light of Modern Thought*. Grand Rapids: Eerdmans, 2002.

Qimron, Elisha. *The Hebrew of the Dead Sea Scrolls*. Atlanta: Scholars, 1986.

Rae, Simon H. "Gospel Law and Freedom in the Theological Ethics of Karl Barth." *SJT* 25 (1972) 412–22.

Rahner, Karl. *The Trinity*. Translated by Joseph Donceel. New York: Crossroad, 1997.
Rauscher, Frederick. "Kant's Social and Political Philosophy." Stanford Encyclopedia of Philosophy, edited by Edward N. Zalta & Uri Nodelman, Feb. 13, 2024. https://plato.stanford.edu/entries/kant-social-political/#FreBasSta/.
Ravenscroft, Ruth Jackson. *The Veiled God: Friedrich Schleiermacher's Theology of Finitude*. Leiden: Brill, 2019.
Raz, Joseph. *The Morality of Freedom*. Oxford: Oxford University Press, 1988.
Reeling Brouwer, Rinse H. *Karl Barth and Post-Reformation Orthodoxy*. Burlington, VA: Ashgate, 2015.
Rey, Jean-Sébastien. *The Dead Sea Scrolls and Pauline Literature*. Leiden: Brill, 2014.
Richards, E. Randolph. *Paul and First-Century Letter Writing: Secretaries, Composition, and Collection*. Downers Grove, IL: IVP, 2004.
Richardson, Kurt Anders. *Reading Karl Barth: New Directions for North American Theology*. Grand Rapids: Baker, 2004.
Riches, John. *Galatians Through the Centuries*. Malden, MA: Wiley-Blackwell, 2013.
Ricoeur, Paul. *Hermeneutics and the Human Sciences: Essays on Language, Action and Interpretation*. Edited and translated by John B. Thompson. Cambridge: Cambridge University Press, 2016.
———. *Philosophical Anthropology*. Edited by Johann Michael and Jerome Poree. Translated by David Pellauer. Cambridge, UK: Polity, 2016.
Ridderbos, Herman. *Paul: An Outline of His Theology*. Translated by John Richard De Witt. Grand Rapids: Eerdmans, 1975.
Rodin, R. Scott. *Evil and Theodicy in the Theology of Karl Barth*. New York: Peter Lang, 1997.
Rosato, Philip J. *The Spirit as Lord: The Pneumatology of Karl Barth*. Edinburgh: T&T Clark, 1981.
Rosner, Brian S. *Paul and the Law: Keeping the Commandments of God*. Downers Grove, IL: IVP, 2013.
Rotelle, John E., ed. *The Trinity*. The Works of Saint Augustine 5. Translated by Edmund Hill. New York: New City, 1991.
Runia, Klaas. *Karl Barth's Doctrine of Holy Scripture*. Eugene, OR: Wipf & Stock, 2018.
Rupp, Gordon. *The Righteousness of God: Luther Studies*. London: Hodder & Stoughton, 1963.
Sanders, E. P. *Paul: The Apostle's Life, Letters, and Thought*. Minneapolis: Fortress, 2015.
———. *Paul and Palestinian Judaism: A Comparison of Patterns of Religion*. 40th anniversary ed. Minneapolis: Fortress, 2017.
———. *Paul, the Law, and the Jewish People*. Philadelphia: Fortress, 1983.
Sandnes, Karl Olav. *Paul—One of the Prophets? A Contribution to the Apostle's Self-Understanding*. Tübingen: Mohr Siebeck, 1991.
Schaff, Philip, ed. *The Apostolic Fathers with Justine Martyr and Irenaeus*. Grand Rapids: Christian Classics Ethereal Library, 2002.
Schoeman, Ferdinand David, ed. *Responsibility, Character, and the Emotions: New Essays in Moral Psychology*. Cambridge: Cambridge University Press, 1988.
Schreiner, Thomas R. *Galatians*. Grand Rapids: Zondervan, 2010.
Schweiker, William. *Responsibility and Christian Ethics*. Cambridge: Cambridge University Press, 1995.
Schweitzer, Albert. *The Mysticism of Paul the Apostle*. London: A&C Black, 1931.
Schwöbel, Christoph, and Colin E. Gunton, eds. *Persons, Divine, and Human: King's College Essays in Theological Anthropology*. Edinburgh: T&T Clark, 1991.

Segal, Alan F. *Paul the Convert: The Apostolate and Apostasy of Saul the Pharisee*. New Haven, CT: Yale University Press, 1990.

Seitz, Christopher R. *Figured Out: Typology and Providence in Christian Scripture*. Louisville: Westminster John Knox, 2001.

Sellers, R. V. *The Council of Chalcedon: A Historical and Doctrinal Survey*. London: SPCK, 1961.

Shauf, Scott. "Galatians 2.20 in Context." *NTS* 52 (2006) 86–101.

Silva, Moisés. *Biblical Words and Their Meaning: An Introduction to Lexical Semantics*. Grand Rapids: Zondervan, 1994.

———. "Galatians." In *Commentary on the New Testament Use of the Old Testament*, edited by G. K. Beale and D. A. Carson, 1273–313. Grand Rapids: Baker, 2007.

———. *Interpreting Galatians: Explorations in Exegetical Method*. 2nd ed. Grand Rapids: Baker, 2001.

Simopoulos, Nicole M. "Who Was Hagar? Mistress, Divorcee, Exile, or Exploited Worker: An Analysis of Contemporary Grassroots Readings of Genesis 16 by Caucasian, Latina, and Black South African Women." In *Reading Other-Wise: Socially Engaged Biblical Scholars Reading with Their Local Communities*, edited by Gerald O. West, 63–72. Atlanta: SBL, 2007.

Smedes, Lewis B. "Being in Christ." In *Major Themes in the Reformed Tradition*, edited by Donald K. McKim, 142–54. Eugene, OR: Wipf & Stock, 1998.

Smiles, Vincent M. *The Gospel and the Law in Galatia: Paul's Response to Jewish-Christian Separatism and the Threat of Galatian Apostasy*. Collegeville, MN: Liturgical, 1998.

Smith, Aaron T. *A Theology of the Third Article: Karl Barth and the Spirit of the Word*. Minneapolis: Fortress, 2014.

Sölle, Dorothee. *Christ the Representative: An Essay in Theology After the "Death of God."* London: SCM, 1967.

Sonderegger, Katherine. *The Doctrine of God*. Systematic Theology 1. Minneapolis: Fortress, 2015.

———. *The Doctrine of the Holy Trinity: Processions and Persons*. Systematic Theology 2. Minneapolis: Fortress, 2020.

———. *That Jesus Christ Was Born a Jew: Karl Barth's "Doctrine of Israel."* University Park, PA: Pennsylvania State University Press, 1992.

Soulen, R. Kendall. "YHWH the Triune God." *MT* 15 (1999) 25–54.

Sparks, H. F. D., ed. *The Apocryphal Old Testament*. Oxford: Clarendon, 1984.

Spencer, Archibald James. *Clearing a Space for Human Action: Ethical Ontology in the Theology of Karl Barth*. New York: Peter Lang, 2003.

Sprinkle, Preston M. *Law and Life: The Interpretation of Leviticus 18:5 in Early Judaism and in Paul*. Tübingen: Mohr Siebeck, 2008.

Stanley, Christopher D. *Arguing with Scripture: The Rhetoric of Quotations in the Letters of Paul*. London: T&T Clark, 2004.

———, ed. *The Colonized Apostle: Paul Through Postcolonial Eyes*. Minneapolis: Fortress, 2011.

Steinmetz, David C. *Luther in Context*. Bloomington, IN: Indiana University Press, 1986.

Steyn, Gert. "'Retrodiction' of the Old Testament in the New: The Case of Deuteronomy 21:23 in Paul's Letter to the Galatians and the Crucifixion of Yehoshua ben Joseph." *HTS Teologiese Studies* 71 (2015) 1–8.

Stone, Michael, trans. *The Testament of Abraham: The Greek Recensions*. Atlanta: SBL, 1972.

Stowers, Stanley Kent. *Letter Writing in Greco-Roman Antiquity*. Philadelphia: Westminster, 1986.
Sumney, Jerry L. *"Servants of Satan," "False Brothers" and Other Opponents of Paul*. Sheffield, UK: Sheffield Academic, 1999.
Sweeney, Marvin A. "Structure, Genre, and Intent in the Book of Habakkuk." *Vetus Testamentum* 41 (1991) 63–83.
Swinburne, Richard. *The Coherence of Theism*. 2nd ed. Oxford: Oxford University Press, 2016.
Talbert, Matthew. "Moral Responsibility." *The Stanford Encyclopedia of Philosophy*, Mar. 26, 2014. Edited by Edward N. Zalta and Uri Nodelman. http://plato.stanford.edu/archives/sum2014/entries/moral-responsibility/.
Tannehill, Robert C. *Dying and Rising with Christ: A Study in Pauline Theology*. Reprint ed. Berlin: DeGruyter, 2020.
Tanner, Kathryn. "Creation and Providence." In *The Cambridge Companion to Karl Barth*, edited by John Webster, 111–26. Cambridge: Cambridge University Press, 2000.
Terblanche, M. D. "Jeremiah 31:31–34: A Prospect of True Transformation." *Acta Theologica* 32 (2021) 258–74.
Thiselton, Anthony C. *The First Epistle to the Corinthians: A Commentary on the Greek Text*. Grand Rapids: Eerdmans, 2000.
Thomas, Gunter. "Sin and Evil." In *The Oxford Handbook of Karl Barth*, edited by Paul Dafydd Jones and Paul T. Nimmo, 354–72. Oxford: Oxford University Press, 2019.
Thomas-Smith, Karen. "Seeing Through the Eyes of Our Sister, Hagar: An Expository Sermon on Genesis 16:1–16, 21:1–21 and John 4:5–14." *Review & Expositor* 105.1 (2008) 135–38.
Ticciati, Susannah. "The Future of Biblical Israel: How Should Christians Read Romans 9–11 Today?" *BI* 25 (2017) 497–518.
Tillich, Paul. *The Courage to Be*. New Haven, CT: Yale University Press, 1980.
———. *Systematic Theology: Three Volumes in One*. Chicago: University of Chicago Press, 1967.
Tomson, Peter J. *Paul and the Jewish Law: Halakha in the Letters of the Apostle to the Gentiles*. Assen, NL: Van Gorcum, 1990.
Torrance, Alan J. *Persons in Communion: An Essay on Trinitarian Description and Human Participation, with Special Reference to Volume One of Karl Barth's Church Dogmatics*. Edinburgh: T&T Clark, 1996.
Torrance, James B. "Covenant or Contract? A Study of the Theological Background of Worship in Seventeenth-Century Scotland." *SJT* 23 (1970) 51–76.
Torrance, Thomas F. *Karl Barth, Biblical and Evangelical Theologian*. Edinburgh: T&T Clark, 1990.
———. *Space, Time, and Incarnation*. Edinburgh: T&T Clark, 1997.
———. *Theology in Reconstruction*. Grand Rapids: Eerdmans, 1996.
Torrell, Jean-Pierre. *Christ and Spirituality in St. Thomas Aquinas*. Translated by Bernhard Blankenhorn. Washington, DC: Catholic University of America Press, 2011.
Trible, Phyllis, and Letty M. Russell, eds. *Hagar, Sarah, and Their Children: Jewish, Christian, and Muslim Perspectives*. Louisville: Westminster John Knox, 2006.
Trick, Bradley R. *Abrahamic Descent, Testamentary Adoption, and the Law in Galatians: Differentiating Abraham's Sons, Seed, and Children of Promise*. Leiden: Brill, 2016.

van Inwagen, Peter. *God, Knowledge and Mystery: Essays in Philosophical Theology.* Ithaca, NY: Cornell University Press, 1995.

van Nes, Jermo. "Faith(Fulness) of the Son of God?: Galatians 2:20b Reconsidered." *Novum Testamentum* 55 (2013) 127–39.

Vanhoozer, Kevin J. *First Theology: God, Scripture and Hermeneutics.* Downers Grove, IL: IVP, 2002.

Vanhoozer, Kevin J., et al. *Theological Interpretation of the New Testament: A Book-by-Book Survey.* Grand Rapids: Baker, 2008.

Vermès, Géza. *The Dead Sea Scrolls in English.* 3rd ed. New York: Penguin, 1987.

von Balthasar, Hans Urs. *The Dramatis Personae: Persons in Christ. Theo-Drama: Theological Dramatic Theory 3.* Translated by Graham Harrison. San Francisco: Ignatius, 1992.

———. *The Theology of Karl Barth: Exposition and Interpretation.* Translated by Edward T. Oakes. San Francisco: Ignatius, 1992.

von Rad, Gerhard. *Deuteronomy: A Commentary.* Louisville: Westminster, 1966.

Wainwright, Geoffrey. *Doxology: The Praise of God in Worship, Doctrine, and Life.* Oxford: Oxford University Press, 1980.

Wakefield, Andrew H. *Where to Live: The Hermeneutical Significance of Paul's Citations from Scripture in Galatians 3:1–14.* Atlanta: SBL, 2003.

Ward, Timothy. *Word and Supplement: Speech Acts, Biblical Texts, and the Sufficiency of Scripture.* Oxford: Oxford University Press, 2002.

Warfield, Benjamin Breckinridge. *The Inspiration and Authority of the Bible.* Edited by Samuel G. Craig. Phillipsburg, NJ: Presbyterian and Reformed, 1948.

Watson, Francis. *Paul and the Hermeneutics of Faith.* London: T&T Clark, 2004.

Webster, John. *Barth's Ethics of Reconciliation.* Cambridge: Cambridge University Press, 1995.

———. *Barth's Moral Theology: Human Action in Barth's Thought.* London: T&T Clark, 2004.

———. *Holy Scripture: A Dogmatic Sketch.* Cambridge: Cambridge University Press, 2003.

Wedderburn, A. J. M. "Some Observations on Paul's Use of the Phrases 'in Christ' and 'with Christ.'" *JSNT* 25 (1985) 83–97.

Weima, Jeffrey A. D. *Paul the Ancient Letter Writer: An Introduction to Epistolary Analysis.* Grand Rapids: Baker, 2016.

Wengert, Timothy J., ed. *Harvesting Martin Luther's Reflections on Theology, Ethics, and the Church.* Grand Rapids: Eerdmans, 2004.

Wenham, Gordon J., et al., eds. *New Bible Commentary: 21st Century Edition.* Downers Grove, IL: IVP, 1994.

Werpehowski, William. "Command and History in the Ethics of Karl Barth." *JRE* 9 (1981) 298–320.

———. *Karl Barth and Christian Ethics: Living in Truth.* Burlington, VA: Ashgate, 2014.

———. "Narrative and Ethics in Barth." *TT* 43 (1986) 334–53.

Westphal, Merold. *Kierkegaard's Concept of Faith.* Grand Rapids: Eerdmans, 2014.

Whitehouse, W. A. "Providence: An Account of Karl Barth's Doctrine." *SJT* 4 (1951) 241–56.

Wikipedia. "Nicene Creed." https://en.wikipedia.org/wiki/Nicene_Creed.

Wilcox, Max. "'Upon the Tree': Deut 21:22–23 in the New Testament." *JBL* 96 (1977) 85–99.

Bibliography

Wilder, William N. *Echoes of the Exodus Narrative in the Context and Background of Galatians 5:18*. New York: Peter Lang, 2001.

Wiley, Tatha. *Paul and the Gentile Women: Reframing Galatians*. New York: Continuum, 2005.

Willis, Robert E. *The Ethics of Karl Barth*. Leiden: Brill, 1971.

Willitts, Joel. "Context Matters: Paul's Use of Leviticus 18:5 in Galatians 3:12." *TB* 54 (1966) 105–22.

Wilson, Todd A. *The Curse of the Law and the Crisis in Galatia: Reassessing the Purpose of Galatians*. Tübingen: Mohr Siebeck, 2007.

Wisse, Maarten. "The Inseparable Bond Between Covenant and Predestination: Cocceius and Barth." In *Scholasticism Reformed: Essays in Honour of Willem J. Van Asselt*, edited by Maarten Wisse, et al., 259–79. Leiden: Brill, 2010.

———. *Reinventing Christian Doctrine: Retrieving the Law–Gospel Distinction*. London: T&T Clark, 2023.

Witherington, Ben, III. *Grace in Galatia: A Commentary on St. Paul's Letter to the Galatians*. Grand Rapids: Eerdmans, 1998.

Wittman, Tyler R. *God and Creation in the Theology of Thomas Aquinas and Karl Barth*. Cambridge: Cambridge University Press, 2019.

Wold, Benjamin G. "Revelation's Plague Septets: New Exodus and Exile." In *Echoes from the Caves: Qumran and the New Testament*, edited by Florentino García Martínez, 279–98. Leiden: Brill, 2009.

Wolterstorff, Nicholas. *Divine Discourse: Philosophical Reflections on the Claim That God Speaks*. Cambridge: Cambridge University Press, 1995.

———. *Justice: Rights and Wrongs*. Princeton: Princeton University Press, 2008.

Woo, B. Hoon. *The Promise of the Trinity: The Covenant of Redemption in the Theologies of Witsius, Owen, Dickson, Goodwin, and Cocceius*. Göttingen, DE: Vandenhoeck & Ruprecht, 2018.

Woodard-Lehman, Derek Alan. "The Law as the Task of the Gospel: Karl Barth and the Possibility of an Apostolic Pragmatism." *JJE* 2 (2016) 62–85.

———. "Reason After Revelation: Karl Barth on Divine Word and Human Words." *MT* 33 (2017) 92–115.

Wright, N. T. *The Climax of the Covenant: Christ and the Law in Pauline Theology*. London: T&T Clark, 1991.

———. *Paul and the Faithfulness of God*. Books I and II. Minneapolis: Fortress, 2013.

Wright, Terry J. "Reconsidering *Concursus*." *IJST* 4 (2002) 205–15.

Wynn, Kerry H. "Between Text and Sermon: Jeremiah 31:1–6." *Interpretation: JBT* 68 (2014) 184–86.

Zahl, Simeon. "The Drama of Agency: Affective Augustinianism and Galatians." In *Galatians and Christian Theology: Justification, the Gospel, and Ethics in Paul's Letter*, edited by Mark W. Elliot, 335–52. Grand Rapids: Baker, 2014.

www.ingramcontent.com/pod-product-compliance
Lightning Source LLC
Chambersburg PA
CBHW071231170426
43191CB00032B/1320